15. Mrs Thatcher's rebate, and the cost
    of Mr Blair's concession   92
16. Domestic equivalents of the direct and indirect costs   96

Part Four: The Common and Single Market
17. An overview of UK export growth since 1960   106
18. The success of the Common Market 1973-1992   110
19. The failure of the Single Market 1993-2012   115
20. What would have happened to UK exports
    if there had been no Single Market?   122
21. Have UK goods exporters been losing their touch?   127
22. A club of high unemployment…   130
23. …which is also distinctively severe   134
24. The slow growth of GDP and productivity in
    the Single Market 1993-2013   138
25. A burst of candour from European Commission
    staff about the failings of the Single Market   142
26. Who will measure the performance of the
    Single Market, how, when and for whom?   146
27. Paradox in goods exports: non-members have been
    its major beneficiaries   150
28. Paradox in services: non-members have been its
    major beneficiaries   155
29. Why hasn't 'sitting round the table and helping
    to make the rules' helped UK exports?   159
30. Does a Single Market in services exist?   165
31. Services exports to the EU and other markets   171

Part Five: Trade agreements

32. The Commission as trade negotiator (I):
    A preference for small partner countries   174
33. The Commission as trade negotiator (II):
    The neglect of services   180
34. The Commission as trade negotiator (III):
    The sidelining of the Commonwealth   184
35. Have European Commission trade agreements in
    goods helped UK exports? A scorecard versus Chile,
    Korea, Singapore and Switzerland   188
36. The UK's lost years of freer trade   197
37. Obstacles impeding EU service agreements   202

Part Six: Current debate

38. What does Her Majesty's Government actually know
    about the impact of the EU on the UK economy?   212
39. Does the Bank of England know much more?   223
40. Has the EU's Single Market been a magnet
    for foreign investors?   232
41. Why multinationals' opinions on the EU
    are less than convincing   239
42. Immigration, free movement and welfare   242
43. An academic illusion: research depends on
    an EU 'pot of money'   248
44. Scaremongering to keep the UK in   259
45. We have been here before!   266
46. A *Financial Times* editor apologises
    for urging entry into the euro   269
47. How difficult would it be for post-Brexit UK
    to replace existing EU trade agreements?   273
48. Why the UK would negotiate better services
    FTAs by itself   283

Part Seven: The future

49. Uncertainties of staying   296
50. Uncertainties of leaving   305

Author

Michael Burrage is a director of Cimigo, which is based in Ho Chi Minh City, Vietnam, and conducts market and corporate strategy research in China, India and 12 countries in the Asia Pacific region. He is also a founder director of a start-up specialist telecom company which provides the free telephone interpreter service for aid workers and others where interpreters are scarce.

He is a sociologist by training, was a Fulbright scholar at the University of Pennsylvania, has been a lecturer at the London School of Economics and at the Institute of United States Studies, specialising in the comparative analysis of industrial enterprise and professional institutions. He has been a research fellow at Harvard, at the Swedish Collegium of Advanced Study, Uppsala, at the Free University of Berlin, and at the Center for Higher Education Studies and the Institute of Government of the University of California, Berkeley. He has also been British Council lecturer at the University of Pernambuco, Recife, Brazil, and on several occasions a visiting professor in Japan, at the universities of Kyoto, Hokkaido and Kansai and at Hosei University in Tokyo.

He has written articles in American, European and Japanese sociological journals, conducted a comparative study of telephone usage in Tokyo, Manhattan, Paris and London for NTT, and a study of British entrepreneurs for Ernst & Young. His publications include *Revolution and the Making of the Contemporary Legal Profession: England, France and the United States* (OUP, 2006) and *Class Formation, Civil Society and the State: A comparative analysis of Russia, France, the United States and England* (Palgrave Macmillan, 2008). He edited *Martin Trow: Twentieth-century higher education: from elite to mass to universal* (Johns Hopkins, 2010).

His previous Civitas publications include *Where's the Insider Advantage? A review of the evidence that withdrawal from the EU would not harm the UK's exports or foreign investment in the UK* (July 2014) and 'A club of high and severe unemployment: the Single Market over the 21 years 1993-2013' (July 2015) in the Europe Debate series.

Summary

- The EU has a peculiar form of government that ignores the fundamental conditions for the success of democracies: its rulers are not co-cultural with its voters and there is no autonomous civil society.

- The EU is aware of its lack of democratic legitimacy and spends huge amounts of taxpayers' funds on self-promotion.

- As the EU has grown in size, Britain's representation has inevitably declined.

- The EU is a mechanism for the redistribution of wealth across its member countries. The Commission takes from nine wealthier, more developed members, and after taking roughly six per cent of all receipts for its own expenses, returns some of their contributions back to the nine, and re-distributes the rest to other, generally poorer, member countries.

- The Single Market has been a period of decline, of decelerating growth of UK exports. No rigorous attempt has been made to explain why this happened, probably because, in the UK at least, the Single Market has been continuously portrayed as a success and even as the 'Crown Jewel' of European integration.

- The proportion of goods exports going to the future EU member countries grew rather sharply, by 12 per cent, over the 12 years before the UK entered the Common Market, from 49.6 per cent in 1960 to 61.6 per cent in 1972. However, over the 40 years of EU membership, for all the costs and obligations incurred, for all the treaties negotiated, and for all the immense time and anguish spent arguing about various aspects of the EU project, the proportion of UK exports going to the UK's future EU partners has hardly changed at all.

- Enthusiastic British supporters of the Single Market continually claim that there are invaluable advantages for the UK and other members from sitting at the table and helping to make the rules. This evidence suggests that sitting at the table makes no difference whatever, and that if invited to do so, non-members would be well advised to decline, which they would probably do anyway, when told what their country's taxpayers would have to pay for the privilege.

- Non-members' exports of goods to the Single Market have grown faster than those of the UK or other members. This counter-intuitive and profoundly paradoxical result flies in the face of the claims about the advantages of the Single Market for UK trade that have been made over many years by Britain's political leaders.

- UK exports to many other markets over the same years have grown rapidly, suggesting that UK exporters are not to blame.

- One of the more striking and enduring characteristics of the Single Market is its high rate of unemployment. Moreover, growing up in Europe has meant a distinctively high risk of long-term unemployment, a problem that has not afflicted other advanced societies to the same degree.

- From the beginning, EU membership was supposed to improve UK productivity. There is no evidence that it has ever done so, for the UK or anyone else.

- It is a puzzling paradox that the exporters from non-member countries who do not sit at the table, and help to make the rules of the Single Market, and pay nothing for access to it, have been its main beneficiaries as measured by the growth of their goods exports.

- The services exports to the EU of non-members who have not been 'sitting at the table, helping to make the rules', have grown as fast as those who have.

- Since no-one in the UK has measured the Single Market in services, no one can say whether it has been deepened or extended or by how much. In fact, no-one can say for sure that it exists.

- Over the past 40 years, the largest country with which the European Commission has ever concluded an agreement is the Republic of Korea. It has preferred instead to secure a large number of agreements with small countries.

- UK influence on the EU trade agenda and strategy has been minimal. Services have been overlooked in EU trade agreements, despite the pleas of successive British prime ministers.

- The evidence in the Regional Trade Agreements Information System (RTAIS) in the WTO database shows that the European Commission has been very slow to open trade negotiations with Commonwealth countries.

- Switzerland and Singapore show what the UK might have done had it been able to negotiate its own trade agreements. The years of lost freer trade are estimated by supposing that the UK kept pace with Singapore and Switzerland. Singapore, for example, has benefited from over six more years of freer trade with China, 11 more years with the USA and 12 more with Japan.

- Enthusiasts for the EU make confident claims that British exporters have gained by the UK surrendering the right to negotiate trade agreements, and that the interests of British companies, and the livelihoods of the British people, have been wisely and safely entrusted to the EU, because of the 'negotiating muscle' obtained by negotiating alongside 27 other countries.

- Successive governments have failed to inform the public of the impact of the EU, but they have also failed to inform themselves.

- EU enthusiasts still make confident claims about foreign investors' post-Brexit decisions, despite their mistaken predictions about the euro, despite the European Commission's findings, despite contrary indications and evidence, and despite the known uncertainty of such predictions.

- The notion that the UK gets more research grants than others, or 'more than we put in', is merely the folklore of the research community.

- Claims have been made that post-Brexit UK would face near insurmountable difficulties having to renegotiate the EU trade agreements from which it currently benefits, but the evidence suggests that the problem for post-Brexit Britain would be far more manageable than many have suggested.

- The UK has considerable comparative advantages when negotiating services trade agreements. As a member of the EU they have been ignored. After Brexit, they could be put to use.

Introduction

For the forty years and more that the UK has been a member of the EU, successive British governments have declined to monitor, analyse and report to the people the impact of the EU on the economy. One can only speculate on the reasons for this reluctance, but its consequences will be known to anyone who has listened to prime ministerial and ministerial speeches over the years about the benefits of EU membership and the Single Market. None include substantial evidence to support their arguments.

None refer to the impartial and authoritative databases, of the OECD, UNCTAD and UN Comtrade, the World Trade Organization or the World Bank, which reflect what has actually happened to the UK economy whilst it has been a member of the EU and the Single Market. Instead, they have preferred to tell us what they think has happened, or hope might yet happen, or what some model predicts could or should happen. And the media have not on the whole pushed them to provide or collect evidence for themselves.

Unfortunately, large British and multinational businesses who might well have measured the benefits of membership for their own sectors, or even for the country as a whole, have behaved in much the same manner. They have declined to publish any convincing evidence about their preference for remaining in the EU, even when expressly invited to do so during the Balance of Competences Review in 2013.

Governments and businesses have behaved as if the authority of their positions entitles them to speak off the tops of their heads, believing that their audiences will assume that because they are, or were once, parties to EU decision-making, they have accumulated convincing evidence of the advantages of EU membership. Evidence which cannot, for some undisclosed reason, be passed on to the rest of us. Perhaps they think we would not understand the details.

Once upon a time, circa 1975, voters might have accepted this. Today, voters are rather more sceptical of official, elite depictions of the EU. This handbook is for them, prepared by one ordinary voter for others who would like the relevant evidence about the costs and benefits of EU membership, to help them decide about the merits of continued EU membership.

Its primary aim is to find, report and comment on this evidence, mainly about trade, but also about other events, institutions and policies that are relevant to the decision of whether to remain in or leave. UK governments have kept the people in the dark, failing to establish the impact of EU membership for the British people. The evidence presented here sometimes has to end with unanswered questions, and occasionally an unasked one.

One of the aims of the government in holding the referendum as soon as possible is to prevent all the relevant evidence from being put before voters in time for them to consider it. Publications of this kind are therefore produced under severe time constraints, so it is possible that despite our best efforts, errors may occur. If so, we want to hear about them. The source of the data or documents used is given in every case so it is possible for any reader to verify the data presented. The occasional basic calculations made before reporting findings are also shown so anyone can correct, supplement, or update them.

This study has been compiled in the spirit of the Prime Minister, who described himself in the House of Commons on 22 February 2016 as

> Eurosceptical in the genuine sense: I am sceptical about all organisations and about all engagements. We should always question whether organisations work for us, and we should be doubtful about such things.

One must add, however, that he frequently makes claims about the Single Market that have little or no evidence to support them, while we endeavour to remain rather more consistently sceptical than he has proved to be. As such, what follows are 50 chapters of varying lengths that review, from a sceptical position, the most important issues in the debate on UK membership of the European Union.

Part One

History

1

1971: Her Majesty's Government explains why the UK should join the EEC

Here follows a commentary on the UK Government white paper, The *United Kingdom and the European Communities*, 1971.[1]

In retrospect, this white paper is notable for the amount of attention it gives to the geopolitical environment of the day, both as an explanation of the origins of the European Communities and as a reason for UK entry.

In the paper little time is spent looking back to the Second World War, only mentioning that the six European Community countries had been weakened by it and had suffered invasion, that the war was one of the factors leading to the formation of the original agreements, and that they had lost or were in the process of shedding their imperial links. In addition, the six countries of the European Communities had found the world dominated by new non-European superpowers whose resources none of them could match.

The deeply felt need of the six

The countries of Europe felt the need for something more than the institutions created immediately after the war, to 're-establish the fabric of international co-operation for peace, security and economic collaboration and recovery.' The end of the Second World War saw the creation of organisations like the United Nations, the International Monetary Fund (IMF), the International

---

1 HM Government, *The United Kingdom and the European Communities*, (White Paper, Command 4715), 1971

Bank for Reconstruction and Development, and the General Agreement on Tariffs and Trade (GATT). Each of these involved one or both superpowers, so the European core nations also wanted closer cooperation between themselves. This helped to create the Western European Union alliance, the Council of Europe and the Organisation for European Economic Co-operation.[2]

For greater security and prosperity, they decided they could do more by pooling their economic resources, so in 1951 they formed the European Coal and Steel Community, and in 1957, via the Treaty of Rome, the European Economic Community and the European Atomic Energy Community. In 1967, these three communities were brought together under 'one European Parliament, one Court of Justice, one Council of Ministers and one Commission' by the Merger Treaty.[3]

The white paper notes that the institutions' aims included the 'establishment of the foundations of an ever closer union among European peoples, the furtherance of economic and social progress by elimination of the barriers which divide Europe', improved living and working conditions and so forth. The second article of the treaty affirms the task of 'setting up a Common Market and progressively approximating the economic policies of member states, to promote throughout the Community a harmonious development of economic activities, a continuous and balanced expansion, an increase in stability, an accelerated raising of the standard of living, and closer relations of the member states.' The white paper then declares 'These are objectives to which this country can wholeheartedly subscribe.'[4]

The paper then observes that the programme for a Common Market with free movement of persons, goods, services and capital plus common agricultural and commercial policies had 'unfolded steadily and that the influence of the communities in the economic councils of the world has increased impressively, as has the prosperity of their members.' [5]

---

2   (Command 4715) para 10
3   (Command 4715) para 14
4   (Command 4715) para 13
5   (Command 4715) para 16

Why Britain stayed away

Although the UK participated in many of the European co-operative ventures mentioned, the paper notes that 'the realities of our position in the world... were masked. Our physical assets and our economy had suffered less disastrously than those of most other Western European countries as a result of the war: nor did we suffer the shock of invasion.'[6] For these reasons Britain did not participate in the formation of the European Communities. However, during the 1950s, 'the transformation of our position in the world was increasingly borne in upon us' by economic problems, the 'quickening move to independence among former colonies, and of a sense of diminishing influence in world counsels.'[7]

No free trade area

The paper draws attention to the seldom remembered fact that the UK had sought a trade relationship with the Community. From 1956 some thought, 'it would be possible for other European countries which did not become members of this closer grouping to join with the Community in establishing a wider European free trade area.' However, 'in 1958 it became apparent that the basis of general agreement did not exist.' This led Britain to form the European Free Trade Association (EFTA) with Norway, Austria, Switzerland, Denmark, Portugal and Sweden in 1960. But from the start, 'it was recognised that some members of EFTA might eventually wish to join, and others to seek closer trading arrangements with, the European Communities.'[8]

Later, in discussing the possibility of Britain being part of both a North American free trade agreement and the European Communities, the white paper notes that 'the Six have firmly and repeatedly made clear that they reject the concept that European unity should be limited to the formation of a free trade area.'[9]

---

6   (Command 4715) para 17
7   (Command 4715) para 18
8   (Command 4715) para 18
9   (Command 4715) para 36

UK European policy is bi-partisan

As if to emphasize the bi-partisan support for the present application, the white paper refers to the Conservative government's efforts to negotiate entry in 1961, and those of the Labour Government in 1967, which were both 'baulked in their objective'.[10] But in 1970 the Labour Government was invited to re-open negotiations, which it accepted, so after the present Conservative Government was elected, it merely 'picked up the hand which their predecessors had prepared', and resumed negotiation.[11] It was joined by two other members of EFTA, Norway and Denmark, and by the Republic of Ireland.

Regaining world power status

The political case for membership made in the white paper rested heavily on the idea of regaining a world power status, which no European power could hope to exercise individually, by joining a wider European Community of nations, whose joint strength and influence on the world could be much greater than that of individual members. If we remained outside, we would have had 'to maintain our national interest and develop our national resources on a narrower base.' This would have taken place as European political and economic unity proceeded without Britain in 'a neighbouring Community several times our size.' Here, as elsewhere in the paper, there is a hint that the UK would not be entirely comfortable with a new super-power neighbour, and that it might also be another threat to our security.[12]

The white paper then refers to the political and military predominance of two superpowers, and the emergence of a third, China, while noting that in economic affairs the European Communities and Japan were on the way to superpower status. It then predicted a world of five superpowers where, via the International Monetary Fund (IMF) and GATT, the three non-Communist blocs 'will increasingly and inevitably be the decisive

---

10 (Command 4715) para 21
11 (Command 4715) para 22
12 (Command 4715) para 26

influences.' It argues, 'Individually, no European country can ensure its voice is heeded' but that recent negotiations showed the united Communities were listened to. If we joined, suggested the paper, 'we shall be making sure that British trade and manufacturing interests are represented at the summit of the negotiations where the terms on which we earn our living are decided.'[13]

The paper then notes that, while the Community was then mainly focused on economics, 'it is inevitable that the scope of the Community's external policies should broaden as member countries' interests become harmonised.' If we joined then, following the paper's release, 'we shall be able to influence the process of development' including that 'towards economic and monetary union'. If we were not to join, this would not stop' the Community of Six moving forward in both the economic and political fields.'[14]

An inter-governmental form of government

Throughout the paper, the Community is presented as an inter-governmental body where 'sovereign Governments are represented round the table', but no time is spent wondering how this might be reconciled with the future superpower status it anticipates. On issues which a government considers of vital national interest, the paper claims that 'it is established that the decision [must] be unanimous'. The paper asserts, 'There is no question of any erosion of essential national sovereignty; what is proposed is a sharing and an enlargement of individual national sovereignties in the general interest.'[15]

Little change required in British life

The paper minimizes the change in British institutions and the British way of life that membership will entail: 'The common law will remain the basis of our legal system, and our courts will continue to operate as they do at present. In certain cases however they would need to refer points of Community law to the European

---

13 (Command 4715) para 27
14 (Command 4715) para 28
15 (Command 4715) para 29

Court of Justice. All the essential features of our law will remain'.[16] This includes features like habeas corpus and the principle of presumed innocence. In any case, the paper argues that the political differences between European neighbours 'are insignificant, compared with what we have in common.' The paper goes on, 'In history and culture, in political, legal and social framework, in social structures, in standards of living and in national interests and objectives, the countries of the Communities and the United Kingdom have a European heritage.'[17]

The paper then looks at the way in which membership would reinforce British security, which 'has been bound up with that of our European neighbours for over a thousand years.'[18] The paper mentions NATO and says that the United States feels it is 'now time for Europe to play a larger part in maintaining her own security.' For that reason the US had, argues the paper, consistently supported the development of unity among Western European democracies 'in a more self-reliant community of nations.'[19]

Many of the earlier comments might lead one to think that a European army would be a high priority of the Six. The paper says nothing of this, though this must have been in the mind of every participant and observer at the time given the staged withdrawal of France from the military command, but not political structure, of NATO from 1959-1966.

Commitment to world development

Similarly, the Commonwealth countries had little reason or wish to object to UK membership, according to the paper, since they 'have developed and are still developing with other countries trade and investment arrangements which accord with the requirements of their basic geographical and economic circumstances.'[20] But the paper does mention the threat of abrupt dislocation to Commonwealth and other third country suppliers which Britain sought to mitigate.[21]

---

16 (Command 4715) para 31
17 (Command 4715) para 32
18 (Command 4715) para 2
19 (Command 4715) para 35
20 (Command 4715) para 37
21 (Command 4715) para 77

Moreover, the Community was not intended to be inward looking, and in trade, investment and aid has already shown that it is not. It 'already accounts for 30 per cent of world trade, and its members' trade with the outside world has increased more than two and a half times in the twelve years since its formation'.[22] Similarly, 'aid to the poorer nations by our European neighbours is proportionately greater than ours, and the Community has been the first of the major aid donors to introduce a generalised preference scheme [to provide] for duty-free access for a wide range of goods from the developing countries.'[23]

A stark contrast of economies

The white paper made the economic case for membership by arguing that, while French and German earnings were about the same as British earnings in 1958, by 1969 average earnings there 'were now between a quarter or a half higher on average than those in Britain.' Member countries also had low levels of unemployment, higher investment and balance of payments surpluses, all of which were attributed to the formation of the Community.[24]

In sharp contrast, during the same time the UK had slow economic growth, low investment and repeated balance of payments crises, which add credibility to the common characterisation at the time, in Britain at least, of Britain as the sick man of Europe.

The main advantage of membership for the UK, according to the paper, was 'a permanent, assured, and greatly enlarged market' which will prompt 'a radical change in planning, investment, production and sales effort' in the UK.[25] The British government were, therefore, 'confident that membership of the enlarged Community will lead to much improved efficiency and productivity in British industry, with a higher rate of investment and a faster growth of real wages.'[26]

---

22 (Command 4715) para 38
23 (Command 4715) para 39
24 (Command 4715) para 52
25 (Command 4715) para 44
26 (Command 4715) para 56

Drawbacks

The paper mentioned the costs of membership. We would contribute to the budget. The Common Agricultural Policy (CAP) would increase food prices, and we would also have to contribute to the European Investment Bank, but these costs were all considered manageable because of the improvements in efficiency following accession.

None of the costs which figure in the contemporary debate, such as those of regulation or of ceding the right to negotiate individual trade agreements to the Community, were deemed relevant at the time, except in the context of relations with former colonies and dependencies.

Conclusion: 'The advantages will more than outweigh the costs'

This will be the case 'provided we seize the opportunities of the far wider home market now open to us. If we do, we shall obtain, as the Six have done since the Communities were founded, a substantial increase in trade, investment, growth, real wages and standards of living than we have known in recent years or would be possible if we remained outside the Communities.'[27]

In a wider political perspective, the paper asserts that together 'we can do more and better than any of us could do alone.'[28] It suggests that because members of the enlarged Community could help each other, the 'relationships between Europe and particularly the United States, the Soviet Union and, one day, China would become more evenly balanced. A Europe united would have the means of recovering the position in the world that Europe divided has lost.'[29]

---

27 (Command 4715) para 59
28 (Command 4715) para 60
29 (Command 4715) para 61

2

Labour's re-negotiation in 1975: Real or bogus?

An earlier re-negotiation that was used to mislead voters

This question is of interest because it might also be asked of David Cameron who has recently engaged in a very similar pre-referendum re-negotiation.

In Mr Cameron's case, the answer will have to wait a while, until after the referendum when some of the other participants in the exercise feel free to speak candidly, when the decisions of the European Commission and the European Court tell us whether the EU has, as Mr Cameron claims, been 'reformed'.

In the case of Harold Wilson, prime minister at the time of the Labour Government renegotiations, the question has been settled, once and for all, by Peter Kellner in an article published on 15 November 2015 entitled, 'A split on Europe, a sweating PM: Britain has been here before'. What follows are excerpts from his article:

> Forty years ago, at the time of the last referendum on Europe, I was a young journalist on The Sunday Times. One of my tasks was to monitor the government's attempts to negotiate a new deal with Brussels...

> In the October 1974 general election Labour won a small overall majority. Harold Wilson, the prime minister, promised to negotiate a better deal for Britain from the Common Market — or European Economic Community (EEC) — and put the outcome to an in/out referendum. Then, as now, backbenchers in the governing party were evenly divided and the prime minister was desperate to hold his party together.

The negotiations were completed at a summit in Dublin on March 11, 1975. Wilson declared: "Our renegotiation objectives have been substantially though not completely achieved"...

Had the negotiations made a real difference? On the quiet, researchers at Transport House, Labour's headquarters, were asked to analyse the deal in detail. Their secret report concluded that it made little difference. On one key objective, Britain's future payments to the Common Market's budget, Wilson was accused of making things worse: "The formula finally agreed in Dublin is on the whole decidedly less favourable to Britain than that proposed earlier by the commission."

This damning report was presented to an internal party meeting on March 19. While it was well known that different cabinet ministers held opposing views, the report and the details of that meeting were kept from public view — until a contact in Transport House passed to me the report and the minutes of the meeting. These minutes showed that the public pretence of courteous differences within the cabinet were a fiction. [James Callaghan, Roy Hattersley, Tony Benn and Peter Shore had had a 'blazing row'.] On April 6, 1975 *The Sunday Times* carried my story under the front-page headline "Documents reveal gulf in Labour".[1]

[The ministers in favour of remaining in the European Communities] offered broad-brush reassurance that in practice everything would be fine ... [while those in favour of leaving] quoted the unsettling small print.

Whatever view one took about the merits of voting to stay in or leave, the Transport House analysis and the minutes of the March 19 meeting demonstrated that Wilson had been wrong to say he had "substantially" achieved his objectives.

---

1   The documents concerned whether or not the UK government had regained the power to restrict capital movements to protect the balance of payments, to protect Labour's full employment policies, and whether it had complete control over the price of North Sea oil and could discriminate in support of regional development policies.

In my youthful naivety, I thought my story would have a big impact on the referendum, then just two months away. Here was specific, irrefutable evidence from inside the government party that undermined the prime minister's position.

I was wrong. My story had no effect at all. The "leave" campaigners leapt at what I had disclosed; everyone else ignored it. The "stay" campaigners could not dispute the critique of their position and did not try; they just carried on with a soft-focus campaign that promoted the hope of a peaceful Europe working together.

As for the general public, the dream counted for far more than the detail.'[2]

This article suggests that there should be proper scrutiny of the EU and David Cameron's renegotiation this time around.

What the government then told every household

The question asked in the referendum held on 6 June 1975 was 'Do you think the United Kingdom should stay in the European Community (Common Market)?'

The government produced a pamphlet that was sent to every household in Britain, accompanied by statements by the Yes and No campaigns. Copies of these documents are available on the Civitas website.[3]

The government pamphlet explained that after long, hard negotiations, 'we are recommending to the British people that we should remain a member of the European Community.' It claimed Harold Wilson had won 'significant improvements' in the terms of membership which 'can give Britain a New Deal in Europe.'

Specifically, the pamphlet claimed that:

- The CAP would work more flexibly to the benefit of both housewives and farmers in Britain.

---

2 Keller, P, *A split on Europe, a sweating PM: Britain has been here before*, www.the-sundaytimes.co.uk/sto/newsreview/features/article1632760.ece

3 Civitas, 'The 1975 Referendum', http://www.civitas.org.uk/eu-facts/the-1975-referendum.

- Britain's contribution to the Community has been reduced, but it declined to say what it would be, and Britain stood to get back from the Community up to £125m a year.

- The threat of economic and monetary union had been removed.

- Commonwealth countries wanted us to remain a member.

- Parliamentary sovereignty was not threatened, and ministers representing Britain in the European Communities could veto any proposal for a new law or a new tax.

If we say no, the pamphlet argued that there would be:

- A period of uncertainty.

- A risk of making unemployment and inflation worse.

- Britain would no longer have any say in the future political and economic development of the Common Market.

- We would just be outsiders looking in.

Judging by the number of references to the subject, the most important consideration was that the UK would be a net recipient of various European Commission funds:

> Inside the Market we can work to get more European Community money spent inside Britain…

> More from the Social Fund for retraining workers in new jobs. Since we joined we have benefited from this Fund to the tune of over £20 million a year…

> More from the Community's new Regional Fund, which already stands to bring us £60 million in the next three years…

> More from the Farm Fund when world prices are high. For instance, up to now we have obtained £40 million from this Fund to bring down the price of sugar in the shops…

> More from the Coal & Steel funds and the European Investment Bank. Since we joined, arrangements have already been made for loans and grants of over £250 million…

The pamphlet said nothing about where these funds which were to be distributed to the UK came from, and not a word about the UK contribution to the European Commission budget, nor about how much that sum had been reduced.

It is difficult to imagine a more one-sided referendum campaign. The Yes campaign had the support of all three major parties. It used their resources as well as those of the civil service. It had the support of all the ex-prime ministers, innumerable members of the political, economic and cultural establishments, the CBI and even a good section of the Church of England. The European Commission helped by providing free flights to Brussels for nearly 1,000 pro-European speakers. All national newspapers were on their side. The only national publications which opposed entry were the communist daily *Morning Star* and *The Spectator*. The BBC claimed to be neutral, a claim which the No campaign strongly contested.

The Yes campaign also had ample funds. Its treasurers later recalled, 'when the campaign started, money just rolled in', mainly from business. The umbrella organization of the Yes campaign declared it had spent £1.85m, while the No campaign had less than a tenth as much, just £133,000. The Yes campaign was also helped by the fact that the referendum coincided with just about the worst economic crisis in the UK since the war, with a record rate of inflation which hit 27% in June and with a record trade deficit.

The result of the referendum was that 67.5% of votes were in favour of staying in. When asked in a TV interview why the public had voted as it had, Roy Jenkins, then Home Secretary and later the President of the European Commission, replied, 'They took the advice of people they were used to following.'[4]

---

4   Lahr. J (ed.), The Diaries of Kenneth Tynan (2001) p.248, entry for 6th June

3

The 1992 Maastricht Treaty: Misjudgement or misrepresentation?

Maastricht is now generally seen as the foundation treaty of the EU. In John Major's report it sounds like something else, a renewal of inter-governmental collaboration

The Treaty on European Union (TEU) was signed on 7 February 1992 in Maastricht and came into force on 1 November 1993. The name given to it would seem to indicate the fundamental significance attached to it by most of its signatories, though Union only became the legally correct name after the Lisbon Treaty in 2009.

It marked a new stage in European integration setting the Community on the path to political integration, political union and the formation of a new superstate. It introduced the notion of European citizenship, to which were attached certain rights, notably the freedom to move, reside and be employed anywhere within the Union. It also created a European Central Bank, and set out the timetable of the three stages in the creation of the new currency.

It also defined three pillars of its government: the main Single Market pillar, governed mainly by majority voting; and the two unanimity-governed pillars of Justice and Home Affairs (JHA) and Common Foreign and Security Policy (CFSP).

The central, supranational pillar included all the institutions of the European Community: the Commission, the Parliament, the European Court, the European Coal & Steel Community and the European Atomic Energy Community. It greatly enlarged the 'Community Method' of legislating in which the European Commission proposes legislation, the Council and Parliament consent, the Council normally by qualified majority voting (QMV), while the Commission, with the support of the European Court of Justice, monitors compliance.

The Treaty vastly expanded the Community's areas of competence to include trans-European transport networks, industrial policy, consumer protection, the environment, education, culture, public health, vocational training and youth. In a separate Social Chapter, aspects of employment and social policy were also covered, the most notable being workplace health, equal pay, employee consultation and safety.

The second and third pillars added two new areas of policy co-operation: Common Foreign & Security Policy and Justice and Home Affairs. These were left as areas of policy co-operation, so remained inter-governmental and not the responsibility of the European Commission. Under the Treaty of Amsterdam in 1997, aspects of JHA became the responsibility of the Community and therefore of the Commission and the European Court.

Most observers see the 1992 treaty as a major advance in European integration, laying the foundations of a new European state, and the twilight of inter-governmentalism. John Major saw it differently, as is clear from his account given to the House of Commons, which is shown below. His contribution to the Treaty is mainly remembered as him opting out of stage three of the creation of the new currency, when exchange rates would be irrevocably locked, and also of the Social Chapter, which the UK did not sign at the time.

What follows is an excerpt from a speech made by John Major in the House of Commons on 11 December 1991 regarding the Maastricht Treaty. Commentary is provided in the footnotes:

> With permission, Mr. Speaker, I should like to make a statement on the European Council in Maastricht which I attended with my right hon. Friends the Foreign Secretary and the Chancellor of the Exchequer.

> The European Council has reached agreement on a treaty on European union... Let me set out the main provisions of the agreements we reached.

The treaty covers economic and monetary union and political union. It follows the structure for which the United Kingdom has consistently argued.[1]

The treaty creates a new legal framework for co-operation between member states in foreign and security policy and in the fight against international crime. That co-operation will take place on an intergovernmental basis outside the treaty of Rome. That means that the Commission will not have the sole right of initiative and the European Court will have no jurisdiction.[2]

On defence, we have agreed a framework for co-operation in which the primacy of the Atlantic alliance has been confirmed and the role of the Western European Union has been enhanced.[3]

As the House knows, there was strong pressure over many months for all aspects of co-operation to come within European Community competence. That was not acceptable to this country. Instead, an alternative route to European co-operation has been opened up.[4] I believe that this will be seen as an increasingly significant development as the Community opens its doors to new members, and more flexible structures are required.

---

1   The first sentence describes the main theme of the treaty: the creation of a new supranational governmental structure based on QMV. The second sentence ignores it and diverts attention to the two ancillary inter-governmental pillars.
2   The idea that 'cooperation… on an intergovernmental basis outside the treaty of Rome' was a main provision of the Maastricht Treaty has not occurred to anyone else.
3   Far from the role of the Western EU being 'enhanced', its functions and institutions were subsequently transferred to the EU, mainly in 2005-6 after the Nice and Amsterdam treaties, and it was finally declared defunct on 30th June 2011.
4   Surely, a masterstroke of presentation! Intergovernmental institutions were the traditional means of collaboration between national states and the main purpose of this treaty was to replace as many of the existing ones within the European Community as feasible with supranational governmental institutions, though it was accepted that some would have to remain inter-governmental. Hence the ancillary pillars, Justice & Home Affairs, and Common Foreign & Security Policy.

I turn now to the main features of the text. The treaty provides for the possibility that member states will wish to adopt a single currency later this decade, but they can do so only if they meet strict convergence conditions for which the British Government have pressed from the outset. These cover inflation, budget deficits, exchange rate stability and long-term interest rates.

A single currency may come into being in 1997, but only if a minimum of seven countries meet the convergence conditions, and eight of the Twelve [current member states] vote in favour... It is therefore highly uncertain when such a currency will be created and which countries it will cover.[5]

We have exactly the same option to join a single currency at the same time as other member states if we wish. We shall be involved in all the decisions. But, unlike other Governments, we have not bound ourselves to join regardless of whether it makes economic or political sense.

The treaty text on political union provides for enhanced intergovernmental co-operation on foreign and security policy, on defence policy and in the fight against terrorism, drug trafficking and other crimes.[6]

There was pressure from other member states to take foreign policy decisions by majority voting... The treaty reflects our view. It provides that the Council may, but only by unanimity, designate certain decisions to be taken by qualified majority voting. But we cannot be forced to subject our foreign policy to the will of other member states.

---

5 A rather remarkable misreading of the intentions and determination of other members. Either that, or they had other meetings without him. As we now know, the strict convergence conditions were not met, but in 1999 the currency went ahead anyway.

6 He clearly wanted to convey the notion that the treaty, and the future of the Union was mainly about intergovernmental collaboration, and therefore returned for several minutes to describe the ancillary intergovernmental pillars, both of which were intended at the time to describe the ancillary intergovernmental pillars, both of which were intended at the time to be temporary, though they only finally disappeared in the Treaty of Lisbon in 2009.

We are agreed that Europe must do more for its own defence. We should build up the Western European Union [a non-EU defensive alliance] as the defence pillar of the European Union, but the treaty embodies the view set out in the Anglo-Italian proposal two months ago, and endorsed at last month's summit of the North Atlantic Treaty Organisation that whatever we do at European level must be compatible with NATO. The WEU must in no way be subordinate to the European Council. It is not. We have avoided the danger of setting up defence structures which would compete with NATO.[7]

In these negotiations, we put forward a series of proposals designed to be of direct benefit to the European citizen. All of them were accepted. The Community has agreed to increase the accountability of European Community institutions; to strengthen the European Parliament's financial control over the Commission; to allow the European Parliament to investigate maladministration and to appoint a Community ombudsman accessible to all Community citizens; to build up the role of the Court of Auditors, which becomes an institution of the Community; and to ensure compliance with Community obligations by giving the European Court of Justice power to impose fines on Governments who sign directives but subsequently do not implement them.[8]

We wanted – and secured – a sensible enhancement of the role of the European Parliament. We did not accept the proposal made by other member states for a power of co-decision between the Parliament and the Council.

I also said then that we were prepared to consider some blocking power for the European Parliament. That has now been agreed. The treaty sets up, in a limited number of areas, a conciliation procedure where there is disagreement between the Council and Parliament. In the last analysis, the Parliament would be able to

---

7 Another serious error of judgment. The other members were plainly ready to abandon the Western European Union. Given the importance he attaches to it here, it is odd that he does not mention it at all in his memoirs.

8 Community, community, he clings to the name, though the treaty is to transform it into a union.

block a decision in those areas, but only if an absolute majority of its members turned out to vote the proposal down.

The House has been rightly concerned at the creeping extension of Community competence over the last few years. The Commission has often brought forward proposals using a dubious legal base, and the Council has found it difficult to halt that practice in the European Court. We have taken significant steps to deal with that problem.

First, the structure of the treaty puts the issues of foreign and security policy, interior and justice matters and defence policy beyond the reach of the Commission and the European Court.[9]

Secondly, the treaty itself embodies the vital principle of "subsidiarity", making it clear that the Community should only be involved in decisions which cannot more effectively be taken at national level.[10]

Thirdly, in some areas – notably health protection, educational exchanges, vocational training and culture – we have defined Community competence clearly for the first time. Fourthly, there will be no extension of Community competence in employer-employee relations – the so-called social area.

---

9   But for how long? They have all subsequently become Union competences after other treaties were agreed, suggesting that he seriously misjudged the forces behind 'the creeping extension of Community competence'.

10 He makes light of, indeed ignores, the vast expansion of the powers of the Commission authorized by this Treaty. It is doubtful whether the 'vital principle' of subsidiarity has ever been used to restrain the Commission or to allow national governments to retrieve powers from it. In his memoirs this 'vital principle' is mentioned only in passing.

11 But all the other members think there is a reason for the Union 'to get involved in employment legislation' and they also supported the massive extension of Community competence in transport, vocational training education, consumer protection, industrial policy, and culture. The UK was the exception. One of his achievements was to opt out of the Social Protocol or Chapter, and the new currency. One of his failings was to mislead to the House about just how isolated and at odds with other members the UK was.

[We] recognise the Community's social dimension... But there is no reason for the Community to get involved in employment legislation, which must be for each country to decide for itself.[11]

At British initiative, we committed ourselves at Maastricht to the further enlargement of the Community... [And we made commitments] to the successors of the Soviet Union, to respect the rights of minorities, to implement international agreements on arms control and nuclear non-proliferation...

Our role has been to put forward practical suggestions – and sometimes to rein in the larger ambitions of our partners. Where we believed their ideas would not work, we have put forward our own alternatives. Those can be found throughout this treaty. As with all international negotiations, there has been give and take between all 12 member states. But the process was one in which Britain has played a leading role, and the result is one in which we can clearly see the imprint of our views.

This is a treaty which safeguards and advances our national interests. It advances the interests of Europe as a whole. It opens up new ways of co-operating in Europe. It clarifies and contains the powers of the Commission.[12] It will allow the Community to develop in depth. It reaches out to other Europeans – the new democracies who want to share the benefits we already enjoy. It is a good agreement for Europe, and a good agreement for the United Kingdom. I commend it to the House.

A different view of Maastricht from the House of Lords

Two brief excerpts follow from the speeches of former prime minister, Margaret Thatcher, and of Lord Lawson in the Lords debate on an amend on the bill that,[13] in the words of Lord Blake, 'In plain language seeks to ensure that the Maastricht Treaty

---

12 This is a curious way of describing the vast extension of powers of the Commission.

13 *European Communities (Amendment) Bill,* HL Deb, 14 July 1993, vol 548 cc239-334.

takes effect only after a referendum has been established as to whether or not the people want it.' Margaret Thatcher made the following points:

> Some people say that Maastricht does not have a big constitutional issue attached to it. Let us look at what the treaty itself says: 'By this Treaty, the High Contracting Parties establish… a European Union… This Treaty marks a new stage in the process of creating an ever closer union among the peoples of Europe'. It creates the Union. It gives it all the structures of a sovereign state. That is why we have citizenship, European and monetary union, common defence policies, common foreign policy, and so on. It is something quite different. In addition, it adds many more powers which can be decided by qualified majority voting. One should be very careful before extending those powers, except for a specific purpose. With qualified majority voting, the Commission has the only power—monopoly power—of proposing legislation. No one else has it. Only the Commission can propose legislation. It can do it by a simple majority vote: nine votes to eight. It can bring forward something to go to the Council of Ministers. The Council of Ministers is under majority voting; and there are 111 other examples of areas in which majority voting can apply.

Some time later the former Chancellor, Lord Lawson, spoke. Midway into his speech he made the point below:

> Those who claim that the objective of the architects of the Maastricht Treaty is to replace the European Community of nation states by a single European superstate are clearly right. There is nothing disreputable about such an objective, although for my part, as a longstanding proponent of European unity, I believe it to be profoundly mistaken and, if it were ever to be imposed on the peoples of Europe, a blueprint for disaster. But I repeat: there is nothing disreputable about it. All that might perhaps be considered disreputable would be to deny that that is the objective of the architects of the Maastricht Treaty, since it manifestly is so.

Part Two

A peculiar form of government

4

Flying in the face of the global principle of political legitimacy

The primary principle of political legitimacy in the modern world is that those who make laws and give orders should be co-cultural with those who they expect to obey them. This is a principle that underpins every government but one in the modern world. It is the foundation of every democratic society. Indeed, the construction of a democratic polity will only begin after it is known that whoever might emerge as its rulers must be co-cultural with its citizens.

The most visible political apparatus in the modern world that hopes to resist this principle of political legitimacy is the European Union. This may, according to taste, be considered courageous and innovative, or foolhardy, absurd and dangerous, but it has most certainly been attempted with a blithe disregard for the forces that transformed the political structures of the world over the second half of the twentieth century and for those forces which have led to the formation of numerous new states in the twenty-first, and still threatens to either reshape and split many apparently secure and stable polities.

In the second half of the twentieth century this principle triumphed right across the globe, mainly because of the dismantling of colonial empires, followed by the break-up of the Soviet Union, which led to the formation of 15 new countries, and of Yugoslavia, which led to the formation of five countries. All of these new polities were founded on the co-cultural principle, though some of them were further divided when the people themselves had the opportunity to apply the principle, and to decide who exactly they were co-cultural with. Abkhazia and South Ossetia broke away from

Georgia, Montenegro and Kosovo from Serbia. Meanwhile, there were numerous other splits elsewhere in the world. Namibia split from South Africa, Eritrea from Ethiopia, Timor-Leste from Indonesia, and South Sudan from Sudan. We may yet see new boundaries based on this principle emerge from the rubble and slaughter in Syria.

Seemingly secure, stable and relatively long-established states such as Canada, China, Spain and the United Kingdom were not immune from the same forces, as aggrieved sections of their populations questioned the legitimacy of their national governments. This was not because of any particular failings of governance on their part, though the aggrieved naturally prepared lists of grievances, but simply because those who made the laws and exercised power over them were not thought, in one way or another, to share their culture to an acceptable degree.

The EU stands firmly against the principle by which the rest of the world lives. They have done so because of a distinctive interpretation of Europe's history, or at least of that part of Europe to which the founding countries belonged. It is emblazoned on the wall of the visitor centre of the European Parliament.[1]

Everywhere else in the world where the co-cultural principle of political authority has triumphed, it has been supported, to varying degrees, by popular movements. When the European Union asserted its unique principle of political authority, by contrast, there was not the least indication of any kind of popular or mass movement in support of a new supranational construct that would curtail their existing national governments or boundaries. As the principle has been advanced and institutionalized, most indicators or expressions of popular feeling suggest considerable and growing resistance towards the idea.

---

1   'National sovereignty is the root cause of the most crying evils of our times… and of the steady march of humanity back to tragic disaster and barbarism… The only final remedy for this supreme and catastrophic evil of our time is a federal union of the peoples…'

Quoted in the European Parliament Visitor Centre. From: P. Kerr, 'The Ending of Armageddon', 11th Marquess of Lothian, British Ambassador to the United States, on the failure of the League of Nations to halt the Second World War, 26 June 1939.

From the very beginning, this new form of government has been a project of European elites. Many members of these elites are themselves rather trans-national or supranational, equally at ease in meeting other members of the European elite in gatherings in Brussels, other capital cities and in their own country. They may well therefore be tempted to see themselves as the pioneers and exemplars of a brave new pan-European culture. While those who resist it, and insist that their laws be made by their fellow countrymen and women, applied by courts and judges of their own country, must therefore seem to be simply ill-informed, uneducated or misled by irresponsible, populist politicians.

The main question is whether such a unique system of political authority, so at odds with the rest of the world, will continue to work? And in particular, will it continue to work for the UK?

The experience of the rest of the world is unanimous and says it won't, and no other group of countries is conducting or contemplating such an experiment.

5
A synthetic civil society

In English-speaking countries the essential preliminary to democratic government has been an active civil society consisting of groups formed spontaneously and voluntarily to pursue some common interest. This could be religious, economic, professional, charitable, recreational, educational or moral.

Most of these groups had no initial political interests. Their only concern was to organize and govern themselves in the manner they thought best enabled them to fulfil their primary function, and they only became political when some attempt was made to interfere with their freedom of action. In this apolitical and even selfish manner, civil society became the first defender of the liberties of the English people. These voluntary institutions also taught the manners of democratic elections, governance, debate and rule making, how to deliberate and decide despite disagreements, and then act. In so doing, they were constructing the infrastructure of a democracy under the rule of law.[1]

In time they were joined by associations whose aims were to raise public awareness of some political or moral issue or a social problem they considered important, and sought to use their collective voices to bring pressure on members of parliament to bring about some legislative reform. Still later they were joined by political parties which selected and supported candidates for elective office which, when organized nationally, supported or sought to change the government of the country.

---

1 The different, and somewhat chequered, history of civil society in France, Germany, Italy, Portugal, The Netherlands and Belgium is described in N. Bermeo and P. Nord, *Civil Society before Democracy: Lessons from Nineteenth Century Europe*, Maryland, Lanham, 2000.

Under late British imperial rule, colonies' civil societies grew and developed the infrastructure of representative government. This is why one American scholar seeking to find all the possible social, political and economic prerequisites and correlates of democratic government around the world found that 'recent statistical analyses of the aggregate correlates of political regimes have indicated that having once been a British colony is the variable most highly correlated with democracy'.[2]

The supra-national government of the EU has no foundation in civil society. The elite who created the original European Community were primarily concerned with creating an executive arm of government that might exercise supranational authority, which they first accomplished by creating the High Authority of the European Coal and Steel Community in 1951. After the Treaty of Rome in 1957, it became the European Commission, which has remained the central pillar of European government to this day.

Although the elite were not particularly concerned that its supranational institutions should be democratically accountable, they realised from the beginning that if it was to survive, it would require some democratic legitimation beyond that indirectly brought to it by the elected heads of government in the periodic meetings of the European Council and Council of Ministers.

The Treaty of Rome in 1957 therefore provided for an Assembly to which elected members of national parliaments were nominated by their governments, and where debates on Community issues would occur, as if it were a European Parliament, though with no legislative powers. The Treaty also created the European Economic and Social Committee (EESC) to serve as a bridge between Europe and civil society, so that the voices of employers, employees and other organized interests might be heard by the Commission. The Assembly was later renamed a Parliament and in 1979 became directly elected, though it still has no power to initiate legislation. The EESC remained as a bridge even if few came across it.

The Commission remained in the dominant position that it had been placed in by the founding fathers and accumulated

---

2   S.M. Lipset et al., 'A Comparative Analysis of the Social Requisites of Democracy', *International Social Science Journal*, vol. 45, 1993, pp. 155-175.

more and more powers, especially after the Maastricht Treaty of 1992. Commissioners were not drawn from the Parliament, nor routinely accountable to it, but nominated by their governments, and assigned their portfolios by the President, and then approved en bloc by the Parliament. The President of the Commission only required the majority approval of the heads of the member governments until 2014 when majority approval of the members of the European Parliament was also required.

Civil society had taken no part whatever in the construction of this governmental apparatus, since there were hardly any professional, trade, religious, educational, recreational or charitable associations which drew their support and membership from across several member countries, and no pan-EU pressure groups or parties. Europe's civil societies remained stubbornly national.

This only became of interest to the European Commission in the years after the Maastricht Treaty. The Community became a Union and the foundations were laid for the creation of the new European superstate, and it was hoped it might be a democratic one. Turnout in EU elections continued to decline, favoured policies were rejected in referendums, and there were unmistakeable signs of falling popular support in polls including Eurobarometer, and of increasingly organized and popular euroscepticism.

The Commission then became increasingly interested in educating its citizens in the virtues of European integration, and in creating the NGOs and associations of an organized pan-European civil society that had failed to emerge spontaneously. In a discussion paper in 2000, Commission President Romano Prodi and Vice President Neil Kinnock argued that NGOs would help to promote 'European integration in a practical way and often at grassroots level... and their networks and national members can serve as additional channels for the Commission to ensure that information on the European Union and EU policies reaches a wide audience.'[3]

In contrast with the evolution of democracy in English-speaking democracies, the new European polity has evolved backwards, with

---

3   R. Prodi and N. Kinnock, 'The Commission and Non-Governmental Organisations: Building a Stronger Partnership', Commission Discussion Paper, 2000, Available from: http://ec.europa.eu/transparency/civil_society/ngo/docs/communication_en.pdf

an executive and court preceding a legislature, which is still nominal, with civil society very much an afterthought, owing its existence largely to the sponsorship and financial support of the executive branch of government. It cannot therefore perform quite the same functions as the voluntarily and spontaneously organized civil societies of the English-speaking world. They felt free to inform, monitor, scold, shame or challenge elected and appointed state officials. The synthetic civil society of Brussels version is, as its sponsors intended, rather better at receiving information from the Commission. A Commission white paper in 2001 proposed greater co-operation between European Commission & NGOs to get citizens more actively involved in achieving the Union's objectives.[4]

Some of the organized interests in this emergent pan-European civil society are authentic, spontaneous, self-financed representatives of their own interests, most notably the multi-national companies subject to European Commission regulation. After some initial hesitation, they were followed by trade unions whose symbolic international affiliations go back to the early twentieth century. They were at last able to live up to their long-proclaimed, and long-ignored, internationalist ideals as fellow lobbyists for their members in Brussels. A few religious associations also have authentically pan-European affiliations which long precede everyone else's.

There are, however, a host of other political, environmental and recreational lobbies, pressure groups and charitable associations who appear to owe their existence entirely to the goodwill and the funding of the Commission.[5] Some examples have been taken from the breakdown of the 2002 EU budget below:

- Our Europe Association – A study and research group which sponsors and organises seminars on European issues. Their funding was €600,000.

---

4   European Commission, European Governance: A White Paper, COM (2001) 428, Brussels, 2001, p. 15, Available from: http://aei.pitt.edu/1188/1/european _governance_wp_COM_2001_428.pdf.
5   M. Ball et al., 'Federalist Thought Control: The Brussels Propaganda Machine', Bruges Group, June 2002, http://www.brugesgroup.com/media-centre/pa-pers/8-papers/786-federalist-thought-control-the-brussels-propaganda-machine

- European Union Youth Forum – A non-profit international association that acts as a political platform to facilitate and stimulate their participation in the European decision-making process. It lobbies the EU on issues affecting young people by organising conferences and other activities. Their funding was €2,000,000.

- Journalists in Europe – This organisation runs an annual training programme for young journalists from around the world, focussing on the EU and on political, economic and social developments in Europe. Their funding was €250,000.

- European Women's Lobby – An organisation which lobbies the EU on issues of concern to women in Europe and is considered an essential adjunct to EU measures in support of women. Their funding was €650,000.

There are in total some 250 odd recipients in the year. The serious-engaged pressure groups, like those listed, receive the large five or six-figure grants. Budget line B3-500 allocated €7 million to trans-European political parties which 'contribute to forming European awareness'. However, there is also a large tail of other recreational associations such as orchestras, artist co-operatives, operatic groups, conscientious objectors, pharmaceutical, engineering and other student groups, museums and sports clubs who receive grants of under €10,000 with no apparent political goals. At first sight therefore, funding leaves the impression of a representative cross-section of civil society, except that it appears to be trans-national in some respect.

A researcher from the Institute of Economic Affairs, Christopher Snowdon, conducted an investigation into EU communications, activities and funding. He found those receiving the larger grants tend to be of the centre-left politically and use a distinctive vocabulary of 'stakeholders', 'sustainability', 'capacity building', 'active citizenship', 'awareness' and 'identity'. The word 'subsidiarity' is not commonly used. Snowdon's data on the proportion of their income from the European Commission suggests many of them would not exist were it not for the EU. The European Women's Lobby was granted €911,677 which was 83 per cent of their income for the year, and the European Network

Against Racism €1,081,164, 81 per cent of that year's income. As these examples indicate, funding recipients often take the form of umbrella organizations for authentic national societies. Some effort is made to reach the professionals of such societies by supporting the Euclid Network and the European Council for Non-Profit Organisations (CEDAG), which was granted €120,000, 80 per cent of their annual income.[6]

Some of the funding promotes worthy causes that have little popular support, such as the homeless, the disabled, foreign aid, fat taxes or minimum alcohol pricing, and a good number support the EU's own environmental and climate change agenda. However, despite appearances, this is not quite a random and representative cross-section of civil society, since none of them have ever shown any sign of doubting or questioning the EU's direction of travel, the case for closer European integration, more EU regulation or larger EU budgets. Snowdon, not unreasonably, dubs them 'sock puppets'.[7]

Thus the European Commission and the European Parliament have finally been joined by a civil society of sorts, carefully selected organised interests who can be relied on to say what the Commission wants to hear, and at times even to protest against it. Even then they only demand that a policy on which the Commission has already embarked upon should be pursued with more vigour and determination, and with more funds.

There is, however, a price to be paid. In English-speaking countries, voluntary associations monitor, inform, warn, pester and challenge governments, and civil society counter-balances the power of government. It makes it difficult for elected governments to ignore public opinion for long. The sock puppets surrounding EU government increase the power of the Commission and make it rather easier for it to ignore public opinion.

---

6   C. Snowdon, *Euro Puppets: The European Commission's remaking of civil society*, Discussion Paper No. 45, IEA, 2013, p.23, Available from: http://www.iea.org.uk/sites/default/files/publications/files/DPaper_Euro%20Puppets_amended_web%202014%20update.pdf

7   Snowdon has also documented contemporary home-grown versions in the UK, so it is a matter of degree not of kind.
C. Snowdon, *Sock Puppets, How the government lobbies itself and why*, Discussion paper No.39, IEA, 2012, Available from: http://www.iea.org.uk/sites/default/files/publications/files/DP_Sock%20Puppets_redesigned.pdf

6

Intensive self-promotion

In the previous chapter, we saw how the governmental institutions of the EU have been surrounded by a civil society of a peculiar sort. Alongside well-organized multinational firms, trade union federations with offices and professional staffs, and a host of accounting, legal and public relations consultancies, there is a third sector of civil society which has been largely constructed by the Commission itself.

All three types are listed, annually, in print and online, in stakeholder.eu: the directory for Brussels. The Integrity Watch website of Transparency International EU is useful for those who want to learn about what these organized lobbies and interests are doing in Brussels, their funding, and their meetings with EU Commissioners, director-generals and other senior officials.[1] It was launched in October 2014 and, though still under development, this website promises a significant advance in making the European Commission more accountable.

The European Commission sometimes justifies financial support for this third sector on the grounds that they counterbalance already well-organized and funded corporate interests. In one respect, however, they are not a counter-balance at all, but a strong reinforcement: all three sectors sympathize with increased centralization and ever closer union of member countries.

If the ever closer union was completely fulfilled, and all trading standards across the Union were harmonized to the point of complete uniformity, large multinationals would, it seems safe to say, be delighted. Standardization, uniformity and centralization also has a strong appeal to trade unions, especially when it can be

---

1   http://www.integritywatch.eu/about.html

used to outflank and embarrass a national government that is bent on unwelcome measures against some aspect of union activity. Subsidiarity can be a real nuisance to both organized business and trade unions. Moreover, it seems unlikely either group would be in favour of cutting the EU budget since they are both regular recipients of European Commission grants.[2] When the sock puppets, who are also on the EU payroll, urge more centralization, European civil society must appear from Brussels at least to be consistent supporters of further integration even though they disagree about the merits of particular policies.

Unfortunately, whenever the wider grass roots of member countries have been able to express their views via elections, referendums, opinion polls, or through newly-organised political parties, they have often proved less than enthusiastic, or even hostile to the whole idea of further European integration, irrespective of the merits of any particular policy.

Since Maastricht, one or other of these signs of disaffection in the wider civil societies of member countries has frequently recurred. However, when faced with them, the Commission and Parliament have responded not by reconsidering their policies or by re-assessing the merits of inter-governmentalism and subsidiarity, but by criticising themselves for failing to communicate effectively the benefits of European integration, as if the only reason people could disagree with the goal of further integration was that they were ill-informed, or perhaps distracted and misled, by irresponsible media reports or xenophobic populist politicians.

The favoured solution therefore has been for the Parliament and Commission to redouble their efforts to inform citizens of the past and future benefits of the integration, and therefore to increase the budgets devoted to promoting European awareness and spelling out the past and future benefits of ever closer union in a simple, straightforward and convincing manner.

The strategy of persuading the population, in particular children, students and the so-called 'opinion multipliers', became a high priority within the Parliament and the Commission for many

---

2   EU Transparency Register, available at ec.europa.eu/transparencyregister/public/homepage.do

years, and the subject of intensive analysis and review in a succession of influential parliamentary reports, notably:

- The 1985 Adonnino Report[3] favoured further steps to promote an EU identity. EU branded driving licences and passports should be followed by a flag, an anthem, citizenship, an ombudsman and EU postage stamps, all of which, bar postage stamps, later came to pass.

- The 1993 de Clercq Report[4] is perhaps the most explicitly informed by marketing techniques and vocabulary. It wanted EU communication to evoke 'the maternal care of Europa for all her children'. Specifically, it hoped to personalize the advantages of the EU for women 'since they are the most receptive of receivers and the more active of the relays'. Further still it hoped to make youth 'a primary target for persuasion and conviction... since it is strategically wise to go where resistance is least' but also to target the 'particularly relevant multipliers', of journalists, editors and programme directors.

- The 1998 Pex Report[5] sought to promote 'awareness of the European citizenship and the commitment of young people to the development of the Union', as well as 'help to fight for respect for human rights and to combat racism, nationalism, anti-Semitism and xenophobia' by transnational voluntary service.

These were followed by a succession of Commission white papers and action plans giving operational details and indicating the progressively increasing emphasis on communication as described in the European Commission Information Providers Guide. [6] There were two Commission white papers in 2001 which discussed how communication might 'generate a sense of belonging to Europe' and help policy makers stay in touch with public opinion. In an action plan from 2005 communication was formally declared a strategic objective of the EU and was followed by further plans

---

3 http://aei.pitt.edu/992/1/andonnino_report_peoples_europe.pdf
4 http://aei.pitt.edu/29870/1/DE_CLERCQ_REPORT_INFO._COMM._POLI-CY.pdf
5 http://www.europarl.europa.eu/sides/getDoc.do?type=REPORT&reference=A4-1998-0115&language=EN
6 http://ec.europa.eu/ipg/basics/policy/index_en.htm

and papers in 2007, 2011 and 2012, refining operational details to support this strategic objective.

As a result, all Directorates General, EU civil service departments, not just the Directorate General of Communication, gave a great deal of careful attention to the presentation of their work, made use of every contemporary form of advertisement and communication, and also made extraordinarily precise plans of when, how, and to whom they intend to speak and convince.

The example given below is taken from a 2014 plan of the Directorate-General for Regional and Urban Policy,[7] whose main responsibility is the distribution of the EU's Structural and Investment funds. This plan marked the start of the new seven year budgetary period, 2014-2020. It identifies priority themes, countries (the UK being deemed one because of its relatively low levels of awareness) and audiences. It then goes on to specify the 'short and simple' messages that will be given to each of its five audiences: core stakeholders, opinion leaders, regional and local media, beneficiaries, and young people. The message for young people will tell them that the EU 'invests in the future of your region', 'helps to create jobs', and that 'you may be eligible for funding'. Older people are not a priority audience.

An excerpt from a 2014 plan of the Directorate-General for Regional and Urban Policy is given below:

> Traditionally, REGIO's primary audience has been the "core stakeholders" that are directly or indirectly involved in the implementation of Operational Programmes (managing authorities, regional and local administrations, economic and social partners, civil society...).
>
> Through its events, communication products and media outreach, REGIO also aims to reach "opinion leaders" who take an interest in regional economic development (Brussels-based journalists, other EU institutions, academics and researchers, teachers, political parties, think tanks, international organisations).

---

7 http://ec.europa.eu/regional_policy/sources/dgs/complan_2014.pdf

While continuing to serve these audiences in 2014, REGIO will aim to raise the profile of Cohesion Policy by developing specific communication activities and tools that target the following groups and multipliers:

- Regional and local media (people's top source of information about regional policy, according to the Eurobarometer survey)

- Beneficiaries of EU funding (potentially the most credible ambassadors for the policy, if we can provide them with opportunities to share their stories)

- Young people (whose future job prospects and quality of life will be impacted by EU investments)

It then spells out how various 'channels and tools' are to be used: internet and social media; press and media relations, including invitations to accompany the Commissioner on trips to various regions; the diary of conferences, seminars, awards and events for the year; a long list of publications and 'information products' including posters, PowerPoint presentations, videos, working papers for academics and stakeholder audiences; a cartoon book for young people; the use of 'documentation centres of European Universities'; contributions to the Euronews TV series called 'Real Economy'; developing its own team of specialist Team Europe speakers; and mobilizing its own staff as ambassadors.

At the end of the plan it gives 50 performance indicators, with the results for 2013 beside the targets for 2014. In 2013, for example, there were 15 new videos added to the InfoRegio website, while the goal for 2014 was 30. There were 1,467 tweets sent in 2013, so in 2014 their goal was 1,500. There were 33 articles, forewords and interviews written in the name of the Commissioner, so in 2014 their aim was 50. There were 11 Euronews programmes produced in 2013. In 2014 their plan was for 13, and the audience grew from 5.5 million to 6 million.

It is difficult to convey the full scale of this effort across all the directorates and the EU in a short note. Some of the better-known channels and tools will be described below, and conclude with estimates of the communications effort's costs.

A few of the better-known 'channels and tools'

1. Monnet professors, networks and actions

Apart from the institutions that the European Commission owns and manages, like the College of Europe and European Institute in Florence, universities are involved in the EU's information and communication strategy in three ways. First, by Jean Monnet professorships, second, by establishing three-year networks of Jean Monnet European Centres of Excellence, that is university level institutions recognized by the European Commission for high quality research and teaching topics related to European integration, and third, by funding Jean Monnet projects or actions, meaning teaching modules or research projects which 'deal specifically and entirely with the issue of European integration.'

The professorships were started in 1989 and are jointly funded with the host university. In 2009, there were 1,500 Monnet professorships worldwide. There is no annual report on their activities or bibliography of their publications.

They appear to be selected by academic merit and to respect academic freedom. However, when one considers their responsibilities set out on the EU website,[8] it is clear that they also have functions which are not dissimilar to that of Captain Euro and other channels and tools of the EU's information and communication strategy. 'They are supposed', it says:

- To publish at least one book within the University Press during the grant period. The grant will cover part of the publication and, if need be, part of the translation costs.

- Participate in dissemination and information events at European and national level.

- Organise events (lectures, seminars, workshops) with policy makers at a national, regional and local level, as well as with organised civil society and schools.

- Disseminate the results of their activities via the organisation of seminars or lectures geared and adapted to general public and civil society representatives.

---

8 http://eupa.org.mt/erasmus-programme/jean-monnet-activities/jean-monn-et-chairs/

- Network with other Jean Monnet Chairs, academic modules, centres of excellence, label holders and supported Institutions.

- Apply Open Education Resources, publish the summaries, content and schedule of their activities as well as the expected outcomes.

Monet networks have a duration of three years and those in Europe require the participation of universities in three different countries. In 2015, 15 UK universities were designated Centres of Excellence, whilst the US had 22, and the rest of Europe had only ten.[9]

Monnet actions are intended to promote excellence in teaching and research in the field of European studies worldwide. This 'discipline', as the European Commission describes it, places 'particular emphasis on the European integration process... [and] also covers the role of the EU in a globalized world and in promoting an active European citizenship and dialogue between people and cultures.'[10]

2. Town twinning

This is intended to show the benefits of European integration at a local level, and to forge a European identity. Over past years towns and cities in the UK have, however, sometimes veered off script and displayed a rather global vision, and for a mixture of reasons have chosen to twin with towns in Nicaragua or Africa or the United States or even China.[11] Moreover, the spontaneous and voluntary ties formed through the Commonwealth Local Government Good Practice Forum appear to be of more practical value than EU sponsored efforts.[12]

3. The 'opinion multipliers'
The European Journalism Centre
Located in Maastricht, the European Journalism Centre describes itself as an independent, non-profit centre which provides 'services for journalists and other media professionals at all career stages'.

---

9   http://www3.ul.ie/~ceuros/jeanmonnet_centresofexcellence.htm
10   http://ec.europa.eu/education/opportunities/jean-monnet/index_en.htm
11   Clarke N (2011) 'Globalising care? Town twinning in Britain since 1945', Geoforum 42: 115-125 http://eprints.soton.ac.uk/169119/1/Globalising_care_F AVPPR.pdf
12   http://thecommonwealth.org/organisation/commonwealth-local-government-forum-clgf

It also has a range of 'grant based activities'. The latter appear to be largely or wholly European Commission funded. However, since it does not publish its accounts the significance of the European Commission's involvement in its varied activity areas (such as 'dissemination of European research activities' and 'web-based resources and services for journalists, including Brussels correspondents', and 'media watch') cannot be assessed. Nor can we say how far its involvement in various events, seminars, conferences, field trips and awards for journalists have an EU inspired mission. Some awards are rather more explicit. The Salvador de Madariaga Prize for European Journalism in Spain recognises the personal work of journalists from the Spanish media (written press, radio and television), which have helped increase awareness of European integration and European policies.

Troll Patrols

In 2013, *The Daily Telegraph* obtained a confidential document of the administrative bureau of the European Parliament entitled, 'Political guidelines for the institutional information and communication campaign.'[13] It described a plan to conduct 'qualitative media analysis' and 'public opinion monitoring tools', in particular in countries that have experienced a surge in euroscepticism.

'Parliament's institutional communicators must' the guidelines said, 'have the ability to monitor public conversation and sentiment on the ground and in real time, to understand "trending topics" and have the capacity to react quickly, in a targeted and relevant manner, to join in and influence the conversation, for example, by providing facts and figures to deconstructing myths.' Parliament officials were to be trained for this work.

4. Captain Euro, 'kick-starting the new European enlightenment'

Captain Euro is a comic superhero. Created in 1999 because, according to its creator, 'there were no attractive popular European culture icons' and because 'the EU did not have the right narrative to help people identify with Europe'. Initially he was intended to promote the euro, but he now has a wider mission to 'help combat public scepticism and enlighten the public of the merits of a united

---

13 http://www.telegraph.co.uk/news/worldnews/europe/eu/9845442/EU-to-set-up-euro-election-troll-patrol-to-tackle-Eurosceptic-surge.html

Europe.'[14] He is a Superman look-a-like and has a blond female assistant, Europa. They do battle with Eurosceptic terrorists led by the sinister Dr. D. Vider, whose current master plan is Brexit, and broadcasts such messages as:

> Across Europe we are wasting our time with national political infighting, while other blocs are preparing for global domination... Join me in my mission.

The captain is part of Brand EU, 'the independent brand marketing think tank of the EU' which is working 'to re-invent the EU's brand vision & kick-start the new European enlightenment. Brand EU is generating a people movement for the millions that believe in European Unity and want to engage actively to innovate and reinvent Brand Europe.'[15]

5. Euronews

Euronews was created in 1993 by a group of ten European public broadcasters to present information from a European perspective. Its major shareholder (53%) is an Egyptian businessman but the original ten and a further 13 broadcasters are also co-owners. It is based in Lyon. The CEO is French, and the Executive Board and Management Committee are in the main French. It is available in 170 million European households, 350 million worldwide, by cable, satellite and terrestrial TV and by multimedia platforms and apps.

It clearly enjoys an amiable working relationship with the Commission, from whom it receives regular payments, whether for specific services or as a subsidy. The European Commission seems to look on it as a sympathetic and supportive outlet.

How much does it all cost?

1. The 2008 estimate of €2.4bn: out-spending Coca Cola

More than seven years ago, Open Europe investigated the EU's self-promotion expenditures.[16] After a detailed breakdown of

---

14   www.captain-euro.com

15   www.brandeu.eu

16   Open Europe "The Hard Sell: EU Communication Policy and the Campaign for Hearts and Minds", Research by Lee Rotherham and Lorraine Mullally, London, 2008. https://ia600504.us.archive.org/10/items/TheHardSell/TheHardSell.pdf

every line of the EU budget in 2008, it concluded that in that year this expenditure totalled €2.4bn. This figure includes only those budget lines which referred to the Information & Communication strategy of the European Commission which explicitly indicate expenditures 'for fostering European citizenship or promoting a common European culture.' It should therefore be regarded, the authors say, 'as an absolute minimum amount'.

Many other similar expenditures are, they point out, 'hidden deep inside the EU budget', but since they were ostensibly for another purpose, they were excluded. Most importantly, the €2.4bn figure did not include the funding to the civil society organizations mentioned in the previous chapter which are assumed to have political or charitable functions.

To give some idea of the scale of this self-promotion budget, they pointed out that €2.4bn is larger than the total global advertising spending of Coca Cola. In the same year, the UK government 'spent around £190 million on advertising in press, TV, radio and digital media advertising, out of the Central Office of Information's £392 million budget.'[17]

2. The 2014 estimate of €3.9bn: more than is spent on trade negotiations and disputes

In 2014, Business for Britain conducted a similar study using exactly the same methodology. It also distinguished three categories of European Commission spending: primary, where the primary use of the funds is for self-promotion which totalled €664 million; secondary, where the allocated amount is to be spent on both EU promotional activities and other initiatives (€2.1bn), and tertiary, where some of the allocated amount may be used for self-promotion (€1.1bn).[18] This comes to €3.9bn if we take the maximum assumptions.

To illustrate how secondary and tertiary budgets may be used for promotional spending, it was pointed out that funding for EU

---

17 COI annual report http://www.coi.gov.uk/documents/coi-annualreport2007-8.pdf See also *Telegraph*, 10 November 2008

18 'How much does the EU spend on promoting itself?' BfB Briefing Note 10 http://forbritain.org/propagandapaper.pdf

comic books, so-called 'Brussels Beanos', which had attracted some attention at the time, did not come from a primary budget.

The budget of the Directorate-General for Communication in 2016 was €204 million. It employed 1,016 people, and had a bigger budget and larger number of employees than the Directorate General for Trade, which had 607 staff and a budget of €107 million.[19]

---

19   Official Journal of the European Union, Vol.59, February 2016

Staff figure from http://ec.europa.eu/civil_service/docs/europa_sp2_bs_dist_staff_en.pdf European Commission, Statistical Bulletin, 01/02/2016

7

The chancelleries of Europe devise a government

Which of the world's great democracies have been created by diplomats?

The foreign offices of Europe create a government

The government of the European Union has emerged from successive diplomatic negotiations rather than from constitutional conventions, or by piecemeal adaptation of pre-existing inter-governmental institutions. The powers and jurisdictions of its various institutions and their relationships with one another have been defined by treaties. They can only be changed in any significant way by another treaty.

Diplomatic negotiations have certain characteristics which distinguish them from the meetings, assemblies and debates which might be expected to precede the creation of democratic governmental institutions. They are conducted in secrecy until their conclusion, not infrequently involving some deceit, and no wider or popular participation can influence the course of negotiations. Because they are conducted in secret without minutes for subsequent publication, the national representatives who participate in them become de facto plenipotentiaries. They emerge to provide their own inevitably self-serving interpretations of the concessions made and the rival interests satisfied, which none of those they claim to represent can contest. They are only held accountable by the results, by the terms of the treaty they have negotiated. They can, however, interpret these rather freely, and limit further debate since a treaty is a *fait accompli*, which cannot be amended. They must either be ratified or rejected.

For the most part, the successive treaties that have created the EU's governmental institutions have been ratified by parliamentary rather than popular votes. As a result, they have received a democratic mandate which complies with the formal practice of most member governments, in regard to the ratification of treaties which define future relationships with foreign powers. These EU treaties are, however, rather different since they are negotiating fundamental changes to their own form of government, limiting the sovereignty of their own parliament by creating institutions that may override it or assume functions which it previously performed. These treaties thereby permanently disenfranchise their own electorates in certain respects, since they subject them to a supranational government which they are effectively powerless to change. This kind of treaty would seem to deserve something more than ratification by a whipped parliamentary elite if democracy is to mean more than periodic elections.

A few member states recognize that fact, and have not allowed these EU treaties to be ratified by parliamentary votes alone, and have required them to have a wider popular and fully democratic ratification. This has on occasion brought this method of creating government institutions by diplomatic negotiations to a halt. After two such occasions, when the Danes voted no to the euro in September 2000 and when the Irish initially voted against the Nice Treaty in June 2001, in the face of steadily declining turnout in European elections, the EU heads of government seemed to recognize that something was wrong with the institutions they had created. At Laeken in 2001, they formally declared that European institutions 'must be brought closer to the citizens' and proposed a Convention on the Future of Europe, consisting of ministers and representatives of national parliaments who would 'define the powers of the Union and member states' and 'create more democracy, transparency and efficiency'.

Launching a democracy

In the event, the Convention took upon itself to write a European Constitution, which gave the Union its own legal personality, redefined and reinforced the provisions of previous treaties, increased the powers of the Commission in a number of ways and emphasized the primacy of Union law over that of the member states. They also incorporated a Charter of Fundamental Rights, and declined to return any powers to member states.[1]

In October 2002, this Convention produced a draft constitution though, according to one observer, 'it was never clear where it came from or who had drafted it.'[2] Given its title, ambition and scope, many member states decided that this could not be ratified as just another EU treaty. There was therefore the prospect of a Union-wide test of the democratic legitimacy not simply of the proposed constitution, but also, since it incorporated past treaties, a retrospective test of the institutions which had been created by diplomatic negotiations over the preceding thirty years or more. In February 2005, a referendum in Spain accepted it, but in May it was decisively rejected by the people of France and in June by the Dutch. In the UK the Blair government then cancelled the proposed referendum.

Reverting to the method they trust

This setback prompted a long 'period of reflection',[3] after which, guided by a nominated 'wise group of politicians and officials'[4] consisting of past members of the EU elite, European leaders decided to repackage the substance of the constitution as a treaty, and thereby avoid any more referendums about its substance. The British Prime Minister, Tony Blair, welcomed this subterfuge and argued that, since it was now called a treaty, there would be no need for a referendum in the UK. The constitution duly appeared as the Treaty of Lisbon and was ratified by the UK parliament in 2008.

---

1   Its proceedings have been described by two participants. G. Stuart, *The Making Of Europe's Constitution*, Fabian Society, Norwich, Crowes complete print, 2003, p. 109-126, Available from: https://www.fabians.org.uk/wp-content/uploads/2012/04/TheMakingOfEuropesConstitution.pdf

2   D. Heathcoat-Amory, *Confessions of a Eurosceptic*, Barnsley, Pen & Sword Books Ltd, 2012, P. 119.

3   P. Wintour, 'EU scraps timetable for ratifying constitution', *The Guardian*, 17 June 2005, http://www.theguardian.com/politics/2005/jun/17/eu.politics, (accessed 20 April 2016).

4   H. Mahony, 'Select group of politicians to tackle EU constitution', *EUobserver*, 28 September 2006, https://euobserver.com/institutional/22527, (accessed 20 April 2016).

The Treaty of Lisbon definitively demonstrates that diplomatic negotiations, the treaties which conclude them and the parliamentary processes which ratify them, provide European political elites with an alternative means of constructing and developing governmental institutions for the people of Europe without their participation in the process. The failed attempt to ratify the constitution electorally is a landmark. However, the Union will continue to develop, amend and extend its governmental institutions by diplomatic negotiations and treaties for the foreseeable future, avoiding the participation of the people whenever it is able to do so.

A number of contemporary polities mimic democratic forms of government, and the EU has cleverly defined its own imitation by adapting traditional methods of conducting relationships between states, defining a relationship between this new state and its citizens while endeavouring to replace in many respects the authentic democracies of its member states. It is a *tour de force* that never confronts democratic principles, and circumvents them whenever it can. Democratic states are defined less by force of arms or treaties than by a daily tacit plebiscite of their citizens who accept the authority it exercises over them. The authority of this new EU state has, by contrast, been defined over generations by diplomatic elites who claim to speak in the name of their own people, but have been reluctant to ask them to confirm what they have done in their name.

The European Union's governmental institutions are necessarily far removed from its citizens, its activities are conducted in a language foreign to most of it's citizens, by leaders who are rarely fellow nationals, and it has demonstrably failed over many years to pursue policies which have improved their livelihoods. The institutions therefore seem destined to live for a very long time with a low degree of democratic legitimacy, except that which they can borrow from the governments of their member states, probably with a body of opinion in many member countries that will permanently refuse to accept its legitimacy.

One should not be too surprised by this. The founders of the European Union were not endeavouring to create a democratic form of government. They had other goals: to prevent a resurgence of national rivalries and another war in Europe, and to unite so that it could resume what they thought was Europe's rightful place in world politics, alongside the then superpowers of the United States and Soviet Russia. The institutions they created had no particular democratic mission. They had witnessed democratic mandates given to Hitler and Mussolini and wanted a form of government that could override national democratic governments. They took no pains to check or counter-balance the executive arm of the first supra-national government they created: the High Authority of the European Coal and Steel Community in 1952, which morphed into the European Commission in 1958. They were indifferent to the powers that the permanent career officials of their own secretariat would inevitably accumulate from the centre of the communication network of member countries, organizing their own meetings, setting their own agendas, left to interpret and implement their decisions, and to greet their successors when their term of office came to an end.

Declaration of the rebels at the Constitutional Convention 2003

A minority of members were dissatisfied with the way the constitutional Convention conducted its business, and its conclusions. They organized themselves as the Democracy Forum and after the convention had published its draft constitution issued this press release.[5] They later issued a minority report:

> As members of the Convention on the Future of Europe, we cannot endorse the draft European Constitution as presented to the European Council. It does not meet the requirements of the Laeken Declaration of December 2001, which set up the Convention and established its terms of reference.
>
> Laeken describes the Union as *"behaving too bureaucratically"*.

---

5   Recorded in L. Rotherham, *Plan B for Europe*, the Bruges Group. pp. 67–68, Available from: http://www.brugesgroup.com/images/issues/civil_liberties/plan_b_for_europe_lost_opportunities_in_the_eu_constitution_debate_pdf.pdf (accessed 23/05/2015).

The draft Constitution fails to address the 97,000 pages of the acquis communautaire, and proposes a new legal instrument, the 'Non Legislative Act', whereby the Commission can pass binding laws.

Laeken says *"the Union must be brought closer to its citizens"*.

The transfer of more decision-making from member states to the Union, concerning criminal justice matters and new areas of domestic policy, will make the Union more remote.

Laeken adds that *"the division of competences be made more transparent"*.

But the new category of 'shared competences' gives no assurance about how power is to be shared, particularly as member states will be forbidden to legislate in these areas if the Union decides to act.

Laeken calls for the *"European institutions to be less unwieldy and rigid"*.

But the Constitution gives more power to all the existing EU institutions and creates a Europe of Presidents, with more jobs for politicians and less influence for the people.

Laeken highlights the importance of national parliaments, and the Nice Treaty *"stressed the need to examine their role in European integration"*.

National Parliaments lose influence relative to the Commission and the European Parliament. Their proposed new role in 'ensuring' compliance with the subsidiarity principle is in reality no more than a request which the Commission can ignore.

Laeken calls for *"more transparency and efficiency"* in the Union.

The Constitution concentrates more executive and budgetary power in the very EU institutions which have been the subject of repeated and continuing scandals over mismanagement, waste and fraud.

Laeken emphasises simplification: *"if we are to have greater transparency, simplification is essential"*.

The draft constitution runs to over 200 pages. The institutional provisions are the result of contorted compromises. It is hardly a document of clarity and inspiration.

Laeken suggests the possibility of a constitution: *"The question ultimately arises as to whether this simplification and reorganisation might not lead in the long run to the adoption of a constitutional text of the Union."*

The concept of the Treaties as an inter-governmental construct being transformed into a monument for European ambition was rapidly seized upon, but without any study of either the alternatives on offer or the long-term consequences of such an act.

Lastly, *Laeken's overriding aim was a Democratic Europe.*

The draft Constitution creates a new centralised European state, more powerful, more remote, with more politicians, more bureaucracy, and a wider gap between the rulers and the ruled.

8

How much legislation comes from Europe?

In debates about the EU a 2010 research paper of the House of Commons Library,[1] which tried to answer this question, is frequently quoted and often misquoted. Here are key passages from it:

> In the UK data suggest that from 1997 to 2009 6.8% of primary legislation (Statutes) and 14.1% of secondary legislation (Statutory Instruments) had a role in implementing EU obligations, although the degree of involvement varied from passing reference to explicit implementation.[2]

However, later on in the report it is noted:

> These figures do not take account of EU "soft law" or the overwhelming majority of EU regulations, which apply uniformly across all member states, and are several times the number of directives.[3]

It also reports that in the UK, although some regulations are implemented by statutory instruments,

> most (are implemented) by administrative rules, regulations, departmental notes and documents, guidelines on procedures etc.[4]

Furthermore,

> All measurements have their problems and it is possible to justify any measure between 15% and 50% or thereabouts.[5]

---

1   V. Miller, *How much legislation comes from Europe?*, House of Commons Library Research Paper, 10/62, October 2010, Available from: http://researchbriefings.parliament.uk/ResearchBriefing/Summary/RP10-62#fullreport
2   Ibid, p.1.
3   Ibid, p.22.
4   Ibid, p. 22.
5   Ibid, p.24.

According to the report, it is possible to,

> estimate what proportion [of] EU regulations and EU-related UK laws form out of the total volume of UK laws, including all EU regulations, regardless of how or whether they are formally implemented.[6]

The proportion was 45% in 1997 and 53% in 2009.

Some other estimates are mentioned in the paper:

- In 2002, the OECD estimated that 40 per cent of all new UK regulations with a significant impact on business were derived from EU legislation.

- In 2005, the UK government estimated 9 per cent of all national law.

- In 2006, the British government estimated that around 50 per cent of UK legislation with a significant economic impact has its origins in EU legislation.

- In 2006, the British government estimated that about half of all UK legislation with an impact on business, charities and the voluntary sector stems from legislation agreed in Brussels.

One estimate showed that the influence of EU law varied widely by government department. Between 2003 and 2004, in reply to a parliamentary question, it became clear that the proportion varied between the Department for Environment, Food and Rural affairs at 57% and the Ministry of Defence and the Cabinet Office at 0%.

Estimates from other member countries

The paper directly quotes a similar study of the Netherlands which concluded that 'clearly, a case can be made that the EU has a very large impact on national policies if all those 'products' of the European integration, formal and informal, are taken into account'.[7]

It also reviews similar studies in a number of other member countries. Their estimates of the proportion of national laws in

---

6   Ibid, p.24.
7   M. Bovens and K. Yesilkagit, 'The EU as Lawmaker: the Impact of EU Directives on National Regulation in the Netherlands', *Public Administration*, Vol. 88, No. 1, 2010, p. 23.

their own countries which are based on EU laws ranged from around 6% to 84%. While the figures differ, it is clear that a high proportion of UK law is influenced to some degree by the EU.

Caveats

Throughout the research, warnings are given about the difficulty of measuring legislation. They may be summarized as follows:

1. It is extremely difficult to measure the influence of EU legislation since it can be incorporated into UK law in different ways, either directly by legislation, or by amendments, or by administrative means. Moreover, EU regulations, unlike EU directives, are not usually transposed into legislation at a national level, but rather into quasi-legislative measures, administrative rules, regulations or procedures which do not pass through the UK national parliamentary process. How, then, can one be worked out as a proportion of the other?

2. EU 'soft law' measures under the so-called 'Open Method of Coordination' are difficult to quantify as they often take the form of objectives and common targets. Analyses rarely look at such EU soft law, and the role of EU standard setting or self-regulatory measures.

3. Governments might have intended to implement legislation in areas in which the EU decides to act, and might have legislated in anticipation of the adoption of an EU law. These do not then show up as EU-based, even though they might well have been EU influenced.

4. The figures do not give an insight into the relative importance or salience of EU or national legislative acts, nor give information on how EU laws affect the daily lives of citizens or businesses – the relative material impact. There are EU regulations, for example, relating to olive and tobacco growing which are unlikely to have much impact in the UK.

5. Statutory instruments as a measuring tool do not reflect the Europeanisation of policies in the Common Foreign and Security Policy or the former Justice and Home Affairs area, where the EU's influence has largely not been exercised by legislation but by member states acting inter-governmentally.

One caveat may be added: there is a difference between laws, whether hard or soft, that are derived from EU regulations and directives, and those that are created domestically. The former cannot be repealed or amended easily. They are effectively irreversible without the approval of the other 27 members.

The Justice Secretary's experience

The following is an excerpt from an article written by Michael Gove in *The Daily Telegraph*:

> As a minister I've seen hundreds of new EU rules cross my desk, none of which were requested by the UK Parliament, none of which I or any other British politician could alter in any way and none of which made us freer, richer or fairer.
>
> It is hard to overstate the degree to which the EU is a constraint on ministers' ability to do the things they were elected to do, or to use their judgment about the right course of action for the people of this country. I have long had concerns about our membership of the EU but the experience of Government has only deepened my conviction that we need change.
>
> Every single day, every single minister is told: 'Yes Minister, I understand, but I'm afraid that's against EU rules'. I know it. My colleagues in government know it. And the British people ought to know it too: your government is not, ultimately, in control in hundreds of areas that matter.[8]

---

8   M. Gove, 'EU referendum: Michael Gove explains why Britain should leave the EU', *Daily Telegraph*, 20 February 2016, Available from: http://www.tele-graph.co.uk/news/newstopics/eureferendum/12166345/European-referen-dum-Michael-Gove-explains-why-Britain-should-leave-the-EU.html

9

European government in action: five examples

These brief accounts of five recent episodes of EU government are intended to illustrate its mode of government. The merits or demerits of these actions or regulations are not debated or decided, though they inevitably raise the question of whether national governments might have handled these issues more effectively and in a more democratic manner.

Olive oil: organized growers versus restauranteurs

On 14th May 2013,[1] seemingly out of the blue, the people and governments, and more importantly the restauranteurs, of the EU were informed by a Commission official that 'From the first of January next year, we can guarantee the quality and authenticity of olive oil .... And we do that by having new rules on labelling, concerning the category and origin of olive oil.' After explaining that the new rules will force restaurants to serve sealed, throw-away bottles of oil to customers instead of refillable flasks or bowls, he concluded by saying that 'This is good news for consumers in Europe.'[2]

The sudden ban on a traditional way of serving olive oil provoked widespread press, political and public protest in a number of countries, and, in those like the UK where olive oil was a less central part of daily cuisine, ridicule. Nine days later, the Commission withdrew the proposal.[3]

---

1   Commission implementing regulation (EU) No 29/2012 on marketing standards of olive oil [14 January] OJ L 12

2   http://www.pri.org/stories/2013-05-22/spaniards-outraged-new-strict-eu-regulations-olive-oil 22nd May 2013

3   Waterfield, B. (2013) EU drops olive oil ban after public outcry, *Daily Telegraph*, 23 May [online]. Available at: http://www.telegraph.co.uk/news/worldnews/europe/eu/10076201/EU-drops-olive-oil-jug-ban-after-public-outcry.html

The episode raised a number of questions about the nature of the EU's legislative process, and about the power of organized lobbies. However, before illustrating these, it is fair to point out that widespread anger and protests after the regulation was announced gave a brief glimpse of a rare sight in the EU: a European demos, or a section of it at least. On this rather narrow issue, press and people in several member countries felt and spoke as one, and their voices led to the withdrawal of the regulation.

The ban originated in Portugal in 2004. Olive growers had long tried to stop restauranteurs passing off cheap oil as a quality product, and in 2005 persuaded the government to pass legislation requiring tamper-proof, non-refillable olive oil bottles in cafés and restaurants. Failure to do so was an offence punishable by fines.

Casa do Azeite, Portugal's olive oil association, said that the legislation had helped to boost consumption of extra virgin olive oil. In 2006 Italy passed similar legislation. Following the economic crisis in 2008, European extra virgin olive oil was losing market share to cheaper products, some imported from North Africa and Turkey.[4] In June 2009 the EU's Advisory Group on Olives and Derived Products, whose meetings are not open to the public or press, looked for a strategy to combat falling prices. In April 2012 Interprofesional del Aceite de Oliva Español, which represents Spain's olive oil producers, met with Dacian Ciolos, the then EU Agricultural Commissioner, and suggested a series of measures to revive the olive oil industry, among them the proposal that olive oil in restaurants be served in labelled tamper-proof non-reusable bottles.

In February 2013 the proposal was voted on by a 'comitology' committee called the Management Committee for the Common Organisation of Agricultural Markets, which has the power to implement directives without the need for a vote in the European Parliament. However, the committee failed to agree to it, until it came back before the committee on 14 May 2013, when, with the support of the Commissioner Ciolos, it was passed.

The measure was presented, as we have seen, as a consumer protection measure. Since the sealed, throwaway bottles were to

---

4   Mendick, R. (2013) The great olive oil farce, *Daily Telegraph*, 26 May [online]. Available at: http://www.telegraph.co.uk/foodanddrink/foodanddrinknews/10080827/The-great-olive-oil-farce.html

replace bowls and refillable jars of olive oil in every café, bar and restaurant across the EU, it seems likely that the Brussels lobbyists of companies who bottle, label and distribute olive oil or other sauces and condiments were involved, since it would transfer the business of thousands of local olive oil growers, and family-based supply chains, into their hands.

Indeed, after the proposal was dropped, COPA-COGECA, a federation of agricultural lobby groups, emerged to express its 'serious regret' about the reversal of a measure that 'has been discussed for over a year and was supported by 15 Member States and passed through all the correct legal procedures.'[5] These procedures did not, it seems, involve the European Parliament.

Vaping: public health and the fate of an infant industry

On 3 April 2014 the Commission proposed to update the Tobacco Products Directive (TPD) of 2001 ostensibly to harmonise tobacco regulation, ensure the smooth running of the Single Market and a high level of health protection for consumers.[6] Later in the same year it was approved by the European Parliament and Council, and has to be fully implemented in each member state by 20 May 2016.

However, the revised TPD was rather more than an update since Article 20 includes strict regulation of an industry that did not exist in 2001, that of e-cigarette regulation: All ingredients contained in the device and its emissions have to be measured and disclosed by the manufacturer; the liquid inside is not allowed to contain more than 20mg/ml of nicotine; refill cartridges are limited in size to 10ml for liquid cartridges and 2ml for disposable e-cigarettes; most vaping advertisements are banned; and it imposes a six-month standstill period for new vaping products, following notification by the manufacturer of an intention to sell a product. According to the

---

5   COPA-COGECA, Committee of Professional Agricultural Organizations in the EU Press release 23rd May 2013 http://www.copa-cogeca.be

6   European Parliament and Council Directive 2014/40/EU on the approximation of the laws, regulations and administrative provisions of the Member States concerning the manufacture, presentation and sale of tobacco and related products and repealing Directive 2001/37/EC [3 April] OJ L 127/1. The original directive 2001/37/EC.

Commission, these new regulations will ensure that e-cigarettes are safer and of better quality.

According to some observers, safety and quality are not the only reasons for these regulations since they happen to be extremely beneficial for big tobacco companies, since this new competitor will be regulated more severely than they are. E-cigarette manufacturers will, for example, have to measure and list all the ingredients in their product's emissions, whereas tobacco companies only have to test for three emissions: tar, carbon monoxide and nicotine. The size rules on cartridges happen to hit the most popular e-cigarettes, and the content rules means that the e-cigarette will be an exceedingly weak cigarette substitute. The mandatory standstill and advertising ban will obviously hinder and obstruct the emergence of the only significant direct competitor tobacco companies have ever faced.[7]

Most of these new companies are start-ups without representation in Brussels. However one of them, Blackburn-based Totally Wicked, decided to challenge Article 20 in the European Court.[8] A decision was expected in early 2016, but as as this book went to print no decision has been made. The Commission seldom loses before the European Court, so it will be an important one. If Totally Wicked fails, the Commission, aided by big tobacco firms, will have crushed an infant industry.

The issue is complicated by the fact that research was still emerging as the Commission was deciding to legislate. However, well before the European Parliament voted on the Commission's proposed directive, 15 leading researchers in the field wrote to the EU's health commissioner Tonio Borg. According to them, many of the proposed regulations were 'of no benefit to consumers… would incur large unnecessary costs' and 'since they were not required of from cigarette or tobacco manufacturers would create a market advantage for the much more dangerous tobacco cigarettes.'[9]

7   Ridley, M. (2015) 'No smoke without fire in this EU nightmare', *The Times*, 28 September [online]. Available at: http://www.thetimes.co.uk/tto/opinion/columnists/article4569316.ece

8   http://article20legalchallenge.com/media/

9   Scientific errors in the Tobacco Products Directive: a letter sent by various scientists to the European Union, 17 January 2014 [online]. Available at: http://www.ecigarette-research.com/web/index.php/2013-04-07-09-50-07/2014/149-tpd-errors

Their final sentence read: 'If wisely regulated, electronic cigarettes have the potential to obsolete cigarettes and to save millions of lives worldwide. Excessive regulation, on the contrary, will contribute to maintain the existing levels of smoking-related disease, death and health care costs.' [10]

Journey to work: the Tyco windfall for mobile workers

Travelling to and from work is not normally considered working time. However, a 2015 ruling by the Court of Justice of the European Union (CJEU) states that for workers who have no fixed place of work it is working time, and must therefore be paid as such.[11] The UK has to ensure that its legislation complies with this ruling.

The ruling originates from a case in 2011 involving Tyco, a Spanish security company. It closed all of its regional offices, and controlled all its employees from its headquarters. Before these closures, working time started and ended when an employee checked into and out of the regional office. After the closures, employees travelled directly from their home to customers. Tyco decided that working time would begin from the moment an employee reached their first assignment of the day and would end when they left their last assignment of the day.

Employees, believing that Tyco had breached Spanish working time rules, brought a complaint to the Spanish High Court. The Spanish National High Court referred the case to the CJEU to rule on whether Tyco had breached the EU's Working Time Directive (WTD).[12]

The Court decided that it had, and that the time non-fixed workers spend travelling between their home and their first and last place of work constitutes working time under the Working Time Directive.

---

10 Ibid.
11 Case C-266/14 Federación de Servicios Privados del sindicato Comisiones obreras (CC.OO.) v Tyco Integrated Security SL, Tyco Integrated Fire & Security Corporation Servicios SA [2015] Opinion of AG Y.Bot.
12 European Parliament and Council Directive 2003/88/EC concerning certain aspects of the organisation of working time [4 November] OJ L 299

Working time therefore began when they closed their own front door. According to the Court, the journey constitutes working time because it is an integral part of providing services to customers, and during these journeys the worker is at the employer's disposal.[13] Also, the workers' journeys at the beginning and end of the day to and from customers were regarded as working time by Tyco before the closure of the regional offices. Because Tyco previously deemed these journeys as part of working time, driving to and from the first and last customer is part of the employee's job role. Also, forcing employees to bear the burden of Tyco's decision to close the offices would go against their health and safety.

The judgement will mean difficult decisions for employers and employees of UK companies with mobile workers.[14] When travelling hours are added onto existing hours, some employees would be exceeding the WTD regulation of an average working week of 48 hours, varying of course according to the distance they travelled to their first appointment. The Court recognized employers are free to determine payment for the opening and closing travelling time, but could not, of course, exempt them from minimum wage legislation.

This ruling is more consistent with traditional continental labour relations, where the state has commonly intervened to enforce or impose agreements on both sides, usually because the trade unions were incapable of doing it by themselves. Traditional British practice was for the two sides to negotiate, agree and enforce their own agreements. However, as their membership has declined, British trade unions have become more willing to accept intervention by the European state on their behalf, and especially windfalls like this Tyco decision.

It has yet to be seen how firms will adjust to the new regime. They may invite employees to voluntarily exempt themselves

---

13 CJEU Press Release, 99/15 (Sep. 10, 2015). Available at: http://curia.europa.eu/jcms/upload/docs/application/pdf/2015-09/cp150099en.pdf

14 Javaid, M. (2015) What the European Court travel ruling means for UK employers, CIPD, 15 September 2015 [online]. Available at: http://www.cipd.co.uk/pm/peoplemanagement/b/weblog/archive/2015/09/15/what-the-ecj-travel-ruling-means-for-uk-employers.aspx

from the WTD[15], invent bogus regional offices, or simply accept that their mobile work force must spend less time at the premises of work, to account for travel time, and raise prices to compensate for this drop.[16]

The European Arrest Warrant: faster extradition at a price

When first proposed by the European Commission in 2001, the European Arrest Warrant (EAW) was primarily a part of European state-building, of a piece with the euro. There was no public clamour about the large number of German criminals who could not be extradited from the UK, or British offenders living in France. No doubt, as today, a fair number of the British criminal classes preferred to live on the Costa del Sol, out of sight of British police, but they were not protected from extradition.

The 2001 proposal of the European Commission was presented simply as a means of simplifying the process of extradition between EU member states, by obliging member states to extradite on request the citizens of another to stand trial or serve out a sentence.[17] The proposal was approved by the European Parliament on 6 February 2002 and formally adopted by the Council on 13 June 2002.

The UK implemented the EAW Framework Decision via parts one and three of the 2003 Extradition Act, which came into force on 1 January 2004, though its operation has forced the UK to make constant amendments to this Act.[18]

---

15 British responses to EU labour market regulation as a whole are described in HMG (2014), Review of the Balance of Competences between the United Kingdom and the European Union Social and Employment Policy [online]. Available at: https://www.gov.uk/government/consultations/ review-of-uk-and-eu-balance-of-competences-call-for-evidence-on-social-and-employment-policy

16 Ensuring this particular voluntary opt out was once considered part of David Cameron's renegotiation, but subsequently appears to have been forgotten, perhaps because it has been widely accepted in the UK. 'Business groups cry foul as EU rules commuting time is 'work', *Daily Telegraph* 10 Sept 2015

17 European Commission proposal (COM/2001/0522) for a Council framework Decision on the European arrest warrant and the surrender procedures between the Member States [27 November] OJ C 332E.

18 Dawson, J. Lipscombe, S. (2015) The European arrest warrant, House of Commons briefing paper 07016 [online]. Available at: http://researchbriefings.parliament.uk/ResearchBriefing/Summary/SN07016#fullreport

Its main, and perhaps sole, merit is that it has reduced the time taken for extradition. In 2013 it took on average 10 months to arrange extradition from a non-EU state, and only 3 months from another EU country.[19]

One disadvantage is that the UK receives far more EAWs than it issues, many for relatively minor crimes which are thought to be a waste of police time and costly for the taxpayer. Poland has, for example, sent the UK extradition requests in connection with piglet rustling, exceeding a credit card limit, and the theft of a wheelbarrow, teddy bear and a pudding.[20]

However, the most important objection is that it requires the UK to accept a foreign warrant without an extensive enquiry into the facts or circumstances behind that warrant. It therefore requires the UK to arrest the person named in the warrant without affording them many of the protections that have been provided under English and British law for centuries, and to send them to jurisdictions where there is no legal limit on pre-trial detention. It is a clash of fundamentally different legal systems, or as Wheeler put it, the death of Magna Carta.[21]

As a result, many British nationals have served lengthy pre-trial detentions abroad. Andrew Symeou spent 10 months in pre-trial detention in Greece, before being acquitted. He told the House of Commons Committee:

> You cannot imagine what it has done to me and what it has done to my family. It has changed our lives and it is unacceptable.[22]

In July 2013 the Home Secretary set out specific proposals to tackle these issues. These proposals were implemented in part 12 of the Antisocial Behaviour, Crime and Policing Act 2014.[23] To tackle the

---

19 HM Government, Decision pursuant to Article 10 of Protocol 36 to the Treaty on the Functioning of the European Union, July 2013, Cm 8671, page 94

20 House of Commons Home Affairs Committee Pre-Lisbon Treaty EU police and criminal justice measures: the UK's opt-in decision Ninth Report of Session 2013–14 Report, together with formal minutes, oral and written evidence. 29 October 2013 http://www.publications.parliament.uk/pa/cm201314/cmselect/cmhaff/615/615.pdf

21 Wheeler, S. (2015) Eight hundred years later, the death of Magna Carta, Civitas [online]: http://www.civitas.org.uk/ content/files/europedebateno5.pdf

22 Q133. House of Commons, op.cit.

23 Antisocial Behaviour, Crime and Policing Act 2014, part 12. Available at: http://www.legislation.gov.uk/ukpga/2014/12/contents/enacted/data.htm

large number of EAWs submitted to the UK for minor crimes, the Act states that an arrest warrant can be refused by the UK for minor crimes. To stop British citizens facing lengthy pre-trial detentions, the Act states that extradition can only occur if the requesting country has already confirmed that they will charge and try the suspect. However, how these measures will play out in the future is unclear.

Bats: do they need EU protection and regulation?

Adopted in 1992, the Habitats Directive (92/43/EEC) seeks to enhance the conservation of rare, threatened or endemic animal and plant species.[24] It acts alongside the 2009 Birds Directive (2009/147/EC) to enhance wildlife and nature conservation. It also establishes the EU Natura 2000 ecological network of protected areas, which are safeguarded against potentially damaging developments.

The Habitats Directive is based on an international treaty: the Agreement on the Conservation of Populations of European Bats. It was ratified in 1991 by Germany, The Netherlands, Norway, Sweden, and the UK. In 2001 the Agreement became part of the United Nations Environment Programme (UNEP). There was no evidence that this programme was defective in any respect, but nonetheless the European Commission felt it necessary to supplement and specify its provisions, meaning that the UK is now constrained by both international and EU texts, whereas non-EU states could refer to just the original international agreement.

This has led to problems with UK bat legislation, since the EU Directive does not create different solutions for dealing with the different roosting behaviours of bats. In some member states, such as the UK, bats tend to roost in churches, whereas in Germany they prefer trees.[25] It is generally more costly to obey legislation when bats roost in buildings, especially old buildings with complex regulations.

---

24 European Council Directive 92/43/EEC on the conservation of natural habitats and of wild fauna and flora [22 July] OJ L 206.

25 p.412, Chapter 13 Agriculture and Rural Communities. In: Change or Go, Business for Britain, 2015 [online]. Available at: http://businessforbritain.org/change-or-go/

Some UK property owners have had to pay for expensive surveys, a European Protected Species Mitigation Licence, employ an ecologist, and even install a bat flap.[26]

Legislation made at the national level, in accordance with the UNEP, might be better able to take into account bats' varied roosting behaviours and countries' varied building regulations. Does the EU benefit from having a uniform wildlife conservation regulation? And more importantly, do European bats?

---

26 The bat industry has no doubt been helped by EU regulation but it appears to be a British rather than EU phenomenon. Coleridge, N. (2013) Holy bat protection! That's cost me £10,000, *Daily Telegraph*, 25 January [online]. Available at: http://www.telegraph.co.uk/news/earth/wildlife/9827052/Holy-bat-protection-Thats-cost-me-10000.html

10
Do the British have much influence?

Influence is extremely difficult to measure, but that does not stop participants in the Brexit debate making lots of claims about it.

Those who want the UK to remain a member make two claims in particular. First, that as a member we have considerable influence within the EU, because 'we sit at the table and help to make the rules'. Secondly, this gives Britain influence in the wider world. If we were to leave, our influence within the EU would be nil, and it would also decline in the wider world.

For the sake of this argument one has to assume that influence, that is the ability to persuade others to do what we wish without the use of either a carrot or stick, is a valuable resource, and the more we have of it the better. This is not a view that would be universally shared by the British people, especially in regard to influence in the wider world at least. Many would appear to be quite happy if the UK had influence proportional to its population, its economic and military resources, and its talents, and would probably wonder why, and for what purpose, its leaders want any more.

However, here we are discussing influence within the EU, where it is more reasonable to think that it is of some use and some benefit. We must now ask how is it to be measured? If there are no agreed measures, anyone can make any claim about Britain's rising or falling influence, for some reason or other, which no one can verify or contest. There is then no debate, just an exchange of impressions and press reports.

Many British observers are convinced that the UK has exercised disproportionate influence in EU policy-making. The CBI manifesto of 2013 is peppered with comments such as the UK has been 'leading the drive towards a more outward-facing EU'[1], that it 'shapes the research priorities'[2], and that it is 'effective at building alliances and rarely finds itself isolated'.[3] However, evidence is needed to support this rather flattering self-image, preferably from an external source.

In this note, we will try to capture and measure influence in three ways, by the UK's formal representation in EU institutions, by its leaders' success in achieving their stated goals, and by examining policy outcomes to see whether there are signs of British influence. However, before reviewing some evidence on these three counts, it is necessary to recall that the UK has over the years opted out of many agreements that bind all or most of the other EU member countries. Although, it has been joined on some of these opt outs by one or more other members, it now has more opt outs than any other member.

Can a member state with the most opt outs expect to wield much influence? The UK has five major enduring opt outs.

The Schengen Area
The Thatcher Government did not participate in the Schengen Agreement in 1985, which was not negotiated under EU auspices. Under it, five of the then ten EU member countries agreed to remove border checks and controls between each other. It became part of EU law through the Treaty of Amsterdam in 1997. As a result, most members except the UK and Ireland are now obliged to join it.

The euro
The UK declined to make any commitment to the timetable agreed by other members in the negotiations at Maastricht in 1992. The decision not to join was confirmed by the Blair Government in 1997, 2003 and 2007. There are now nine non-euro member countries, but all of them, apart from the UK, are obliged to join eventually.

---

1 CBI, 'Our Global Future: the business vision for a reformed EU', 2013, p.58, Available from: http://news.cbi.org.uk/reports/our-global-future/our-global-future/
2 Ibid, p. 74.
3 Ibid, p. 13.

The Charter of Fundamental Rights

In the negotiations that led to the Lisbon Treaty, the UK, along with Poland, negotiated an opt out that limited the right of the European Court of Justice to declare any law or institution of the UK inconsistent with this Charter, and declared that the rights in it are not justiciable in the UK. Lawyers disagree about whether this protocol has significant legal effect.

Justice and Home Affairs (JHA)

In October 2012, the Coalition Government exercised its previously-negotiated right to opt out of the provisions of the Lisbon Treaty in regard to JHA, and declared that it would selectively opt back into certain measures at later dates of its own choosing. Ireland negotiated an identical opt out.

Ever closer union

In his renegotiations David Cameron announced that he had negotiated an exemption for the UK from this cardinal principle of the European Union which dates back to the Treaty of Rome, and has been assumed or confirmed in subsequent treaties. He claims it will be written into the next EU Treaty. No other state has asked for such an exemption.

The UK is plainly an unusual, even unique, member state, and perhaps is best described as a reluctant, or half-hearted or even semi-member of the European Union. The Prime Minister says that, following his renegotiations, the UK has achieved a 'special status' in the EU, though whether this special status will increase UK influence in the EU seems unlikely. Other member states might reasonably see the UK's special status as a good reason why it should not be allowed to influence significant policy decisions within the Union in the future.

The inevitable decline of British representation in EU institutions

The first of the three ways one may assess UK influence is by looking at formal representation in EU institutions. As the number of member states has grown, from nine to 28 countries, UK representation has necessarily shrunk, along with that of all the other founder or early members.

In the first European elections in 1979, the UK had 20 per cent of the seats in the European Parliament. By 2015, that had declined to 9.5 per cent (73 of 751 members). Likewise, while the UK had 17 per cent of the votes in the Council of Ministers in 1973, that has declined to 8 per cent (29 of 352 votes). Within the Commission itself, there has also been a decline. In 2004, the number of UK commissioners, along with those of other large countries, was reduced from two to one. The number of British nationals working in the Commission fell from 9.6 per cent in 2004 to 3.6 per cent in 2016.[4] This latter however is not due to an increase in the number of member countries or to any attempt to preserve a balance of nationalities. It is entirely due to a lack of suitable applicants. Britain has 12.8 per cent of the EU population.

National representation does not, however, quite tell the whole story. There has been a simultaneous decline in national vetoes, and a corresponding increase in qualified majority voting (QMV). About 80 per cent of all legislation is now by QMV.[5] Thus the influence of Britain, and all other member countries, has shrunk since they cannot veto as many unwelcome proposals and policies as they once did.

Moreover, influence depends on the degree to which the British representatives sympathize with, can find common cause with and therefore ally with other representatives of other member countries. A majority of British MEPs are in the smaller political groupings of the European Parliament meaning that they probably have less chance of creating working alliances to influence votes, and also less chance of electing a future president. However, there seems to be no study of how groups and their alliances shape the work and votes of the European Parliament.

Business for Britain has analysed in some detail the voting in the 1,936 motions put before the European Parliament over the years

---

4   Business for Britain, Change or Go, London, 2015, p.331, Available from: http://businessforbritain.org/change-or-go/. The figures for British nationals in the Commission are from http://ec.europa.eu/civil_service/about/fig-ures/index_en.htm
5   Consilium, 'Qualified Majority', http://www.consilium.europa.eu/en/coun-cil-eu/voting-system/qualified-majority/

2009-2014. They found that 576 of these motions were voted against by the majority of British MEPs.[6] However, 485 of these motions nevertheless passed, a failure rate of 84 per cent. In party terms, UKIP failed to block 95 per cent of the motions they opposed, the Conservatives failed to block 87 per cent, Labour 53 per cent, and Liberal Democrats 36 per cent. This does not suggest strong influence, but then there were 1360 other motions, in which a majority of British MEPs were not opposed, and it is possible that these were on issues that some British MEPs were able to influence results.

In view of the significant opt-outs mentioned above, it seems unlikely that British nationals will ever fill the five most important jobs in the EU: the presidencies of the Commission, the European Council and the Parliament, and they can hardly be selected as President of the European Central Bank or the Eurogroup. The Presidency of the Council of the EU rotates among members and if the UK votes to stay it will take up the role in July 2017.

Prime ministers' influence in European Council decision-making

British prime ministers usually declare their goals before meetings and key decisions of the European Council. Hence whether or not they have achieved their declared goals is a rough measure of the influence of the UK. Decisions taken by four prime ministers which might be taken to demonstrate their influence within the EU are listed below, though it is an open list, so that plausible suggestions can be added to it.

Mrs Thatcher's rebate on the UK subscription obtained at the Fontainebleau summit in 1984 is a clear case of a prime minister exercising on behalf of the UK a very considerable influence in council decision-making, since it was not only initially opposed by other members, but also to their financial cost, and to the immense benefit of the British people.

John Major's reservations about joining the euro, as well as opting out of the Social Chapter, count less as exercising influence

---

6   Business for Britain, 'How much influence does Britain have in the European Parliament?', Briefing Note 5

in the EU, than as declining to be influenced by others, which is creditable no doubt but not quite the same thing. In his memoirs he does not point to any EU policy or programme which he proposed and influenced, or any contemporary EU institution or policy which owes anything to his influence.

Tony Blair's declared goals with respect to the EU, on becoming prime minister were: to secure legally binding rights to keep frontier controls, to oppose the integration of the WEU with the EU, and to honour a campaign pledge and curb foreign vessels fishing for British quotas. The first two were soon lost, and forgotten, even in his memoirs, and fishermen got an agreement that boats using British quotas had to land 50% of their catch in British ports.[7]

His better known EU policy decisions, however, were to have surrendered the Social Chapter opt-out of the Maastricht treaty and to have conceded a reduction in the UK rebate, both examples of being influenced rather than exerting it. The rebate concession is important because it was, according to his speeches at the time, though not his memoirs, a *quid pro quo* for reform of the CAP, which never happened. This suggests that even under the favourable circumstances of the UK presidency, the UK at the time had little influence. Blair's major foreign policy decisions, Kosovo and Iraq, reinforce this conclusion and suggest that he had far more influence in the U.S. Like Major, he does not claim in his memoirs to have influenced the EU in any particular policy or direction.

David Cameron's veto of treaty change to help the stricken euro in 2011 did not change the plans of other members in any respect. His attempts to persuade the Commission to cut its budget and significantly reduce its staff in 2014 were announced as a success but subsequently have been shown to have failed.[8] His recent

---

7   C. Booker and Richard North, The Great Deception: Can the European Union Survive?, London, Continuum, 2005, p.412.

8   At an EU Budget summit on 7/8 Feb 2013, Cameron and other EU leaders agreed a €908 billion limit for the seven-year period 2014 – 2020. This was 3 per cent lower than in the previous seven-year period. Hence his claim. However, a few months later this decision was overturned, and the EU budget, and the UK contribution sharply increased. Source: Tim Congdon's open email 30th September 2014 quoting evidence from the Office of Budget Responsibility, the Office of National Statistics and the HM Treasury White Paper, European Union Finances, 2014.

renegotiations also fell well short of his declared goals. They are nonetheless a high water mark of British influence which is unlikely to be repeated, since his hand was strengthened by the forthcoming referendum. Their significance can, however, only be finally judged post-referendum, and after the European Court has its say.

Policy and programme outcomes

The most direct way of measuring UK influence would be to discover the number of EU regulations or directives, where the UK has taken a distinctive position which other members were initially not inclined to support, but where British representatives eventually prevailed to the benefit of UK exporters, taxpayers and consumers.

This method has a respectable pedigree in political science, though it is not readily applied to the EU. The UK Permanent Representative in Brussels sought patiently to explain the extraordinarily complex web of relationships that form the EU legislative process to members of the Commons European Scrutiny Committee.[9] Parts of it are confidential and completely hidden, so it seems doubtful whether any researcher could identify who was responsible for any of the more than three thousand EU directives and regulations that together form the Single Market.[10] One academic expert, who is 'very strongly supportive of the European Union', observed of its decision-making that 'It is not clear who is responsible for what. It is not clear what coalitions governed on what issues, what the majority was on what issues, or who were the winners and losers.'[11]

Financial regulation is one field in which there has been a thorough examination of earlier decision-making to assess British

---

9   It took him a couple of hours, and it is doubtful whether any outsider could have followed it. Sir Jon Cunliffe, UK Permanent Representative to the EU, Minutes of Evidence HC 109-I *House of Commons Oral Evidence taken before the European Scrutiny Committee*, Wed 8 May 2013.

10 'As of 1 October 2012, 1,420 directives and 1,769 regulations were in force to ensure the functioning of the Single Market.' Source: Internal Market Score-board. European Union, 2013, p.9.

11 Professor Simon Hix, *Uncorrected Transcript of Oral Evidence*, to be published as HC 109-ii, taken before the European Scrutiny Committee in the House Of Commons 12 June 2013, Q.454.

influence. It was conducted by Europe Economics and referred to EU efforts 'to create/deepen the Single Market' during its Financial Services Action Plan 1998-2006, focusing specifically on the Markets in Financial Instruments Directive (MiFID) of 2004. This is an area in which one might expect the UK to exercise great influence within the EU given that its financial sector is much larger than any other in the EU. Europe Economics concluded that EU policymakers, at that time, had decided that British practice was best.[12] The MiFID therefore 'closely reflected British norms and policy theories', and in many respects 'mimicked UK practice'. It might therefore be taken as a telling example of the UK's influence within the EU.

Europe Economics went on to point out, however, that the UK was able to exercise such influence largely because of favourable circumstances at the time: the EU was then seeking to liberalize financial services, and the UK was then thought to embody international best regulatory practice. After the financial crisis, circumstances changed fundamentally. The EU is now seeking to restrict and control the financial sector, and is no longer looking to the UK for inspiration or guidance. Far from it. Hence, the second half of Europe Economics' analysis largely consists of explaining why UK influence is likely to be insignificant or negligible in the foreseeable future, and why it should probably expect to be regularly overruled or outvoted, as it already has been on the bonus cap, the Financial Transactions Tax and Solvency II.[13]

The recent Bank of England report corroborates this conclusion and does not convey much confidence in the UK's ability to influence EU policymakers. On the contrary, they see the possibility of 'problematic' regulation in the future, which is one reason why in his renegotiations, the Prime Minister was anxious to secure some

---

12 Europe Economics, *Optimal Integration in the Single Market: A Synoptic Review,* A Europe Economics report for BIS, April 2013, pp.82-94. This directive 2004/39/EC was the product of an EU Committee of Wise Men on the Regulation of European Securities Markets 2001 chaired by Alexandre Lamfalussy which reported in 2001. One of its seven members was British, Nigel Wicks, a Treasury mandarin at the time. http://ec.europa.eu/internal_market/securities/docs/lamfalussy/wisemen/final-report-wise-men_en.pdf.

13 For a fully documented account of the decline of UK influence in financial services regulation see Business for Britain, Change or Go, pp.325-342.

kind of protection for non-euro countries being put at a disadvantage by decisions within the Eurogroup. Whether he has, or could ever obtain such protection remains to be seen. The Eurogroup will undoubtedly have to caucus without the non-euro members. The betting must be, as Europe Economics found, that the UK influence in this area will remain insignificant or negligible.[14]

Trade agreements

Many British observers have claimed that, left to themselves without British influence, EU members would have resisted the global trend to freer trade and would have remained a protectionist bloc, which may be true but is difficult to demonstrate. What is not difficult to demonstrate is that the EU has preferred agreements with small trading partners, has neglected Commonwealth countries and a relatively low proportion of its agreements include services. This suggests that the UK has had little influence over its trade negotiating strategy for the past 40 years. Even the present TTIP negotiations seem long overdue, by about 20 years, and a major concession had to be made to France before these negotiations could begin to exclude all audio-visual products from the negotiations, so that French culture might be protected from an American onslaught. It so happens that this is a rather strong sector in the UK.

The distribution of R&D funds

According to three global measures of academic excellence of universities, citation impact studies of researchers as well as by Nobel prizes, the UK research community is far and away the EU leader.[15] One might therefore suppose that the UK had a strong influence on its programmes to support scientific research.

---

14 Europe Economics, *Optimal Integration in the Single Market: A Synoptic Review*, A Europe Economics report for BIS, April 2013.
15 Three global measures of academic excellence of universities:
    The Shanghai Academic Ranking of World Universities, http://www.shanghairanking.com/ARWU2014.html
    The *Times Higher Education* rankings of the world's top 100 universities, https://www.timeshighereducation.com/world-university-rankings
    The *CWTS Leiden* rankings, http://www.leidenranking.com/

Many spokespersons for the research community support this claim by saying it has obtained disproportionate research funds from the European Commission, more in fact than the UK has put in. These claims are, however, folk myths of the research community. The evidence shows quite clearly that the leaders over the 15 years 2000-2014 in the distribution of funds per researcher have been Belgium and Spain, neither of whose universities appear very often in world rankings. In the ordinal rankings of funds distributed per researcher, the UK ends up in 8th position and Germany in 10th, which does not suggest that the UK exercises disproportionate influence in these programmes.

Part Three

Finance

11

The European Commission power elite: pay and pensions

The calculation of European Commission staff's pay is immensely complicated. The table below outlines the basic annual pay of the president, commissioners and officials working in the EU commission, showing tax, pension and 'solidarity levy' deductions from their annual salary

Table 11.1	Basic Pay (£) p.a[1]				
The Commission	**Annual Salary**	**Deductions**			**Total Take home pay**
		Tax Rate[*2]	**Pension Contribution****	**Solidarity Levy*** **	
President	225,910	12.5%	22,817	12,556	166,819
High Representative, Foreign Affairs,	212,814	12.5%	21,494	11,835	157,240
Vice-President	204,628	12.5%	20,667	11,385	151,252
Commissioner	184,166	10.0%	18,601	10,524	139,823
Civil Servant top[3]	163,703	10.0%	16,534	9,204	124,588
Civil servant average[4]	72,724	8.0%	7,345	3,607	57,621

* After tax free allowance of 803 EUR and subject to a) 10% abatement for occupational and personal expenses b) Twice the amount of dependent child allowance for every dependent child of the person liable.
** 10.1% of monthly salary. Amounts to 1/3 of overall pension contribution, 2/3 tax payer funded
***In effect until 31 December 2023. The solidarity levy was introduced during the 1970s oil crisis as a way for the commission to demonstrate sympathy with the financial struggles of EU citizens and so that the institutions would seem less detached and privileged. After the financial crisis, it was decided to increase it for the period 2014-2023 to 6%/7%. This is explained in the 2013 amendment - http://eur-lex.europa.eu/legal-content/EN/TXT/?uri=celex%3A32013R1023

1 All figures have been converted from euros using the exchange rate in April 2016 at time of writing (1.39)
2 Regulation (EEC, EURATOM, ECSC) No 260/68, 29 February 1968 - http://eur-lex.europa.eu/legal-content/EN/TXT/PDF/?uri=CELEX:31968R0260&from=EN
3 Grade 16, third tier. As of 1 July 2015. Annual update to Staff Regulation Article 66 (2015/C 415/04). There are 37 officials on AD/AST grade 16 as of 1st February 2016. 158 officials on grade 15 - lowest annual salary £133,251; 550 on grade 14 –salary £117,772; 2293 on Grade 13 - salary £104,091; and 1763 on Grade 12 - salary £91,999. Total - 4,801 officials, in exclusively administrative positions (>grade12), earning minimum £92,000 p.a salary pre-allowances. http://ec.europa.eu/civil_service/docs/europa_sp2_bs_nat_x_grade_en.pdf
4 Mean average of 16 pay grades (2015/C 415/04). There are 23,022 officials on AD/AST grades 1-16 as of 1st February 2016, -http://ec.europa.eu/civil_service/docs/europa_sp2_bs_nat_x_grade_en.pdf

Table 11.2

The Commission	Total Take home pay p.a	Allowances (£) p.a:				Family Allowances			Total income (pay + allowances) Per year in office	Income over a typical 5 year term
		Expatriation	Entertainment	Installation and Resettlement ****	Daily Subsistence allowance	Household allowance	Dependent Child <27	Education, Child <27 yrs		
President	166,819	35,968	12,242	75,303	30 per day away from institution	10,556	3,320	2,253	231,158	1,231,091
High Representative, Foreign Affairs,	157,240,	33,925	7,868	73,121	30 per day away from institution	10,032	3,320	2,253	214,638	1,144,126
Vice-President	151,252	32,648	7,868	71,756	30 per day away from institution	9,705	3,320	2,253	207,046	1,103,439
Commissioner	139,823	29,456	5,246	68,346	30 per day away from institution	8,886	3,320	2,253	188,984	1,006,309
Civil Servant top	124,588	27,276	Determined by appointing authority	64,936	5,113	3,450	3,320	2,253	166,000	884,566
Civil servant average (mean average of 16 pay grades)	57,621	12,428	Determined by appointing authority	24,241	5,113	2,198	3,320	2,253	82,365	436,067

**** Assumed at 2 months basic pay pcm. Set at 2 months if official is also entitled to household allowance ie. Married. If not entitled then Installation and Resettlement are set at 1 month

Note: all allowances are detailed in REGULATION No 422/67/EEC, 5/67/EURATOM OF THE COUNCIL

EU salaries are recorded in euros per calendar month in the Staff Regulations so have been converted into pounds per year. In addition to their basic pay, all officials are entitled to a large number of untaxed allowances which substantially increase their total income. These allowances apply in different combinations and circumstances. Table 11.2 provides a comprehensive and up to date list (at the time of writing) of the allowances which Commission officials are entitled to, as well as a breakdown of what a typical official earns in both a single year of office and at the end of a typical five year term. At the end of their employment, when they leave or retire, a 'transitional allowance' of 40-65% of their final salary is paid for a maximum of three years. During this time, family allowances are retained. From the age of 66 officials also receive generous pensions. Top level officials (President to Commissioners) receive 4.275% of their final salary for every year served. Civil servants, receive 1.8% of their final salary for each year served.

It is not possible to show all of the different variations of allowances entitlements. The tables show a typical entitlement, each official has been assumed to be married and have one dependent child under the age of 27.

12

Cost of MEPs and MPs in 2011

In 2012 Lord Stoddart of Swindon asked the government for the annual total costs of the House of Lords, the House of Commons and the European Parliament.[1]

The table below from the Treasury[2] sets out the annual cost, number of members and average cost per member for the House of Commons, House of Lords and European Parliament. It shows that even per member the cost of the European Parliament is more than twice that of the two UK chambers of government:

Table 12.1	Annual cost £ million	Number of Members	Expenditure per member £ million
House of Commons	385	650	0.59
House of Lords	109	821-831	0.13
European Parliament	1,332	736	1.79

1   House of Lords Business, Tuesday 11 December 2012, HL4062 http://www.parliament.uk/search/results/?q=HL4062
2   The figures for the House of Commons are taken from the House of Commons annual accounts 2011-12 (for both administrative and Members budgets) and the Independent Parliamentary Standards Authority annual accounts 2011-12. The House of Lords figures are taken from the House of Lords annual accounts 2011-12. For the European Parliament, figures are taken from the European Union Budget of 2011 financial report. The European Parliament increased from 736 Members to 754 from 1 December 2011. Reported annual cost of €1,555 million, converted at the December 2011 exchange rate of €1.18 = £1
    http://www.parliament.uk/business/publications/commons/resource-accounts
    http://parliamentarystandards.org.uk/About%20Us/ Corporate%20Publications/Annual%20Report%20and% 20Accounts%202011-%202012.pdf
    http://www.publications.parliament.uk/pa/ld/ldresource/35/35.pdf
    http://www.europarl.europa.eu/aboutparliament/en/ 00059f3ea3/The-budget-of-the-European-Parliament.html

A reply was prompted by UK press reports of these figures. It pointed out that the European Parliament is polylingual, moves between two locations, not by choice, but under the terms of EU treaties, and that it has to rent its office space.

It also took issue with the claim in some reports that the European Parliament did not hold 'proper debates' by pointing out that it is 'constantly grilling' commissioners, that MEPs steer bills through several readings, and argued that they have 'significantly more legislative powers than the average British backbench MP', and that they are not bound by whips.[3]

This response does not take account of the fact that the European Parliament is unable to introduce legislation. It can only approve, amend or reject legislation introduced by the Commission.

---

3   http://www.europarl.org.uk/en/media/euromyths/mep_costs.html

13

Givers and takers:
the EC's redistribution of
nine members' contributions

Whatever else it may be, the EU is a mechanism for the redistribution of wealth across its member countries. The Commission takes from nine wealthier, more developed members, and after taking roughly 6 per cent of all receipts for its own expenses, returns some of their contributions back to the nine, and re-distributes the rest to other, generally poorer, member countries.

This chapter reviews these decisions over the years 2000-2014 taking the evidence from the annual financial reports on its budget, which is fairly easy to do from 2000, since the data over these years is presented in a standard excel document. Earlier years are more difficult for various reasons, but a full account going back to 1973 is being prepared.

Of 28 member countries, 19 have been net beneficiaries over the fifteen years, in the sense that the funds received for projects in their country exceeded the contribution they made to the European Commission budget. Nine have been net contributors or donors.

Since member countries vary considerably in size, Table 13.1 presents these figures in the more intelligible form of the total sum received *per capita* over the entire 15 years. Member countries are listed with the largest beneficiary, Luxembourg at the top, and the largest contributor, the Netherlands, at the bottom. An alternative, more user-friendly, bar chart version is also given below.

Over this period the status of beneficiary or contributor has been remarkably stable. Finland became a net beneficiary in 2000, 2002 and 2003, but these now look like aberrations. They have not been a net contributor since. Ireland became a net contributor in 2009 and 2014, but not enough time has passed to determine whether this is a permanent change in its status from beneficiary to contributor. Cyprus looked like it had made the transition from beneficiary to contributor in 2007 and continued as a contributor till 2012, but in 2013 became a beneficiary once more. Given the general stability of member countries' status, it is surprising that it has not crystallized into a widely acknowledged distinction within EU debates.

The appearance of all the former Soviet countries in the net recipients section of the list is not unexpected, nor is the cluster of the wealthier Northern European countries among the net contributors. It is the anomalies that attract interest and curiosity. Simply so that they may be recognized more easily, the GDP *per capita* of the 28 countries in 2000 has been added in the right hand column. This makes it easier to see the order in which EU expenditure would have been allocated had it been done purely on the basis of need, equity or to create a level playing field.

The greatest anomalies, Luxembourg and Belgium, will be discussed in a moment. There are several other unexpected results. Ireland, for instance, is slightly surprising. It was a 1973 EU entrant, and has, over many of the years under review, also been by far the highest recipient of FDI *per capita* in the EU. Even in 2000 it had a higher *per capita* GDP than the Netherlands, the largest contributor. It is therefore odd that it should nevertheless have remained high among the recipients. However, as noted above, it became a net contributor in 2014, suggesting that, after it has resolved its financial problems, it may become a permanent contributor. Portugal and Greece also appear to have been fortunate recipients given their GDP in 2000.

All these are modest anomalies by comparison with the striking and curious position of Luxembourg at the top of the table of beneficiaries, since it means that the country with the highest GDP per capita at the start of the period, is also the country that received the highest proportion of the funds distributed by the Commission over these 15 years. In Luxembourg's case, the Commission has not been redistributing income from the wealthier to the poorer, but taking from the wealthier to give to the wealthiest.

Table 13.1: Net Beneficiaries of, contributors to, funds distributed by the Commission over 15 years, 2000-2014

Total net receipts or net contributions per capita over the 15 years, in euros

Net recipients per cap in current €		GDP per cap in 2000	
Luxembourg	31759.26	1634	Bulgaria
Greece	5936.92	1662	Romania
Portugal	4081.28	3308	Lithuania
Lithuania	3894.04	3267	Latvia
Estonia	3486.05	4070	Estonia
Latvia	2988.58	4488	Poland
Ireland	2872.53	4614	Hungary
Hungary	2863.58	4920	Croatia
Poland	2056.30	5402	Slovakia
Malta	1944.59	5995	Czech Rep
Belgium	1891.93	10227	Slovenia
Slovakia	1632.76	10377	Malta
Slovenia	1614.44	11961	Greece
Czech Rep	1604.56	11502	Portugal
Spain	1436.09	13422	Cyprus
Bulgaria	1244.25	14788	Spain
Romania	968.40	20059	Italy
Cyprus	320.85	22466	France
Croatia	247.51	23152	Belgium
Net contributors per cap		23685	Germany
Finland	-912.02	24253	Finland
Italy	-973.14	24517	Austria
France	-1080.76	25958	Netherlands
Austria	-1202.72	26101	Ireland
UK	-1331.81	26296	UK
Denmark	-1930.60	29283	Sweden
Germany	-1977.16	30744	Denmark
Sweden	-2367.62	48827	Luxembourg
Netherlands	-3403.05		

Source:European Commission Financial statement 2014

This is, one imagines, somewhat embarrassing for the present President of the Commission when arguing about the budget and budgetary allocations with the UK or other states, given that he himself is from a state that, despite having the highest GDP per capita in the Union, has not contributed a single euro to it over the past 15 years.

The position of its neighbour Belgium amongst the ex-Soviet beneficiaries is barely less curious than that of Luxembourg, especially as the Netherlands, the country making the highest net contribution *per capita*, is its neighbour.

The funds distributed by the Commission do not include, one must add, plant and administrative costs of EU institutions of which there are, of course, a good number in both Luxembourg and Belgium. These costs are accounted for in the six per cent taken by the Commission from all the revenue received from member countries. The presence of many EU institutions cannot therefore explain why these two countries are major beneficiaries. There must be some other explanation.

The Commission evidently noticed the anomalous status of the two countries, and did its best to explain it, observing in notes accompanying its financial report in 2007 that 'some expenditure allocated to Belgium and Luxembourg might be inflated due to the large number of multinational consultancies or ad-hoc companies based in these two Member States.'[1]

The puzzle remains. One of the fundamental questions for whomever it is that the Commission is accountable to, must be the rationale, wisdom and equity of all these distributive decisions. Perhaps the European Parliament, or the representative of the UK or some other member country, or the auditors have satisfied themselves that this distribution of funds has been appropriate, though I have yet to discover when and where this is done, or to find a EU document or supporter who can tell me.

I wrote to the European Commission asking for a fuller explanation in December 2015, and received a request for the lines of the budget to which I was referring, but as this book went to print have received no explanation. One cannot help but think that if the EU had a demos, and was subject to active media scrutiny, the privileged status of Luxembourg and Belgium would have long since formed the subject of investigation and analysis either by the Parliament or by muckraking.

---

1   European Commission, *EU budget 2007 Financial Report*, p.29
     http://ec.europa.eu/budget/library/biblio/publications/2007/fin_report/
     fin_report_07_en.pdf

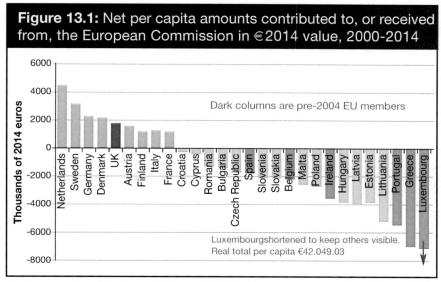

Figure 13.1: Net per capita amounts contributed to, or received from, the European Commission in €2014 value, 2000-2014

From European CommissionFinancial statement 2014, http://ec.europa.eu/budget/financialreport/2014/ calculated in 2014€€ from the EuropeanCentral Bank Inflation dash board https://www.ecb.europa.eu/stats/prices/hicp/html/inflation.en.html

14

EU Budget: the HM Treasury report

Since 1980, HM Treasury (HMT) has reported details of the EU Budget annually to Parliament. It shows the gross and net UK contributions in the recent past, as well as the UK rebate.[1] It gives forecasts for the next few years under the 7-year Multi-Annual Financial Framework (MAFF). This document is the primary source for basic data about EU revenues and expenditures, though it often reads, one must add, like a fiercely partisan brief on behalf of the current UK government.

The current MAFF, agreed in 2013, covers the period 2014-2020, and, according to HMT, 'achieved a real terms cut in the payment ceilings for the first time', so that 'the EU's seven-year budget will cost less than 1 per cent of Europe's gross national income for the first time in its history'[2] – which presumes they know what Europe's or rather the EU's, GNI will be in 2020:

> Overall, the deal agreed represents a better outcome in terms of growth, jobs and competitiveness. Since spending on research, innovation and university funding has increased by over a third... The UK was also clear throughout the negotiations that there could be no change to the UK rebate and no-EU wide taxes could be introduced as new own resource.[3]

The page below, taken from the 2015 HMT report, shows the differing positions of the Commission, Parliament and Council on the 2015 budget. Despite the 'cut' mentioned, one may note that:

---

1   HM Treasury, European Union Finances 2015: statement on the 2015 EU Budget and measures to counter fraud and financial mismanagement (Cm9167, December 2015).
2   (Cm9167, December 2015) p.5
3   Nonetheless approval was obtained a new Own Resources Decision, enabling the European Commissionto raise its own funds. The paper gives no details. (Cm9167, December 2015) p.19

- There is an increase of more than €2bn on the 2014 budget.

- The 2015 budget is closer to the Commission's proposal than to that of the Council.

- The Commission's own budget, that of 'Administration', is increased, in fact rather more than it requested.

- That the original commitment ceiling of €141.9bn in 2015 will rise to €167.6b in 2020, plus inflation.[4]

The details of the UK government's proposal to the European Council remain confidential, so we do not know by how much the UK government's position differed from that of the Council, and therefore whether it should be counted a victory or defeat.

Budgets can, of course, be altered by 'amending budgets', which have been very common in the past.[5]

Table 14.1

Payment appropriations	Financial perspective ceiling	Commission draft 2015 EU Budget	Council position	European Parliament position	Adopted 2015 EU Budget	Final 2015 EU Budget	Final 2014 EU Budget
1. Smart and inclusive Growth		67,185	65,630	70,854	66,923	66,853	65,300
1a. Competitiveness and Growth for Jobs		15,583	14,248	15,893	15,798	15,729	11,863
1b. Economic, Social & Territorial Cohesion		51,602	51,382	54,960	51,125	51,125	53,437
2. Sustainable Growth: Natural Resources		56,907	56,762	56,955	55,999	55,998	56,444
3. Security and Citizenship		1,881	1,853	1,920	1,860	1,929	1,666
4. Global Europe		7,327	6,943	7,512	7,422	7,422	6,841
5. Administration		8,612	8,585	8,672	8,659	8,659	8,405
Total Payment appropriations	141,901	142,137	139,997	146,417	141,214	141,280	139,034

Source: HM Treasury, *European Union Finances 2015: statement on the 2015 EU Budget and measures to counter fraud and financial mismanagement* (Cm9167, December 2015) p.7

---

4 The budget ceiling for 2015 will in the event be €161.8b, rather than €141.9 because a proportion of commitments for programmes in 2014 could not be adopted and were transferred to 2015 by a so called 'expenditure-neutral reprofiling' (Cm9167, December 2015) p.10

5 For guidance on the EU budget, see: http://ec.europa.eu/budget/explained/budg_system/fin_fwk0713/fin_fwk0713_en.cfm

15

Mrs Thatcher's rebate, and the cost of Mr Blair's concession

The UK rebate negotiated by Mrs Thatcher in 1984 has, as shown in the table below, saved the UK £85.9bn up to 2015, which in today's (2015) money amounts to £115.4bn, a rather remarkable return for her 'handbagging'.

Without this rebate, the net UK contribution would have more than doubled over these 28 years, and of course, until the day that a future Prime Minister no longer vetoes its abolition, this grand total will continue to increase. In terms of pounds saved over these years, it amounts to £1424.35, for every man, woman and child of the UK population, or again to put this into today's money, with the help of HMT's deflator, £1929.69 for every man, woman and child in the UK.

Criticism of the UK rebate became more intense after the admission of 10 new members in 2004 and the resulting increased pressure on the EU budget. Before the meeting of the European Council in June 2005 to discuss the budget for 2007-2013, President Chirac had said 'le cheque Britannique' could 'no longer be justified. It is from the past.'[1] He suggested that Britain should give it up as 'a gesture of solidarity for Europe.'[2] One of the aides of Jean Claude Juncker, then president of the Council, said 'It is the key to everything... a psychological key. If it stays where it is, there are quite a few new member states from eastern Europe who would be financing the rebate, and to many eyes that is not quite decent.' The Dutch Finance Minister said it was 'unacceptable'. Peter Mandelson, then trade commissioner of EC, sided with its

---

1   Booker & North, p.548
2   Booker & North, p.558

critics, on the grounds that it was 'wrong to ask new member states to contribute towards it.'[3]

At this meeting Mr Blair robustly rejected all these criticisms, by pointing out that even with the rebate, the UK contribution was still larger than that of France. Supported by the Chancellor and Foreign Secretary, he made it clear that there would be no negotiations about the rebate. The meeting ended with considerable ill-will, especially between Britain and France.

However, immediately after the meeting, the UK assumed the presidency of the Council, and on assuming it, or at some point shortly afterwards, Mr Blair seemed to have a change of heart. The BBC reported him as saying that the rebate was 'an anomaly that has to go.'[4] In his memoirs he observed that 'as Europe enlarged it... became unfair to others. This was not hard to see. The figures were there. Agreed. Clear. In pounds, shillings and pence. Or euros.'[5]

Unfortunately, he has never shared those figures with anyone. His account of the summit at which he agreed to amend the rebate is singularly uninformative. 'We preserved the rebate', he declared, 'tied its demise to the CAP, and agreed a break in the budget period where both could be reformed.'[6] He had agreed to abandon the right to a rebate on non-agricultural spending in member states that joined in or after 2004, apparently in the expectation that CAP funding would fall.[7]

It is still not entirely clear how much Mr Blair's concession has cost and will continue to cost the UK. In the House of Commons on 11th February 2013, Mr Cameron claimed that it had reduced the rebate by 50 per cent. Business for Britain carefully estimated it to be £10.4bn over the years 2007-2013.[8]

However, if we compare the rebates as a mean percentage of the gross total UK contribution over the preceding 22 years with the

---

3   Booker & North, pp. 558-59
4   BBC News "Blair says EU rebate 'has to go'" (June 2005) http:// news.bbc.co.uk/1/hi/uk_politics/4114180.stm
5   Blair, *A Journey* (2011), p.535
6   Blair, p.542
7   The complex formula for calculating the rebate is described pp.376-8, Change or Go. BfB
8   *ibid* p.369. Where the cost of Mr Blair's concession is analysed

mean percentage over the years since 2006, it seems to be rather less than the figure given by Mr Cameron, amounting to an overall reduction of around 10 per cent. This means that, up to 2015, it has cost HM Treasury £12.5bn, or in today's money £13.3bn, and every person in the UK £206.34 (2015).

Or to put it the other way around, had Mrs Thatcher's rebate not been amended, every man, woman and child in the UK would have benefited by £2136.03 in today's money. As a result of Mr Blair's gesture to European solidarity, they have benefited by just £1929.69, though this sum will, of course, increase in the years ahead.

Table 15.1 Year	1. Rebate in current value £m	2. £ per UK inhabitant	3. Rebate in 2015 £m	4. Rebate *per capita* in 2015 £m
1985	559.4	9.89	1402.52	24.80
1986	1240.3	21.88	2980.37	52.58
1987	1143.6	20.13	2612.00	45.98
1988	1581.3	27.78	3409.19	59.89
1989	1150	20.15	2295.28	40.22
1990	1694.2	29.6	3127.51	54.64
1991	2490.3	43.36	4314.05	75.11
1992	1908.9	33.15	3202.23	55.61
1993	2489.5	43.14	4071.25	70.55
1994	1799.7	31.1	2907.65	50.25
1995	1223.5	21.09	1928.90	33.25
1996	2410	41.43	3652.61	62.79
1997	1679.9	28.81	2488.23	42.67
1998	2120.7	36.27	3091.27	52.87
1999	2356.8	40.16	3397.60	57.90
2000	2084.8	35.4	2937.69	49.88
2001	4564.8	77.22	6365.25	107.68
2002	3102.2	52.29	4220.11	71.13
2003	3586.6	60.22	4749.34	79.74
2004	3577.8	60.61	4604.01	77.99
2005	3547.1	59.71	4435.41	74.66
2006	3559.5	59.57	4321.53	72.32
2007	3552.9	59.08	4193.73	69.74
2008	4862	78.51	5578.37	90.08
2009	5392	86.32	6063.00	97.06
2010	3047	48.4	3322.84	52.78
2011	3143	49.5	3357.10	52.87
2012	3110	48.73	3268.79	51.22
2013	3674	57.22	3786.51	58.97
2014	4416	68.38	4468.99	69.20
2015 est	4861.00	75.25	4861.00	75.25
Totals	£85.9bn	£1,424.35	£115.4bn	£1,929.69

16

Domestic equivalents of the direct and indirect costs

It is easy to lose all sense of the scale and real value of the large amounts of UK taxpayers' money sent to the EU every year, and of the many more billions of indirect costs incurred as a result of EU membership, especially as the costs are expressed in such a variety of ways as millions or billions of euros or of pounds, and as percentages of GDP or per capita or per household.

This is an attempt to express these expenditures and costs a little more intelligibly by comparing them with other more familiar national spending, including expenditures such as the Premier League, the Olympics and various items of government spending, including health care, hospitals, housing, the police and the courts, aircraft, submarines and aircraft carriers, universities and R&D. The expenditures are all made in a single year, 2013, which is still the most recent year for which many figures are available, and are given alongside its equivalent as a percentage of GDP.

The direct UK cash contribution of £11.5bn to the EU in 2013 is shaded in dark blue on the chart. All the items listed above that row were smaller expenditures and hence allow one to say that the direct costs of the EU membership in that year were:

- More than the total costs of 100,000 hospital nurses plus 20,000 GPs.

- Considerably more than double the annual cost of six university teaching hospital trusts.

- About the same as all central and local government expenditure on housing in that year.

- More than the total construction costs of 6 Astute class nuclear submarines and 2 QE class aircraft carriers.

- Substantially more than the cost of the 2012 Olympics every year.
- Six times the total wages bill of all 20 Premier League clubs in 2013.

The indirect costs of EU membership can only be estimated. These estimates are given in the lightly shaded rows. They vary depending, among other things, on the costs that the analyst cares to include in the estimate. They are all discussed further in the notes below. In these cases, the validity of the cost comparison depends of course on the credibility of the estimate.

If Open Europe's estimate of the costs incurred by 100 top EU regulations is roughly correct, then they equal the entire R&D expenditure conducted in the UK in that year, by universities, businesses, foundations and defence establishments.

If the European Commission estimates of 'red tape' or 'administrative costs' are anywhere near correct, they far exceed the annual UK defence spending, which includes funding the UK's three armed forces.

And if Tim Congdon's estimate is correct, EU membership costs far more than total NHS expenditure.

These figures might well inform the choice to remain in or leave the EU, though it is worth remembering that only the direct costs are recoverable by the UK government in the event of a Brexit. Savings from the indirect costs are only recoverable by those affected and may help to make a more efficient economy and in that sense we all might benefit. However, the UK would no doubt choose to retain some of them.

The chart enables one to see what alternative expenditures options might be possible, on housing, on education, on R&D, on healthcare and on defence, if the UK decides to leave the EU.

Notes on four estimates of indirect costs

The direct cost of membership, shown in the dark blue shaded row, is rather small by comparison with the indirect costs that result from EU policies such as the CAP and CFP, its environmental and renewable agenda, and from its employment health and safety policies such as the Working Time or Temporary Agency Workers Directives.

Table 16.1 Expenditures in 2013	% of UK GDP	in £b	Sources
100,000 day ward nurses Including salary on costs & all admin and capital overheads	0.3	5.4	p.235 working 42 weeks pa, 37.5hrs pw Unit Costs of Health & Social Care, http://www.pssru.ac.uk/project-pages/unit-costs/2013/#sections
20,000 GPs Including care & admin staff, premises, travel & expenses	0.2	4.1	p190, Unit Costs of Health & Social Care, http://www.pssru.ac.uk/project-pages/unit-costs/2013/#sections
6 major teaching hospitals Total operating expenses	0.3	4.8	Royal Free, £608m, Manchester £886m, Leeds £1021m, UCL £856m, Oxford Radcliffe Oxford £823m, Bristol £549m from 2013 –14 annual reports
6 top universities Total operating & capital costs 2013-14	0.2	4.2	Bristol £0.47b, Cambridge £0.964b, Glasgow £0.49b, Manchester £0.24b, Oxford£1.04b, UCL £1.0b
R&D expenditure Total UK government	0.5	7.5	(PESA Table 5.2 all 10 sectors of public sector R&D expenditure £8.5b) OECD http://stats.oecd.org/Index Main Science & Technology Indicators 2013
2 QE-Class aircraft carriers	0.4	6.2	This is the entire multi-year construction cost as of Nov 2013 http://www.bbc.com/news/uk-28153569
6 Astute Class nuclear submarines'	0.3	4.5	Total multi-year construction costs £747m x 6 http://en.wikipedia.org/wiki/Astute-class_submarine
50 RAF Typhoon fighter aircraft	0.3	4.4	2015 unit production cost £87m x 50 *Daily Telegraph* 19 July 2015 http://www.telegraph.co.uk/finance/newsbysector/industry/defence/11749347/
20 Premier League clubs Total wages bill 2013	0.1	1.8	http://www.theguardian.com/football/2014/may/01/premier-league-accounts-club-by-club-david-conn
Olympics 2012 Total final cost	0.5	8.8	http://www.bbc.com/sport/olympics/20041426
Housing & amenities	0.7	11.3	Table 4.2 PESA 2014 FAQs state Table 4.2 'shows total UK public sector spending, which 'includes spending by devolved administrations, local government and public corporations' as well as central government departments.
International services	0.6	10.1	Includes FCO & the entire diplomatic corps around the world. PESA 2014

Table 16.1

Expenditures in 2013	% of UK GDP	in £b	Sources
EU direct net payments 2013	**0.8**	**11.5**	http://ec.europa.eu/budget/financialreport/2013/lib/financial_report
Transport	1.2	20.2	PESA 2014
R&D Total public & private UK expenditure	1.7	27.8	Of all kinds public & private OECD http://stats.oecd.org/Index Main Science & Technology Indicators 2013
1. Open Europe Net indirect costs of 'Top 100' EU regulations	1.7	27.4	http://openeurope.org.uk/intelligence/britain-and-the-eu/top-100-eu-rules-cost-britain-33-3bn Net of estimated benefits see notes
Public Order & safety	1.8	30.2	Police and courts PESA 2014
Defence	2.2	36.4	PESA 2014
Public Sector debt interest	2.9	48.0	PESA 2014
2. EC 'red tape' estimate 2004	4.0	69.4	The EC estimate in 2004 was 4% of GDP, the figure is 4% of UK GDP in 2013 see notes
3. EU 'administrative costs' (EC estimate 2012)	6.0	104.1	EC Better Regulation website 12 Feb 2012 see notes
Education total expenditure	5.5	90.2	PESA 2014
NHS total expenditure	7.9	129.5	PESA 2014
4. Congdon estimate EU total costs	11.5	185	p.7: http://www.timcongdon4ukip.com/docs/EU2014.pdf see notes.
Social protection All welfare & benefits	15.4	251.3	PESA 2014

Tables 4.3,4.4,5.2, Public Sector expenditure on services by function & as a per cent of GDP 2013-14, pp.62-72, HM Treasury, Public Expenditure Statistical Analyses 2014, July 2014, Cm 8902 https://www.gov.uk/government/uploads/system/uploads/attachment_data/file/223600/public_expenditure_statistical_analyses_2013.pdf

The ultimate costs of these and other measures are often difficult to measure and estimates are subject to large margins of error, and therefore the subject of debate. This is not the place to try to settle those debates. The four estimates of the indirect costs of membership are entered in the lighter shaded rows. These notes simply explain how each of the estimates came to be in the public domain and leave the reader to decide which they find to be more credible.

1. Open Europe's estimate of the costs of the 'Top 100' EU regulations

This estimate starts from Open Europe's analysis of the impact assessments (IAs) conducted by the UK government on regulations and directives proposed by the European Commission. However, apart from the costs, these IAs also attempt to assess the benefits of the proposed regulation. Unfortunately, Open Europe's analysis indicates that the latter are 'almost certainly vastly over-stated'. They give the EU's climate targets as one example of several. Their estimated benefit was £20.4 billion, but this was dependent on a global deal to reduce carbon emissions that never materialized. In fact, Open Europe estimates that 'up to 95% of the benefits envisaged in the UK Government's IAs have failed to materialise.'

Even the most mildly sceptical person would have to acknowledge that the UK government's determination to sell the benefits of EU membership to the British people gives it a strong incentive to provide flattering data about EU activities, or when that becomes difficult, no data at all. This is not, I might add, Open Europe's view. The £27.7billion figure is their final assessment of the costs net of plausible benefits.[1]

2. European Commission's estimate of red tape in 2004

In 2004, speaking to the Confederation of British Industry as EU trade commissioner-designate, Lord Mandelson according to the report in the *Financial Times*:

> ...said the cost of EU red tape is roughly double the economic benefits generated by the Single Market. Regulation amounted to about four per cent of the EU's gross domestic product.[2]

---

1   http://openeurope.org.uk/intelligence/britain-and-the-eu/100-most-expens-ive-eu-regulations/

2   Jean Eaglesham and Frederick Studemann, 'Mandelson calls for Brussels to pick fights', *Financial Times*, 8 November 2004: http://www.ft.com/cms/s/0/bf97ad9a-31c2-11d9-97c0-00000e2511c8.html#axzz3cT0ItOZK. The quotations refer to the FT report, and not to the words of Lord Mandelson.

Lord Mandelson has never repeated this surprising admission. However, in a review of the literature of the costs of the EU, Jonathan Lindsell noted that in the same year the Dutch finance minister gave exactly the same 4 per cent figure for the burden to the Netherlands, which suggests that the figure came from official sources within the EU.[3]

This is therefore included as one estimate of the costs of the EU to the UK, even though it obliges us to assume that what was then true of the EU as a whole, and for the Netherlands, was also true of the UK, that there have been no significant increases or decreases between 2004 and 2013 and we have no idea how it was arrived at.

Such vague and dated estimates have to be included only because we lack anything better, as a result of the reluctance of either the EU or the UK government to undertake regular reliable surveys of the costs of regulation, despite both being committed to reducing them.

3. The European Commission's estimate of administrative costs of 6% GDP in 2012

The Commission figures about the costs of regulation tend to arrive out of the blue. In 2006 Günther Verheugen, Commissioner for Industry & Enterprise, stated that the average cost of regulation for member states was 5.5 per cent of GDP, though in the following year, he revised the figure down to 3.5 per cent, without giving any explanation of where either figure came from.[4]

Another out-of-the-blue estimate came on the Commission's Better Regulation website in 2012. It reported that 'According to estimates it would be feasible to reduce administrative costs by as much as 25 per cent by 2012. This would have a significant economic impact on EU economy - an increase in the level of GDP of about 1.5 per cent or around €150 billion.'[5] If 25 per cent of the

---

3   Jonathan Lindsell, 'Does the EU impede the UK's economic growth?' Civitas, Europe Debate series, No.2, 2014.

4   Ibid.

5   Commission of the European Communities, 'Reducing Administrative Burdens in the EU', Brussels 28 January 2009: http://ec.europa.eu/governance/ betterregulation.The EC did not date its estimates, but given that it is referring, in 2012, to a target 'by 2012', one guesses that it is referring to the study which it had conducted in 2009.

administrative costs amount to €150bn and about 1.5 per cent of GDP, then it seems reasonable to infer that the EU's total administrative costs were €600bn per annum and about six per cent of the EU's GDP. Obviously, it would be preferable to have a direct statement of the total administrative costs, along with an explanation of how they were collected, but in their absence, we have taken this as a second very rough estimate, and again have to assume that what was true of the EU as a whole might also be true of the UK.

4. Tim Congdon's estimate in 2014

This estimate explains its methodology in detail, identifies and explains line by line the costs included, focuses specifically on the UK, and endeavours to measure all the costs of membership, not just those of regulation.[6] His work is based on earlier work by Gerard Batten and has been revised annually some six times, and draws on all the available published research over these years. Congdon concluded that, in 2013, EU membership cost the UK about £185bn or 11.5 per cent of its GDP. Until the UK government, the EU or some other agency sets about the task with as much care and documented detail as Congdon it must be considered the best estimate we have to date.

As he has been an active member of UKIP, it may be as well to add that he is also a distinguished professional economist, and that his method during this research was, as he put it, 'to avoid giving my own opinion, but to use other people's expertise and to cite other sources. With some exceptions (which I made clear in the text), every number was not mine, but that of another authority or individual.'[7]

His estimate of the costs of regulation turns out to be the same as that of the Commission given above, but his total estimate is considerably higher because he includes items which other

---

6   Tim Congdon, 'How much does the European Union cost Britain?' UK Independence Party, Seventh Edition, 2014, p.7: http://www.timcongdon 4ukip.com/docs/EU2014.pdf.

7   Tim Congdon, 'How much does the European Union cost Britain?' UK Independence Party, Seventh Edition, 2014, p.11: http://www.timcongdon4ukip.com/docs/EU2014.pdf.

estimates omit: the higher prices paid by consumers as a result of the Common Agricultural Policy, lost jobs owing to free movement, losses from fraud, waste and corruption and the potential costs for contingent liabilities. Any attempt to provide a comprehensive estimate would, one imagines, address these possible costs.

In my view it ought also to include the potentially enormous losses caused by many lost years of freer trade.

Part Four

The Common and Single Market

17

An overview of UK export growth since 1960

This overview focuses on UK exports and on their growth, as do many of the charts that follow. It does so on the grounds that this is the decisive metric in assessing the merits, from a trade point of view, of remaining in or leaving the EU. Figures on 'trade' alone or 'trade intensity' combine imports and exports, and neither Edward Heath nor anyone else who negotiated UK entry did so on the grounds that the UK could increase its imports.

Figure 17.1 presents the UK exports to 14 countries that were to become members of the present EU from 1960 to 2012, as a percentage of total UK exports to all 22 of the OECD countries for

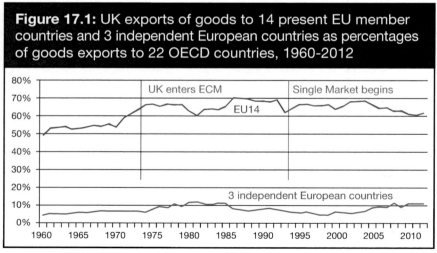

Figure 17.1: UK exports of goods to 14 present EU member countries and 3 independent European countries as percentages of goods exports to 22 OECD countries, 1960-2012

The 14 present EU members are members of the EU up to 1995 following the admission of Austria, Finland and Sweden. The three independent European countries are Iceland, Norway and Switzerland.

Source: *Monthly Statistics on International Trade, Dataset: trade in value by partner countries, United Kingdom.* Since exports to Belgium and Luxembourg were not recorded from 1960-1993 imports from the UK recorded by the Belgium and Luxembourg Economic Union were substituted over these years. Both databases are at www.oecd.ilibrary.org

which we have data over this half century. To provide a comparative marker, it also gives the proportion going to the three European countries that opted to remain independent.

What it shows is that the proportion of goods going to the future EU member countries grew rather sharply, by 12%, over the twelve years before the UK entered the Common Market, from 49.6% in 1960 to 61.6% in 1972. However, over the 40 years of EU membership, for all the costs and obligations incurred, for all the treaties negotiated, and for all the immense time and anguish spent arguing about various aspects of the EU project, the proportion of UK exports going to the UK's future EU partners has hardly changed at all. To be precise, it has fallen by 2%, from 63.9% in 1973, the year of entry, to 61.9% in 2012; 0.5% of the fall occurred during the years of the Single Market, despite the insider advantages the UK was supposedly enjoying.

The overall impression of this graph is, surely, that EU membership and the Single Market changed nothing. Year by year, the proportion has, as the graph shows, fluctuated a little, near 60% in 1981, and touching 70% in 1986-87, and there is an ominous downwards slide since 2004, (some years before the financial crisis one may note), but there is no indication whatever, by this first simple measure, that the EU or the Single Market has had any impact on UK exports of goods at all. It therefore gives no clue as to where the insider advantages might be found.

The green line plotting the proportion of the exports of the three independent countries only makes matters worse. It also fluctuates, but overall it contrasts with exports to the present members of the EU. Instead of continuity and slight decline, exports to these three countries increased during all three periods, before the UK joined the EU and was still a member of EFTA, from 5.1% to 6.5%; over the Common Market years from, 6.0 to 7.6%, and most of all under the Single Market, from 7.0% to 10.7%. Over the half century, therefore, the proportion going to the non-EU members has more than doubled, so the Single Market years have been rather good years for UK exports to them, even though they are not members of it, and have no part in determining its rules. By themselves, these figures suggest that the UK enjoyed more advantages trading with outsiders, albeit outsiders with which the UK or the European Commission had bilateral trade agreements, than with fellow insiders.

Figure 17.2 presents an overview of the UK exports of goods to the other 11 founder members of the EU Single Market since 1960, as a share of UK export of goods to the world. Their share of the UK's total goods exports increased rapidly in the 12 years before entry, to 48% in 1973, and continued to grow rapidly under the Common Market to a peak of 64% in 1989. It reached 68% in 2004 and again in 2007, but since then has been rapidly declining, and was just 36% in 2015 – the same share as it was in 1971, two years before the UK entered the Community.

Figure 17.2: A timeline of UK exports of goods to the other 11 founder members of the Single Market as % of UK world exports 1960-2015

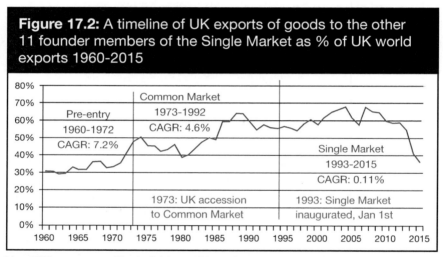

Note: UK imports reported by the Belgium and Luxembourg Economic Union were used in place of the missing figures UK exports to Belgium and Luxembourg up to 1992.The missing entry for exports to Spain in 2013 was assumed to be the same as in 2012. Fourth quarters of exports to the EU 11 and to the World in 2015 were estimated by assuming they were the same proportion of the annual totals as in 2014. Source: OECD iLibrary 1960-2009 *Monthly Statistics on International Trade, Dataset, 2010 -2015* Trade in value by partner countries. Extracted 26 April 2016.

Over the 13 pre-entry years:

- the real value of UK exports to these 11 countries grew by 131%;

- at a compound annual growth rate of 7.2%;

- and their share of the UK's world goods exports increased from 30.6% to 41.8%.

Over the two Common Market decades:

- the real value of UK exports to these 11 countries grew by 136%;

- and at a compound annual growth rate of 4.6%;

- and their share of the UK's world goods exports increased from 48.1 to 57.5%.

Over the 23 years of the Single Market:

- the real value of UK exports to these 11 countries grew by 2.5%;

- and at a compound annual growth rate of 0.11%;

- and their share of the UK's world goods exports fell from 56.0% to 36.3%.

By whatever of these three measures one prefers to use, the Single Market has been an era of decline, in which UK exports to fellow members of the Single Market have sharply decelerated. If one of the goals of the Single Market was to raise UK exports to fellow members it has failed spectacularly.

No serious attempt has been made to explain why this has happened, probably because, in the UK at least, the Single Market has been continuously sold as a success story, and even as the 'Crown Jewel ' of European integration, so no-one really wants to acknowledge that it has serious problems.

18

The success of the Common Market
1973-1992

Before measuring the advantages of membership of the European
Single Market, it will be useful to look back to the Common
Market, which many older voters will say is the market they voted
for 1975.

Setting up a fair comparison

So that we can make fair comparisons of an equal number of 11
member countries, we have to assume that Greece, Spain and
Portugal became members along with the UK, Ireland and
Denmark in 1973, instead of 1981 and 1984 respectively. We also
have to draw a dividing line in 1992 as marking the end of the
Common Market, and 1993 as the start of the Single Market, so
that we can compare two decades of both. In fact, the Single
Market reforms were agreed in the Single European Act of 1986,
and phased in gradually over subsequent years. 1 January 1993
was merely the formal inaugural date.

The illuminating metric

We will take export growth relative to non-member exporters as
the critical index of success or failure. This is a more illuminating
measure than either the absolute value of exports to the EU, or the
proportion of exports going to the EU, since the value and
proportion of UK exports to its near neighbours were both higher
than many non-member countries long before the UK entered the
Common Market. Nor is growth of trade as a whole particularly
illuminating. Nine years out of every ten trade grows in most

countries of the world that are not at war. The volume of trade is the sum of imports and exports so an increase in trade alone might simply mean a large increase in imports and no increase in exports. The UK might be said to have joined the European Community to increase its trade with other members but, more specifically, it hoped to increase its exports to them. Since we wish to know if any observed increase is out of the ordinary, the most important single measure is the increase in the rate of UK exports compared to non-member exports to the same 11 EU members.

Table 18.1 presents a list of the 35 fastest-growing exporters to the 11 members of the EU who were to be the founding members of the Single Market[1] over the two Common Market decades.

It shows that growth of UK exports over the 20 Common Market years increased by 192%, putting it in 15th place overall. However, most of those above the UK on the list were either emerging exporting countries or oil producers. If these were eliminated, the UK would have been very near the top of the list, with Japan ahead, and only Singapore, China and Hong Kong, and possibly Turkey, as contenders for second place, depending on which of them we wish to exclude as start-up exporters.

Moreover, the growth of UK exports in these decades exceeded that of the United States and several other countries that were well-established in the global trading networks at the time: Australia, Argentina, Canada, Switzerland, Norway and South Africa.

The comparison with the United States is especially telling. In 1973, the average monthly value of UK exports of $994m per month was slightly lower than the $1,006m of U.S exports. In 1974, it surpassed them, and then continued to grow at a faster pace until 1992 when, at $9,170m, their value was nearly 50% higher than the $6,108m value of U.S exports. Demonstrating that the country with the highest monthly average value need not invariably have a low rate of growth.

There are, therefore, grounds for thinking that the UK enjoyed certain advantages in exporting to fellow EU members over these years.

---

1   12 members founded the Single Market however the UK has been excluded.

Table 18.1: Top 35 fastest-growing exporters to the Common Market, 1973-1992

Rank	Country	% real growth in US(1973)$	Exports per month in 1973 US(1973)$m	Exports per month in 1992 US(1992)$m
1	Korea	1219	14	584
2	Saudi Arabia	670	28	691
3	UAE	590	14	311
4	Taiwan	494	29	551
5	Bahrain	454	3	45
6	Thailand	431	19	318
7	Singapore	393	30	465
8	China +HK	385	82	1262
9	Qatar	334	3	36
10	Indonesia	256	32	364
11	Japan	212	193	1902
12	Turkey	204	77	741
13	Pakistan	203	15	141
14	Mexico	199	57	540
15	**UK**	**192**	**994**	**9170**
16	Egypt	188	36	327
17	Kuwait	149	17	131
18	India	136	40	298
19	Morocco	125	51	363
20	Chile	113	20	131
21	Israel	102	68	432
22	Vietnam	96	5	28
23	Australia	95	78	483
24	US	92	1006	6108
25	Nigeria	89	42	249
26	Argentina	89	45	858
27	Switzerland	87	643	3806
28	Canada	82	118	679
29	Iceland	75	10	57
30	New Zealand	62	14	71
31	Norway	51	182	873
32	Kenya	14	8	28
33	S. Africa	-2	129	397
34	Bangladesh	-8	10	28
35	Brazil	-15	126	339

The figures vindicate those who voted to remain in the Common Market because they thought free trade would mean an increase in exports to fellow members.

Here is another take on exports over the same common market decades. Figure 18.1 compares the growth in the total value of UK exports of goods to the EU11 with the mean of seven founder or long-standing members of the OECD: Australia, Canada, Iceland, Japan, Norway, Switzerland and the United States, whose trade with EU countries was well-established, and well-documented at the time. Over all the Common Market years, as may be clearly seen, UK exports to the EU grew at a decidedly more rapid rate than those of these seven OECD countries, and by the end of the two decades had grown almost twice as much. This result is still more remarkable when one remembers that the seven OECD countries include Japan, which over this period was at the height of its export-led rapid growth years.

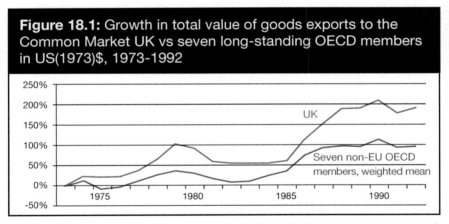

Figure 18.1: Growth in total value of goods exports to the Common Market UK vs seven long-standing OECD members in US(1973)$, 1973-1992

Source: *Monthly Statistics on International Trade, Dataset: trade in value by partner countries*, www.oecd-ilibrary.org.

Over these years, therefore, it is plausible to argue that the UK enjoyed some kind of insider advantage because of membership of the European Common Market.

But what kind of advantage was it? The directives and regulations which have 'harmonised' the member countries under the Single Market were barely under way, and indeed the entire EU institutional apparatus, surrounded by lobbyists/stakeholders and its culture of comitology, were still rudimentary. Apart from the bracing effects of competition within the Common Market, there are three possibilities that first come to mind. First, the strong economic growth in France, Germany and Italy, which may or may not have been a consequence of the Common Market. Second, the one distinctive characteristic of the Common Market over all those years, the rather high common external tariff. Perhaps this tariff restricted the growth of the exports of the seven OECD members, to the advantage of the UK which, as an EU member, was not subject to it.

The third possibility is that other trade costs, and in particular transport costs, were still high. As a result, the UK enjoyed the advantage of being the near neighbour of its customers, whereas the four largest of the other OECD exporters were geographically distant. That, as the popular gravity theory of trade insists, can make a difference. The rule of thumb derived from this theory is 'other things being equal, doubling the geographic distance between countries halves the trade between them.'[2]

Our task here, however, is not to find an explanation of the remarkable growth of UK exports over these years, but the much simpler one of documenting it and providing a marker, helping us to see how well exports have performed later under the Single Market.

---

2   This is taken from the discussion and documentation of the evidence to support this theory in Pankaj Ghemawat with Steven A. Altman DHL Global Connectedness Index of 2011

19

The failure of the Single Market
1993-2012

In terms of the growth of UK exports to other members, the Single Market has been an era of decline, though not for those of non-members. This contrast has attracted little attention from politicians or analysts

We may begin to compare the Common Market with the Single Market decades by again taking UK exports to the other 11 founder members, and compare the growth of these exports with that of 34 non-member countries. The results are presented, as we have previously, in a rank of the top 35 fastest-growing exporters.

Over these decades, a number of smaller countries had entered export markets for the first time. Often they have tiny starting figures and therefore record high growth rates. Simply to keep the list manageable, a minimum requirement of exports to the EU11 of at least $500m per month in 2012 was set for inclusion in the comparison. As in the Common Market ranking, the exports of

Table 19.1: Top 35 fastest-growing exporters of goods to 11 founding members of the EU Single Market, 1993-2012

Rank	Country	% real Growth over 20 years in US(1993)$	Exports per month in 2012 in US(2012)$
1	Vietnam	545	0.5
2	Ukraine*	471	1.2
3	United Arab Emirates	399	2.8
4	China & Hong Kong	398	14.9
5	Kazakhstan	379	0.5
6	Russia	376	8.1

Table 19.1: Top 35 fastest-growing exporters of goods to 11 founding members of the EU Single Market, 1993-2012

Rank	Country	% real Growth over 20 years in US(1993)$	Exports per month in 2012 in US(2012)$
7	Brazil	347	3.4
8	India	311	3.1
9	Turkey*	267	6.0
10	Australia	235	2.6
11	Algeria	211	1.9
12	Chile*	196	0.7
13	South Africa*	195	1.9
14	Nigeria	191	0.9
15	Mexico*	191	2.5
16	Korea*	188	3.0
17	Malaysia	178	1.2
18	Morocco*	166	1.6
19	Singapore	162	2.4
20	Colombia*	158	0.5
21	Lebanon	140	0.6
22	Canada	138	2.3
23	United States	128	23.2
24	Saudi Arabia	119	2.4
25	Venezuela	117	0.6
26	Switzerland*	103	11.5
27	Egypt*	101	1.3
28	Norway*	100	2.6
29	Tunisia*	95	1.1
	EU11	75	140.4
30	Thailand	75	1.2
31	United Kingdom	72	23.6
32	Libya	58	0.6
33	Argentina	57	0.8
34	Japan	53	4.7
35	Indonesia	41	0.8

Source: www.oecd-ilibrary.org.OECD database Monthly Statistics of International Trade

these 34 countries to the UK were subtracted from their totals, since the UK cannot, of course, export to itself.

Twelve of the countries in the table are starred (*) to indicate that they enjoy trading advantages with the EU by virtue of Free Trade Agreements (FTAs) they have negotiated with the EU. These came into force either before or during these decades of the Single Market.[1]

The UK, it may be seen, has fallen from 15th position under the Common Market years to 31st under the Single Market years. This is fractionally below the rate of growth of the rest of the exports of other founding members of the Single Market to each other. 30 non-member countries, many of whom have had to face tariff and non-tariff barriers, have therefore been able to increase their exports to 11 founder members of the Single Market at a faster rate than the UK. In addition, these non-member countries have not been sitting at the table and helping to make the rules.

To some degree, this fall is not unexpected, since even after excluding some 19 mini-exporters, the ranking still includes a number of what UNCTAD calls 'emerging', 'transitional', 'middle-income developing countries' as well as 'petroleum and gas producing countries'. In many cases, the value of their exports was extremely low at the start of the period and they therefore show high rates of growth during it.

In many contexts, one would not want to consider these smaller newly-emerging exporters alongside 'major exporters of manufacture goods', long-established in world trade, like the UK. In the present context, however, it is of some interest to observe how they coped with exporting to the Single Market. They are, compared with the UK, doubly disadvantaged in the sense that they not only face the tariff and non-tariff barriers of the Single Market, but also the obstacles of opening new markets. It is not unusual for UK exporters to complain about the latter. Plainly, many have coped, and even prospered, despite their double disadvantage.

The fall in the UK's rank order position is certainly not due simply to the inclusion of these newly-emerging exporters. The real growth

---

1   The agreements with Norway and Switzerland came into force in 1973, Turkey in 1996, Tunisia in 1998, Mexico and South Africa in 2000, Egypt in 2004, Algeria in 2005, Korea in 2011, Columbia in 2013 and the agreement concluded with Ukraine in 2014, which came into force on January 1st 2016.

of UK exports over these exporters was only 72 per cent, whereas over the Common Market decades it was 192 per cent. That decline is real. More importantly, over the Common Market decades we observed that UK exports had grown more than those of Australia, Argentina, Canada, Switzerland, Norway and South Africa, all of which were already established exporters of the day. In contrast, during the Single Market decades UK exports grew less than all of them except Argentina. That is a second indication of a real decline.

Another take on this decline may again be presented by a graph, similar to that for the Common Market decades, comparing the growth in value of UK exports to the other 11 EU members over the 20 years of the Single Market with that of the same seven OECD, non-EU countries.

Over the first six years, from 1993 to 1999, it may be seen that the value of UK exports still grew at a faster rate than the seven OECD countries, though with nothing like the same lead it enjoyed during the Common Market years. From 2000 to 2004 the differences are slight, but from that year on, the UK slipped behind their rate of growth, and from 2009 more markedly behind, so that by the end of 20 years in 2012, the exports of the seven OECD countries recorded real growth of 124 per cent whereas the UK's was only 72 per cent.

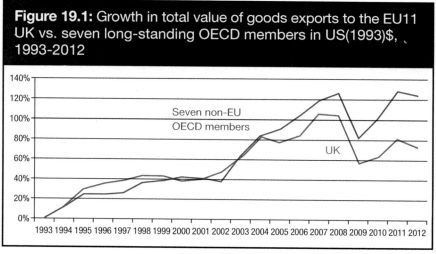

Figure 19.1: Growth in total value of goods exports to the EU11 UK vs. seven long-standing OECD members in US(1993)$, 1993-2012

Source: www.oecd-ilibrary.org.OECD database *Monthly Statistics of International Trade*
The seven non-EU OECD members are Australia, Canada, Iceland, Japan, Norway, Switzerland and the United States.
Missing data for exports from Switzerland to Ireland in 2002, from Iceland to Netherlands 1996-2011 and to Spain in 1997 are estimated as a proportion of exports from the OECD to the EU-11, based in years with complete data.

The American comparison

The comparison with the United States is again especially telling. We have seen how the UK, in total value, overtook US exports in 1973 at the moment of entering the Common Market. The UK then pulled steadily ahead over the next twenty years so that exports were 50 per cent higher in value in the final year of the Common Market. Uncannily, 1992 was to be their high point. Ever since, the differential between the value of UK and US exports has been declining. The US real growth to 2012 was 128 per cent, slightly above the OECD 7 mean, and as a result they had, at \$23.2b per month, almost equalled the value of UK exports (\$23.6b), though still not overtaken them.

These changes in the relative position of the two countries gives reason to question the familiar, rather lazy defence of low UK growth, that since the value of UK exports is high relative to non-members, one must expect its growth to be low. The high value of UK exports in 1973 did not prevent them growing more than those of the US over the next twenty years, and the relatively high value of US exports in 1992 did not prevent them subsequently all but catching up with the UK.

Contrast with the Common Market

The graph of the Common Market years gave grounds for thinking that UK exports had benefited from membership, that there was some kind of insider advantage. We were not altogether sure what it was, and still have to wait on research that takes account of all the many factors that may affect export performance to identify it.

In the case of the Single Market, it is difficult to believe that there are any benefits from membership, or any kind of insider advantage. Even if there were in the early years, it has been disappearing the longer it continued to harmonize, regulate and level the playing field of its members.

It might perhaps be argued that there was and is an insider advantage, which for the moment we cannot identify, and that without it, the growth of UK exports would have fallen below 31st place, registered still less than 72 per cent real growth, and fallen still further behind these other six OECD countries. However, that is only worth considering if we have grounds for thinking that UK exports would have fallen dramatically if the UK had not joined the European Single Market.

Improbable claims

One of the more improbable claims about these opportunities was made by Ed Davey, when Minister of State at the Department of Business, Innovation & Skills. He told the House of Lords Select Committee in 2010 that 'EU countries trade twice as much with each other as they would do in the absence of the Single Market programme.'[2] Another was made by the Centre for European Reform. It constructed an economic model which showed that Britain's EU membership 'has boosted its trade in goods with other member states by 55 per cent'.[3]

These claims refer to trade (i.e. imports plus exports) rather than exports alone, so one must assume they would claim slightly less for the growth of exports, but both have been examined in some detail elsewhere and shown to be far beyond the credible.[4] Applying them roughly to the present evidence, Davey's would mean that, had it not been for the Single Market programme, the real growth rate of UK exports to its members would have been somewhere around 36 per cent over the 20 years of the Single Market. When looking at the CER's claim, had it not been for EU membership, the real growth of UK exports to these countries would have been around 50 per cent. If the former were true, the UK would not have made these rankings at all, and would have had one of the world's

---

2   House of Lords Select Committee on the European Union (Sub-Committee B), Inquiry into Re-launching the Single Market, Oral and associated written evidence, Department for Business, Innovation and Skills, written evidence (EUSM 7), 14 October 2010, p.110, Available from: https://www.parliament.uk/documents/lords-committees/eu-sub-com-b/single-marketinquiry/singlemarketwo.pdf Oral evidence was given on 24 January 2011, pp.119-137.

3   Centre for European Reform, *The Economic Consequences of Leaving the EU*, London, June 2014, p.10, Available from: https://www.cer.org.uk/sites/default/files/smc_final_report_june2014.pdf

4   M. Burrage, *The Myth and Paradox of the Single Market*, London, Berforts Group Ltd, 2016, pp.8-88, pp. 161-167, Available from: http://www.civitas.org.uk/content/files/mythandparadox.pdf

lowest rates of export growth. If the latter were true, it would have been in 34th position. But neither need be taken seriously. They have merely succumbed to the Single Market myth.

In 2005, an HM Treasury team estimated that EU membership had increased UK trade with other members by 7 per cent.[5] This has at least the merit of being within the bounds of the possible.

Possible explanations

This evidence only reports what has happened. It does not explain why the exports of UK goods should have performed rather poorly by comparison with the Common Market decades, and confounded all reasonable expectations, extravagant promises and confident claims about the benefits of the Single Market programme.

Among the plausible explanations are the contemporaneous fall in the level of EU tariff protection and in the trade costs of non-members,[6] as well as the adoption of the euro. From non-members' point of view, the euro is after all a public good. Whatever its disadvantages for member countries, it has been extremely convenient for non-member exporters to have just one unit of account and one rate of exchange for all transactions for all 11 of these countries, given that the Danish kronor is pegged to the euro.

Enthusiastic British supporters of the Single Market continually claim that there are invaluable advantages for the UK and other members from sitting at the table and helping to make the rules. This evidence suggests that sitting at the table makes no difference whatever, and that if invited to do so, non-members would be well advised to decline, which they would probably do anyway, when told what their country's taxpayers would have to pay for the privilege.

---

5   HM Treasury, *EU Membership and Trade*, 2005, p. 7, Available from: https://www.gov.uk/government/uploads/system/uploads/attachment_da ta/file/220968/foi_eumembership_trade.pdf
6   Examples include comprehensive containerisation, more efficient customs procedures, and lower transport and cargo handling charges.

20

What would have happened to UK exports if there had been no Single Market?

'What ifs' are usually intuitive, speculative games, where no two people who play get the same answer. In this case, however, there is a simple, robust method of finding out what would have happened in the absence of the Single Market which any Microsoft Excel user can perform and where everyone will always arrive at exactly the same answer.[1]

It makes only one assumption, that absolutely nothing changed in 1986 or 1993, and that the Single Market had not been thought of. Therefore, there has been no EU directives or regulations regarding the Single Market, and UK exports to the EU have continued to grow between 1993 and 2012 as they had done over the preceding two Common Market decades (1973-1992).

Needless to say, this gives a wholly imaginary reconstruction, though for analytical purposes, when placed alongside what really happened to exports from 1993 to 2012, it is illuminating. It allows us to see how far actual export growth differed from this imaginary export growth curve when all the factors that are known to affect exports such as variations in tariff and exchange rates, raw material, capital, labour and transport costs, and

---

1   Which means that, as we have used publicly available OECD data, anyone can verify or correct the conclusions of the analysis with a few clicks of their mouse. The calculations make use of the Excel growth function which instantly calculates the exponential growth curve through a given set of export values over a given set of years, in this case from 1973-1992. This can then be extended year by year to calculate additional export values, in this case for the 20 years 1993-2012. In all the cases considered below, the linear growth curve differs only marginally from the exponential, usually with a lower best fit R^2 measure.

production technologies, continued to operate exactly as they had done over the preceding decades.

For the sake of this exercise we have taken 1 January 1993 as the formal start date of the Single Market programme, though we know some elements of the programme began to be phased in after the Single European Act came into force in 1987. And to make meaningful comparisons we have also held constant the number of member countries. Three of the founding members of the Single Market, Greece, Portugal and Spain, were not members of the EU in 1973. So we have backdated their entry to 1973.

The blue line in Figure 20.1 shows the actual growth of UK exports to the EU over the 40 years 1973 to 2012 in constant US(1973)$. The red line is the exponential trend line of UK export growth over the first two decades, and as the R^2 indicates, it is quite a close fit with the recorded figures from which it is drawn.

The striking feature of this imaginary extrapolation is the extent to which real UK goods exports to other founding members of the

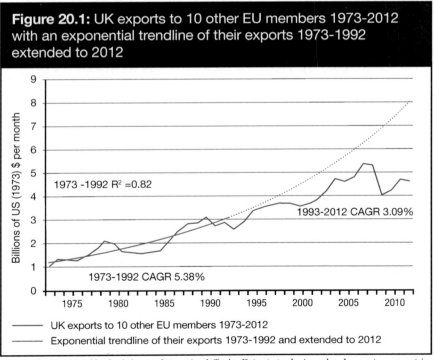

Figure 20.1: UK exports to 10 other EU members 1973-2012 with an exponential trendline of their exports 1973-1992 extended to 2012

1973 -1992 R^2 =0.82

1993-2012 CAGR 3.09%

1973-1992 CAGR 5.38%

Billions of US (1973) $ per month

——— UK exports to 10 other EU members 1973-2012
——— Exponential trendline of their exports 1973-1992 and extended to 2012

Source: OECD, *Monthly Statistics on International Trade, Dataset:* trade in value by partner countries www.oecd.ilibrary.org/statistics (now discontinued in favour of Quarterly, but I continued up to 2012 in Monthly)

Single Market have fallen short of what they would have been had they continued to grow as they had done under the Common Market. It represents a shortfall of 22.6 per cent in value.

If UK exports to other members had continued to grow at the CAGR of 5.38 per cent as they had during the Common Market years, they would have been just short of US(1973)$8bn per month by 2012. In reality, they grew at a CAGR of 3.09 per cent over the Single Market years, and were US(1973)$4.6bn per month by 2012, equating to $23.4bn in 2012 US dollars.

This large shortfall is due in part to the financial crisis. We can calculate their growth up to their peak pre-crisis year in 2007 and assume that the pre-crisis boom was part of the normal growth path of the Single Market. The CAGR from 1993 to 2007 was 5.3 per cent, and therefore only 0.08 per cent below that of the Common Market years. Over the first 15 years of the Single Market, UK exports to other members were almost keeping pace with the growth during the Common Market years. The shortfall in the exports to other members up to 2007 is only 14.6 per cent. This increased to a shortfall of 22.6 per cent over the following five years to 2012.

The UK in a portrait of the Single Market's failure

This analysis is part of a larger study which also compared UK exports to OECD members over the Common Market and Single Market decades, the exports of EU members to one another and to the other OECD members, and the exports of OECD members to EU members.[2] The results are summarized in the chart below.

The dark columns show the growth in the total value of exports over the 20 years of the Single Market. The lighter columns show the same for growth up to the peak year as a percentage of growth under 20 years of the Common Market before the financial crisis, this being 2008 in all cases except for the UK when it is 2007. The figures in the columns give the CAGR over the same periods, and the yellow figures at the base of the dark blue column give the CAGR over the Common Market decades.

---

2   M. Burrage, *Myth and Paradox of the Single Market*, Civitas, London, 2016, Available from: http://www.civitas.org.uk/content/files/mythandparadox.pdf

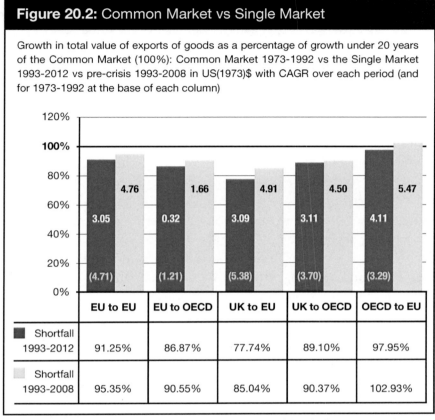

Figure 20.2: Common Market vs Single Market

Growth in total value of exports of goods as a percentage of growth under 20 years of the Common Market (100%): Common Market 1973-1992 vs the Single Market 1993-2012 vs pre-crisis 1993-2008 in US(1973)$ with CAGR over each period (and for 1973-1992 at the base of each column)

	EU to EU	EU to OECD	UK to EU	UK to OECD	OECD to EU
CAGR 1993-2012	4.76	1.66	4.91	4.50	5.47
CAGR 1973-1992	3.05	0.32	3.09	3.11	4.11
(base)	(4.71)	(1.21)	(5.38)	(3.70)	(3.29)
Shortfall 1993-2012	91.25%	86.87%	77.74%	89.10%	97.95%
Shortfall 1993-2008	95.35%	90.55%	85.04%	90.37%	102.93%

Source: OECD, *Monthly Statistics on International Trade, Dataset: trade in value by partner countries* www.oecd.ilibrary.org/statistics (now discontinued in favour of Quarterly, but I continued up to 2012 in Monthly)

The line at 100 per cent represents the exports of all the five exporters analysed if they had continued at the same rate under the Single Market as they had done under the Common Market years.

The exports of every group has grown less than expected had they grown as much as they did over the 20 Common Market years. However, if we eliminate the impact of the financial crisis of 2008, by measuring export growth only to that year (or in the UK case to 2007), they all performed rather better. However, only the exports of the 8 independent OECD countries grew more than they did over the Common Market years. As one might expect, the CAGR in the value of exports after eliminating the impact of the financial crisis is higher in every case than the CAGR over the 20 years of the Single Market from 1993-2012.

The peculiarities of the UK emerge more clearly in this composite comparative profile. Whilst it had the highest rate of export growth under the 20 years of the Common Market, at a rate of 5.38 per cent, growth under the Single Market has fallen further than any other group, whether measured to 2012 or to 2008. UK exports to the EU are therefore also unique in having a CAGR in the pre-crisis years – in the years when the Single Market was working as it was supposed to work and undisturbed by a financial crisis - that is less than that of the Common Market years. Its exports to the EU also appear to have suffered more from the financial crisis than any other, as indicated both by differences between the total value of exports over the 20 years and the pre-crisis years and by the CAGRs over the two periods.

For the UK the Single Market years have been vastly disappointing in terms of the growth of the exports of its goods to other members. It compares unfavourably not only with the growth of its exports during the Common Market decades and with the growth of UK exports to non-member countries, but also with growth of exports to the Single Market of many OECD countries that are not members of the EU.

This final conclusion, that non-members' exports of goods to the Single Market have grown faster than those of the UK or other members, is counter-intuitive, and profoundly paradoxical. It flies in the face of the claims about the advantages of the Single Market for UK trade that have been made over many years by Britain's political leaders.

21

Have UK goods exporters been losing their touch?

By contrast, UK exports to many other markets over the same years have grown rapidly, suggesting that UK exporters are not to blame

There has been a decline in the growth rate of UK exports during the Single Market. According to one explanation, UK exporters have not been smart or nimble enough to profit from the opportunities it offered.

When a comprehensive analysis of all the other factors that might influence UK export performance is available, this will no doubt be considered a possible explanation. However, until that research is undertaken, it is interesting to compare the growth rate of UK exports to Single Market members with exports to non-member countries.

The 33 fastest-growing markets for UK goods exports over 19 years of the Single Market are listed in the table. It shows that UK exports to 25 non-member countries have grown at a faster rate than those to the 11 other founding members of the single market. These results were not seriously affected by the financial crisis. If we stop the clock in 2008, and calculate the growth of UK exports only to that date, the EU only moves up two places. Growth of exports to the Single Market was slow throughout its 16 pre-crisis years.

Of course, the value of exports to the EU11 far exceeds the value of exports to single non-member countries. Some of the EU11 were among the highest value markets for UK exports. This is in no way remarkable since every nation trades more with their neighbours than with more distant countries. The USA's biggest export markets are Canada and Mexico, not China and Japan.

Table 21.1: Top 33 fastest-growing markets for UK goods exports over the life of the Single Market, 1993-2011

Rank	Country	% growthin 19 years measured in US$(1993)	Mean monthly value in $m (2011)
1	Qatar	16141	638
2	Vietnam	5043	222
3	Nigeria	1268	746
4	Turkey*	651	815
5	Bangladesh	628	199
6	Mexico*	545	180
7	Russia	508	974
8	China + Hong Kong	492	4021
9	Algeria*	446	199
10	Canada	428	1582
11	UA Emirates	413	252
12	Kuwait	368	196
13	Sri Lanka	286	107
14	India	269	784
15	Norway*	255	3601
16	Columbia*	244	117
17	Egypt*	190	106
18	Argentina	186	79
19	Israel*	171	291
20	Australia	159	652
21	Thailand	121	332
22	Bahrain	113	218
23	Brazil	112	373
24	S Africa*	100	389
25	Korea*	92	414
26	**EU 11**	**81**	**23897**
27	Pakistan	80	114
28	Switzerland*	66	933
29	Singapore	62	511
30	Taiwan	41	445
31	US	36	4664
32	Indonesia	27	174
33	New Zealand	22	101

* Countries with which the EU has a preferential trade agreement in place.

Source: www.oecd-ilibrary.org. OECD database *Monthly Statistics of International Trade*
doi:10.1787/data-02279

The promise of EU membership was *growth* in trade, and that promise was fulfilled as we saw in the Common Market decades. It has not been fulfilled under the Single Market.

This data also throws some doubt on the claim that UK exporters have not been smart or nimble enough to take advantage of the opportunities presented by the single market. They must have been quite smart and nimble in some of these other extra-EU markets, where they have not enjoyed the advantage of 'sitting around the table helping to make the rules.' These figures also suggest that this advantage has been much over-rated.

22

A club of high unemployment...

One of the more striking and enduring characteristics of the Single Market is its high rate of unemployment

The distinctive characteristics of unemployment in the Single Market can only be seen and analysed in a comparative perspective. The rate of unemployment of its 12 founder members over the entire life of the Single Market is compared here with 10 independent countries, which seem to be most similar, in terms of their labour market institutions and productivity, to those of the EU12 – Australia, Canada, Iceland, Korea, Japan, New Zealand, Norway, Singapore, Switzerland and the United States.

The three European countries among these 10 independent countries, Switzerland, Norway and Iceland, are also given separately from the 10. They are of particular interest in any attempt to identify the impact of the EU, since comparison with them provides the best chance, indeed the only chance, of distinguishing European characteristics from EU ones.

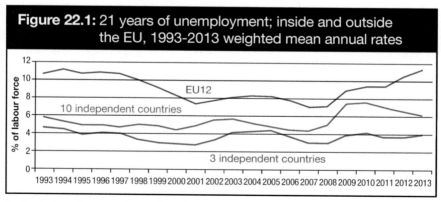

Figure 22.1: 21 years of unemployment; inside and outside the EU, 1993-2013 weighted mean annual rates

The ten independent countries are Australia, Canada, Iceland, Korea, Japan, New Zealand, Norway, Singapore, Switzerland and the United States.
The three independent European countries are Iceland, Norway and Switzerland.
Source: OECD Employment database http://www.oecd.org

Figure 22.1 shows the weighted mean rates of unemployment in the three groups of countries over the years 1993-2011.

Over these 21 years, the 12 EU countries have had a significantly higher rate of unemployment than the 10 independent countries.

The contrast between the unemployment rate of non-EU European countries and that of the EU12 is still more marked. In 18 of these 21 years, EU unemployment has been *more than double* that of these three countries, and in the other three years, 2004-6, it has been only fractionally less than double. This comparison does not therefore support the idea that there is a peculiarly European high unemployment profile. On the contrary, it suggests that high unemployment is a distinctive and enduring EU characteristic, not a European one.

Weighted means of groups may, of course, hide variations within groups, and these may best be seen in Table 22.1 which gives in full the data from which the graph is drawn. The shaded cells of the entries for the EU countries indicate the years in which they have had unemployment rates equal to, or lower than, the mean of the 10 independent countries: Luxembourg and the Netherlands qualify in 13 of the 21 years, and Denmark in 10 of them – but these are a deviant minority, representing just over six per cent of the total labour force of the EU 12. Other EU countries have occasionally joined them, Portugal in six years, the UK in five, Ireland in three and Germany once. Overall, in 52 of the 252 individual years measured, EU members have had unemployment rates equal to or lower than the mean rate of the 10 independent countries.

Deviance on the other side – meaning one of the 10 independent countries having an unemployment rate equal to, or higher than, the mean rate of the EU 12 – is far less common, the exceptions being Australia and Canada in 1993, and the United States in 2009 and 2010. Otherwise, clear blue water separates the independent countries from the EU over all 21 years.

A host of questions

Why is it that unemployment in the EU only began to attract significant media attention when it reached hitherto unimaginable levels in some member states after the financial crisis of 2008? It has been distinctive feature of the Single Market since it began.

Is this distinctively high EU rate of unemployment compatible with the claims of the present Prime Minister, and of several of his predecessors, that the Single Market is good for jobs in Britain?

Why has the distinctive persistence of the EU's unemployment problem not been the subject of continuous investigation, both in the UK, the European Commission and other member countries, so that we might finally understand why it differs from other OECD countries? Why is it in no-one's interest to know?

Who is accountable within the EU? And when and where? No doubt most people will hold their national governments mainly accountable for their continuing high unemployment, but the Commission has a department for dealing with employment which receives substantial funds every year to deal with the problem.[1] But when and how are its various programs evaluated and debated? When have commissioners for employment ever been held personally responsible for them? Why is it that the problem has never figured as a major issue in the elections to the European Parliament?

---

1   The Investment for Growth and Jobs, item 1.2 in the EU Budget, is for the most part administered by the D-G for Employment, Social Affairs & Inclusion. It has increased from €36.9b in 2007 to €54.4b in 2014, and totalled just under €346b for the eight years.

Table 22.1: Annual Unemployment Rates of the 12 founder members of EU Single Market vs 10 independent countries 1993-2013

EU 12 mean annual unemployment shaded cells indicate that the rate equals or is below the mean annual rate of the 10 independent countries

	1993	1994	1995	1996	1997	1998	1999	2000	2001	2002	2003	2004	2005	2006	2007	2008	2009	2010	2011	2012	2013
Belgium	8.1	9.6	9.3	9.5	9.0	9.3	8.6	6.6	6.2	7.5	8.2	8.4	8.4	8.2	7.5	7.0	7.9	8.3	7.1	7.6	8.4
Denmark	10.7	8.0	7.0	6.8	5.4	5.0	5.1	4.5	4.2	4.6	5.4	5.5	4.8	3.9	3.8	3.4	6.0	7.5	7.6	7.5	7.0
France	11.4	12.7	11.9	12.4	12.6	12.1	12.1	10.2	8.6	8.7	8.5	8.8	8.9	8.8	8.0	7.4	9.1	9.4	9.3	9.8	10.4
Germany	7.9	8.4	8.1	8.9	9.8	9.2	8.4	7.7	7.8	8.6	9.3	10.3	11.1	10.3	8.6	7.5	7.7	7.1	5.9	5.4	5.3
Greece	9.0	8.9	9.1	9.7	9.6	10.8	11.7	11.1	10.2	10.3	9.7	10.5	9.8	8.9	8.3	7.7	9.5	12.5	17.7	24.5	28.0
Ireland	15.8	14.8	12.2	12.0	10.3	7.8	5.9	4.5	3.9	4.4	4.6	4.5	4.7	4.6	4.6	5.7	12.0	13.6	14.3	14.7	13.9
Italy	10.0	11.0	11.5	11.5	11.6	11.8	11.3	10.5	9.5	9.0	8.7	8.0	7.7	6.8	6.1	6.7	7.8	8.4	8.4	10.7	12.3
Luxembourg	2.3	3.5	2.9	3.3	2.5	2.8	2.4	2.3	1.8	2.6	3.7	5.1	4.5	4.7	4.1	5.1	5.1	4.4	4.9	5.1	6.9
Netherlands	6.1	6.8	7.0	6.4	5.4	4.3	3.5	3.0	2.5	3.1	4.1	5.0	5.3	4.3	3.6	3.0	3.7	4.5	4.4	5.3	6.7
Portugal	5.3	6.5	6.8	6.8	6.3	4.9	4.4	3.9	4.0	5.0	6.3	6.7	7.6	7.7	8.0	7.6	9.5	10.8	12.7	15.8	16.3
Spain	22.4	23.9	22.7	22.0	20.6	18.6	15.6	13.9	10.5	11.4	11.3	11.0	9.2	8.5	8.3	11.3	18.0	20.1	21.6	24.8	26.2
UK	10.3	9.6	8.6	8.1	7.0	6.1	5.9	5.5	4.7	5.1	4.8	4.6	4.7	5.4	5.3	5.3	7.7	7.8	7.8	7.9	7.7
W'td Mean of 12	10.8	11.4	10.9	11.0	10.8	10.1	9.4	8.4	7.5	7.9	8.0	8.2	8.2	7.8	7.1	7.1	9.0	9.5	9.5	10.5	11.2

10 independent countries annual unemployment rates shaded cells indicate that the rate equals or is above the mean annual rate of the EU 12

	1993	1994	1995	1996	1997	1998	1999	2000	2001	2002	2003	2004	2005	2006	2007	2008	2009	2010	2011	2012	2013
Australia	10.9	9.7	8.5	8.5	8.5	7.7	6.9	6.3	6.8	6.4	5.9	5.4	5	4.8	4.4	4.2	5.6	5.2	5.1	5.2	5.7
Canada	11.4	10.4	9.5	9.6	9.1	8.3	7.6	6.8	7.2	7.7	7.6	7.2	6.8	6.3	6.0	6.1	8.3	8.0	7.4	7.2	7.1
Japan	2.5	2.9	3.2	3.4	3.4	4.1	4.7	4.8	5.0	5.4	5.2	4.7	4.4	4.1	3.9	4.0	5.0	5.0	4.5	4.4	4.0
Korea	2.9	2.5	2.1	2.0	2.6	7.0	6.3	4.4	4.0	3.3	3.6	3.7	3.7	3.4	3.2	3.2	3.6	3.7	3.4	3.2	3.1
New Zealand	9.8	8.4	6.5	6.3	6.8	7.7	7.0	6.2	5.4	5.3	4.8	4.0	3.8	3.9	3.7	4.2	6.1	6.5	6.5	6.9	6.2
United States	6.9	6.1	5.6	5.4	4.9	4.5	4.2	4.0	4.7	5.8	6.0	5.5	5.1	4.6	4.6	5.8	9.3	9.6	8.9	8.1	7.4
Singapore	2.3	2.3	2.4	2.5	2.2	3.4	4.8	2.7	2.7	3.6	4.0	3.4	3.1	2.7	2.1	2.2	3.0	2.2	2.0	2.0	2.2
Iceland*	5.3	5.3	4.9	3.7	3.9	2.7	2.0	2.3	2.3	3.3	3.4	3.1	2.6	3.0	2.3	3.0	7.2	7.6	7.1	6.0	5.4
Norway*	6.0	5.3	4.9	4.8	3.9	3.2	3.2	3.4	3.4	3.9	4.4	4.4	4.6	3.4	2.5	2.6	3.2	3.6	3.3	3.2	3.5
Switzerland*	3.7	3.8	3.3	3.7	4.1	3.6	3.1	2.7	2.5	2.9	4.1	4.3	4.4	4.0	3.6	3.4	4.1	4.5	4.1	4.2	4.1
W'td Mean of 10	7.3	6.6	5.5	5.4	5.7	6.6	6.3	5.6	5.2	5.3	5.0	4.4	4.2	4.1	3.9	4.2	5.7	5.9	5.7	6.5	6.1
W'td Mean of 3*	4.6	4.3	3.9	4.0	4.0	3.2	2.9	2.9	2.7	3.2	3.3	4.1	4.2	3.7	3.0	3.0	3.8	4.1	3.7	3.7	3.9

Source: www.oecd.library.org OECD (2014), "Labour Market Statistics: Labour force statistics by sex and age: indicators", OECD Employment and Labour Market Statistics (database). DOI: 10.1787/data-00310-en

23

...which is also distinctively severe

For a generation, growing up in Europe has meant a distinctively high risk of long-term unemployment, a problem that has not afflicted other advanced societies to the same degree

We can delve further into these figures by comparing the rates of long-term unemployment in the 12 EU countries with independent countries for which there is age-specific data over the years 1993 to 2013. Switzerland and Singapore cannot therefore be included in this comparison.

The results are given in Figure 23.1. Long-term unemployment is here defined as being unemployed for a year or more, and is expressed in the figure, first in the darker lines, as percentages of the total unemployed in the two groups of countries, and second in the lighter lines, as percentages of all the unemployed 15-24 year olds.

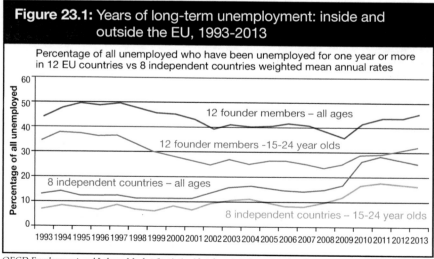

Figure 23.1: Years of long-term unemployment: inside and outside the EU, 1993-2013

Percentage of all unemployed who have been unemployed for one year or more in 12 EU countries vs 8 independent countries weighted mean annual rates

12 founder members – all ages

12 founder members -15-24 year olds

8 independent countries – all ages

8 independent countries – 15-24 year olds

OECD Employment and Labour Market Statistics (database). Labour Market Statistics: Labour force statistics by sex and age: indicators DOI: 10.1787/data-00310-en MB ref UNEMP TABLE 1993-2011 ROW 364

Throughout these years, the proportion of the unemployed of all ages suffering this fate in the EU 12 has been a substantially larger proportion than in the eight independent countries; more than three times larger in the early years, peaking at four times larger in 1998, and then declining reaching its lowest point in 2010, immediately after the financial crisis. The average of the EU weighted mean over the 21 years in the EU is 43.6 per cent, while that of the independent countries is 16.4 per cent, so on average the EU rate has been well over double. That such a large difference has continued over 21 years, reinforces the impression that we are dealing with two sets of economies that differ from one another in some fundamental and enduring manner, which does not seem altogether consistent with the vaunted 'social model' of some EU countries.

When comparing the 15-24 age group, we may first observe that in both cases the rates are at least lower than their elders, but the difference between the EU and the eight independent countries is no less stark. It peaked at five times higher in 1996, and only fell below double the rate in 2010 through to 2013. The average in the independent countries over the 21 years was 10.4 per cent, and in the EU 29.9 per cent. Coming of age and entering the labour market has been a stressful and depressing experience in the EU, and its young people have been almost three times more likely to experience a year or more of unemployment than those in the eight independent countries.

Table 23.1 shows that the weighted means used in the graph are not hiding major variations within each group. Only one EU country, Denmark, has had a lower proportion of long-term unemployed than the mean of the independent countries. Its record over all 21 years is quite distinctive compared with other EU members, but over the four years 2008-2011, and again in 2013, it achieved what no other EU country has ever been able to do: the proportion of its unemployed who remained unemployed for a year or more, was lower than the mean proportion of the eight independent countries.

There are also noticeable variations among the independent countries. Over all 21 years, a distinctively high proportion of Japan's unemployed have been long-term. By itself, given its size,

Japan has been responsible for boosting the weighted average of the group as a whole. By contrast, the US has had a remarkably low proportion of long-term unemployed until 2010 when the proportion shot up, and has remained high until 2013. However, the main point is that over the 21 years not a single independent country has ever had a proportion of long-term unemployed as high as the mean of EU countries, a quite remarkable contrast.

The EU has, therefore, not only suffered from a higher rate of unemployment than independent countries, but its unemployment has been especially severe, as measured by the proportion unemployed for a year or more; especially among young people. The average of the weighted means over the 21 years indicates that about 10.4 per cent of young unemployed people in the independent countries remained unemployed for a year or more, whereas 29.9 per cent of young people in the Single Market countries did so. They have been, in other words, nearly three times more likely to be scarred by this experience.

As the Eurozone crisis has unfolded, UK media has given increasing attention to the previously unimaginable rates of unemployment found in some EU countries, and especially among young people. However, the experience of long-term unemployment is not simply the consequence of that crisis. As the light blue line in the graph indicates, although the rate of long-term unemployment in the 15-24 year old cohort was *declining* over the years 1997-2008, it was always at a higher level than in the independent countries over the pre-crisis years. While recent rates of long-term youth unemployment are astonishingly high, they were almost as high in some countries over the first decade of the Single Market. Unnoticed by the UK media, well over half of young, Italian men and women were unemployed for more than a year over the 11 years from 1993-2003, as were over half of young Greeks over the five years from 1996-2000. More than a third of young people in several other EU countries – Ireland, Portugal, and Spain – had a similar experience, and even, surprisingly, though for fewer years, Belgium and the Netherlands.

Table 23.1: Long-term unemployment in the Single Market 1993-2013:

( ) estimates to fill missing entries.   Shaded cells indicate a rate that is equal to or below that of the mean of independent countries

	1993	1994	1995	1996	1997	1998	1999	2000	2001	2002	2003	2004	2005	2006	2007	2008	2009	2010	2011	2012	2013
Belgium	53.0	58.3	62.4	61.3	60.5	61.7	60.5	56.3	51.7	48.8	45.4	49.0	51.7	51.2	50.4	47.6	44.2	48.8	48.3	44.7	46.0
Denmark	25.2	32.1	27.9	26.5	27.2	26.9	20.5	20.0	22.2	19.1	20.4	21.5	23.4	20.8	16.1	13.5	9.5	20.2	24.4	28.0	25.5
France	33.3	37.5	40.2	38.2	39.6	41.6	38.7	39.6	36.8	32.7	39.2	40.6	41.1	41.9	40.2	37.4	35.2	40.2	41.5	40.4	40.4
Germany	40.3	44.3	48.7	47.8	50.1	52.6	51.7	51.5	50.4	47.9	50.0	51.8	53.0	56.4	56.6	52.5	45.5	47.4	48.0	45.4	44.7
Greece	50.9	50.5	51.4	56.7	55.7	54.9	55.3	56.4	52.8	51.3	54.9	53.1	52.1	54.3	50.0	47.5	40.8	45.0	49.6	59.3	67.5
Ireland	59.1	64.3	61.6	59.5	57.0	(56.0)	55.3	(44.0)	33.1	30.1	32.8	34.9	33.4	31.6	29.5	27.1	29.1	49.1	59.3	61.7	60.6
Italy	57.7	61.5	63.6	65.6	66.3	59.6	61.4	61.3	63.4	59.6	58.1	49.2	49.9	49.6	47.3	45.7	44.4	48.5	51.9	53.0	56.9
Luxembourg	31.6	29.6	23.2	27.6	34.6	31.3	32.3	22.4	28.4	27.4	24.7	21.0	26.4	29.5	28.7	32.4	23.1	29.3	28.8	30.3	30.4
Netherlands	52.4	49.4	46.8	50.0	49.1	47.9	43.5	(38.0)	(32.0)	26.5	27.8	34.2	40.2	43.0	39.4	34.4	24.8	27.6	33.6	33.7	35.9
Portugal	43.5	43.4	50.9	53.1	55.6	44.7	41.2	42.9	38.1	34.6	35.0	44.3	48.2	50.2	47.1	47.4	44.1	52.3	48.2	48.7	56.3
Spain	46.2	52.7	54.6	52.9	51.8	49.9	46.3	42.4	36.9	33.7	33.6	32.0	24.5	21.6	20.4	18.0	23.8	36.6	41.6	44.4	49.7
UK	42.5	45.4	43.6	39.8	38.6	32.7	29.6	28.0	27.8	21.7	21.5	20.6	21.0	22.3	23.7	24.1	24.5	32.6	33.4	34.8	36.3
Wtd Mean	**44.2**	**47.8**	**49.7**	**49.0**	**49.5**	**47.8**	**46.1**	**45.1**	**43.4**	**39.6**	**41.0**	**40.6**	**40.8**	**41.8**	**40.7**	**38.4**	**35.9**	**41.6**	**43.6**	**43.8**	**45.6**

Shaded cells indicate a rate that is equal to or above that of the mean of EU countries

	1993	1994	1995	1996	1997	1998	1999	2000	2001	2002	2003	2004	2005	2006	2007	2008	2009	2010	2011	2012	2013
Australia	36.7	36.1	32.0	28.5	31.2	32.9	31.3	28.3	23.9	22.4	21.5	20.6	18.2	18.1	15.4	14.9	14.7	18.6	18.9	19.0	19.2
Canada	16.5	17.9	16.8	16.8	16.1	13.8	11.7	11.3	9.5	9.6	10.0	9.5	9.6	8.7	7.4	7.1	7.8	12.0	13.5	12.5	12.7
Iceland	12.2	15.1	16.8	19.8	16.3	16.1	11.7	11.8	12.5	11.1	8.1	11.2	13.3	7.3	8.0	4.1	6.9	21.3	27.8	27.9	21.9
Japan	15.6	17.5	18.1	19.3	21.8	20.3	22.4	25.5	26.6	30.8	33.5	33.7	33.3	33.0	32.0	33.3	28.5	37.6	39.4	38.5	41.2
Korea	2.6	5.4	4.4	3.8	2.6	1.5	3.8	2.3	2.3	2.5	0.6	1.1	0.8	1.1	0.6	2.7	0.5	0.3	0.4	0.3	0.4
NZ	33.6	32.9	25.6	21.0	19.8	19.6	21.1	19.8	17.2	14.8	13.6	11.7	9.7	7.8	6.1	4.4	6.3	9.0	9.0	13.2	12.1
Norway	27.2	28.8	24.2	14.2	12.4	8.3	7.1	5.3	5.5	6.4	6.4	9.2	9.5	14.5	8.8	6.0	7.7	9.5	11.6	8.7	9.2
US	11.5	12.2	9.7	9.5	8.7	8.0	6.8	6.0	6.1	8.5	11.8	12.7	11.8	10.0	10.0	10.6	16.3	29.0	31.3	29.3	25.9
Wtd mean	**13.2**	**14.5**	**12.8**	**12.7**	**12.8**	**11.8**	**11.6**	**11.6**	**11.6**	**14.0**	**16.2**	**16.7**	**16.0**	**14.9**	**14.3**	**15.1**	**17.0**	**26.7**	**28.5**	**27.1**	**25.8**

Percentage of the unemployed who have been unemployed for a year or more. 12 Single Market founder members vs 8 independent

Source: www.oecd.library.org OECD (2014), "Labour Market Statistics: Labour force statistics by sex and age", OECD Employment and Labour Market Statistics (database), DOI: 10.1787/data-00309-

24

The slow growth of GDP and productivity in the Single Market 1993-2013

From the beginning, EU membership was supposed to improve UK productivity. There is no evidence that it has ever done so, for the UK or anyone else

One of the main aims of the UK when joining the Common Market was to raise the level of productivity to equal that of its six founder members.[1]

> ... the Government are confident that membership of the enlarged Community will 'lead to much improved efficiency and productivity in British industry.[2]

One of the main goals of the Single Market was to improve the productivity of the labour force in member countries. In 1988 the Cecchini report, its founding charter, predicted GDP gains of up to 6.5 or 7 per cent over five or six years, and confidently referred to the productivity gains that would follow the creation of a Single Market.[3]

World Bank data on real GDP growth *per capita* in $US (2005) over the 21 years, 1993-2013, shown in Figure 24.1, compares the 12 founder members of the Single Market with 10 independent countries, consisting of nine OECD members plus Singapore. The three of these OECD countries in Europe – Switzerland, Norway

---

1   HM Government, *The United Kingdom and the European Communities*, (White Paper, Cmnd 4715, 1971)
2   HM Government, *The United Kingdom and the European Communities*, (White Paper, Cmnd 4715, 1971), p.16
3   'Commission of the European Communities', 'Europe 1992: The Overall Challenge', Brussels, 1988, Paolo Cecchini et al., SEC (88)524. http://aei.pitt.edu/3813/.

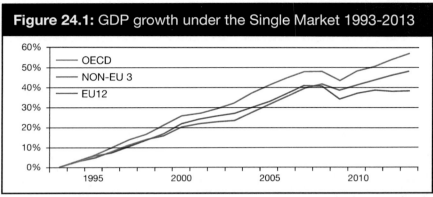

Figure 24.1: GDP growth under the Single Market 1993-2013

Annual percentage growth rate of GDP at market prices based on constant local currency, but the aggregates are based on constant 2005 US dollars. http://data.worldbank.org/indicator/

and Iceland – are also shown separately. It may be seen that real growth of GDP *per capita*, or productivity, of the founder members of the Single Market has been slower than both.

Table 24.1 gives the CAGR of individual countries over the period, and the weighted means of both groups. Only three member countries, Ireland, Luxembourg and the UK have exceeded the mean growth rate of the ten other OECD countries.

On several occasions the Commission staff report of 2007 referred to the lagging productivity growth of member countries compared

Table 24.1: CAGR of GDP Real growth per cap 1993-2013 in US(2005)$

EU 12		OECD 9	
Belgium	1.37	Australia	1.85
Denmark	1.12	Canada	1.59
France	1.13	Iceland	2.08
Germany	1.28	Japan	0.76
Greece	0.78	Korea	4.16
Ireland	3.17	NZ	1.78
Italy	0.39	Norway	1.52
Luxembourg	1.72	Switzerland	1.13
Netherlands	1.48	US	1.54
Portugal	1.07	**Mean**	**1.57**
Spain	1.31		
UK	1.64		
Mean	**1.18**	Source: www.OECDiLIbrary GDP per cap.xls	

with the US. The OECD database provides an updated measure of this productivity gap, by showing, in percentage terms, how far the productivity of each member country falls short of, or exceeds, that of the U.S. This data uses the more familiar measure of productivity as output per member of the labour force, or per hour worked, rather than *per capita*. Table 24.2 shows how the gap has narrowed or widened over the 21 years, 1993 to 2013.

Table 24.2: Are the members of the Single Market closing the productivity gap with the US?

% gap in GDP per hour worked with respect to the USA

	1993	2013	% change
Belgium	11.7	-1.6	-13.3
Denmark	-8.5	-5.7	+2.8
France	-6.5	-6.9	-0.4
Germany	-5.7	-6.9	-1.2
Greece	-45.8	-46.3	-0.5
Ireland	-30.1	-6.8	+23.3
Italy	-13.2	-24.3	-11.1
Luxembourg	41.3	41.9	+0.6
Netherlands	-2.1	-5	-2
Portugal	-52.6	-47.4	+5.2
Spain	-21.4	-23.4	-2
UK	-19.8	-25.8	-6

Dataset: GDP per capita and productivity levels

One member country, Luxembourg, had no productivity gap with the US in 1993, though in comparisons of industrial productivity, as in other respects, it bears more resemblance to an Offshore Financial Centre (OFC) than to a normal industrial economy. Three other member countries have seen the gap narrow: Ireland most strikingly, Portugal by over five percentage points, and Denmark by nearly three points. The other eight member countries, which include the larger EU economies, have all fallen back in terms of productivity versus the US, most by rather small amounts, though Belgium by more than 13 points, Italy by more than 11, and the UK, the third largest decline, by six.

None of this evidence suggests that the Single Market programme has had a distinctive and positive impact on productivity which has been shared by its members, but then there has been no regular analysis of productivity within the Single Market, or why it has fallen short of Cecchini's predictions. It seems to have been just one more of those predictions which has served its purpose once pronounced and used to justify further policies, regulations and directives.

Overall, the wide variations among member countries suggest that the determinants of productivity growth may have rather little to do with Europe or the Single Market, and that they are peculiar to the economic, political and cultural context of each nation. Members' results are no less varied than those of non-member countries. Among non-members, decisive gains were registered by Norway (+27), Korea (+17.8), and Chile (+15.2). Others, such as Switzerland (+1.4) and Australia (0) remained much the same, while New Zealand (-2.9) and Canada (-8.9) both declined.

A further hope, and prediction, of the founders of the Single Market was that as member countries became more integrated they would also become more alike; partly as a result of normal competitive pressures, and partly because they would learn from their fellow members and adopt the best practice found amongst them. This idea recurs frequently in the Lisbon Treaty.[4]

The variance of these measures of productivity gives little support to the idea that member countries have become more alike, and that their productivity has converged. In the first measure, growth of GDP per capita, in $US (2005) the standard deviation was 7,910 in 1993, whereas in 2013 it had risen to 11,964.

By the second measure, the percentage distance from the US productivity, there was a marginal convergence among member countries. In 1993 the mean gap with US productivity was -12.7%, and by 2013 had increased to -13.2%, but the standard deviation of the percentage differences from the US was 24.9% in 1993, and 23.5% in 2013.

---

4   See for example the frequent references to the 'organization of exchange of best practice' in the Treaty of Lisbon, pp c306/82, 83-84, 86, 150, Official Journal of the European Union C306, (Volume 50, 17 Dec 2007).

25

A burst of candour from European Commission staff about the failings of the Single Market

The staff of the European Commission give a more candid assessment of the Single Market than Her Majesty's Government has ever provided, albeit to make the case for still more integration

If one is looking for a candid and thorough assessment of the EU's economic performance over the years of membership, one cannot unfortunately turn to any authoritative studies by the UK government. Over the 40 plus years of membership, Britain has not conducted regular analyses of the EU's impact on UK trade. In 2000 HM Treasury (HMT) published two insightful guides about the research methodologies that should be used to ensure that public policies were evidence-based. However, it has declined to apply any of these methodologies to the one government policy that has had the greatest impact on the livelihoods of the British people – the EU project.

There has been just one exception to this general rule, the studies organized by the Treasury to evaluate five tests to determine whether or not the UK should join the euro. On that occasion, HMT drew on expertise and research from around the world in a spirit of open debate, and published the results as they appeared, before taking the fateful decision. No such research has ever been conducted on the merits of the EU or of the Single Market, probably because the Prime Minister and political elite of the UK had decided that their main task was to persuade the British people of its merits. Empirical research might, as the five tests research showed, go either way.

No research comparable to the five tests is contemplated before the referendum. Hence, it seems likely that the prime minister, ex-prime ministers, ministers and assorted leaders of opposition parties will continue to make claims about the merits of the EU for UK trade, employment and investment, without ever having any evidence, and probably without ever being asked by the media to provide any.

The research of the European Commission, on which the UK government has long relied, is mainly concerned with future prospects and predictions to keep their project moving forward towards ever closer union. It is much less concerned with retrospectively evaluating its own policies, holding itself to account, or explaining why so many of its predictions have fallen short. It is seldom concerned with evaluating the impact of its policies on individual countries, to identify winners and losers.

On one occasion, however, in 2007, it produced a reasonably thorough and critical examination of the Single Market. This was plainly intended to justify and encourage and promote deeper economic integration of the EU. In the present context, the authors' motives and recommendations are unimportant. What is important is that they provided an unusually candid and fair assessment of the Single Market, which can help any undecided UK voter to decide whether it is worth the economic and political costs of membership.

In its own way, the report is a valuable historical document because it was produced in 2007, shortly before the financial crisis. It was therefore analysing the Single Market at its very best, as it was supposed to be, and even on the crest of a wave. All of the subsequent problems of the Single Market can be, and often are, attributed to the crisis.

Problems of the Single Market

These are excerpts from the European Commission report 'Steps towards a deeper economic integration: the Internal Market in the 21st century':

'There has been a slowdown of trade growth within the EU15 and euro-zone relative to trade growth with third partners'

'The trade boosting effect of the introduction of the euro has... been far less pronounced than the trade effect of enlargement.'

'...since 2000 the trade effect of the enlargement process and particularly intra-EU15 trade integration, seem to have stalled.'

'EU product markets remain heavily regulated, business dynamism is insufficient and prices rigidities are persistent.'

'...the share of extra EU suppliers in... consumption... has gradually increased at the expense of domestic production.'

'Not only are EU firms less active in fast growing markets but also they have not managed to improve their performance in fast growing sectors at world level although this was one of the main goals of the 1992 Single Market programme.'

'...the Internal Market... has not led to a sufficient shift of the specialisation of the production sector towards the more technology intensive sectors where EU competitiveness can be more sustainable in the long-run.'

'16.6 per cent of world exports of low technology goods originated in the EU25 while only 8.4 per cent and 1.6 per cent came from the US and Japan. Furthermore, the EU25 reveals a comparative disadvantage in high technology sectors including ICT 52...'

'The Internal Market does not seem to have been a sufficient catalyst for innovation and resource reallocation towards technology intensive activities.'

'...the innovative performance of the EU as a whole and of most EU countries lags significantly behind that of top performers such as the US and Japan... What is more worrying is the widening gap between the laggards and frontrunners and between the EU and other developed economies.'

'Since 2001 the volume of FDI from the rest of the world into the EU25 has gradually declined.'

'...the Internal Market has not been able to deliver in terms of promoting further the role of the EU with respect to global investment flows.'

'The internal market two-fold objective of making the EU a more attractive place for foreign investors and of boosting the presence and competitive position of EU firms in world markets seems far from being achieved.'

'The Internal Market is also losing its attractiveness for international R&D investment. Multinational companies prefer to carry out their R&D activities in the US – and more recently in China and India – rather than in the EU.'[1]

---

1   Fabienne Ilzkovitz, Adriaan Dierx, Viktoria Kovacs and Nuno Sousa, European Economy, Economic Papers, N° 271 January 2007, *Steps towards a deeper economic integration: the Internal Market in the 21st century, A contribution to the Single Market Review* European Commission, Directorate-General For Economic and Financial Affairs, ISSN 1725-3187, http://ec.europa.eu/ economy_finance/index_en.htm

26

Who will measure the performance of the Single Market, how, when and for whom?

After 22 years the European Commission and Parliament are considering measuring the performance of the Single Market, but not it seems to make it more accountable to the press or public

The EU has legitimized its moves towards ever closer union by predictions derived from economic models, which tell of gains in productivity, employment and income, once the next step forward is taken. It is a forever forward-looking mind set which resembles that of Soviet planners, and does not require backward glances to see whether the gains were actually realised, or any explanation or apology if they were not.

The Single Market fits this pattern rather well. It began with predictions of the Cecchini Report that it would increase GDP by 6.5%.[1] It then marked its tenth anniversary in 2003 with celebrations of its astonishing achievements, but without pausing to see whether or not it was living up to Cecchini's predictions or to the high expectations at its launch.

In 2007 a European Commission staff report indicated that all might not be well in some blunt asides (see Chapter 25) but only to show how they made the agenda stated in its title, 'Steps towards a deeper economic integration', that much more urgent.[2]

In 2008 Boltho & Eichengreen, two neutral academic observers, made some informed, but as they admitted, rough estimates, and

---

1 Commission of the European Communities, 'Europe 1992: The Overall Challenge', Brussels, 1988, Paolo Cecchini et al., SEC (88)524. http://aei.pitt.edu/3813/.
2 Fabienne Ilzkovitz et al.

concluded that the Single Market (1993-2002) had been responsible for an increase in EU GDP of between 0.75 and 1.0 per cent of EU GDP.[3]

All the data presented in Chapter 23 about the Single Market's distinctively high and severe unemployment and its distinctively low rate of productivity growth had not formed any part of discussion of the Single Market within the European Commission or Her Majesty's Government (HMG) or its numerous enthusiasts in the UK political elite who argued, without having any evidence one way or the other, that it was the main reason for our membership.

In 2014, discussions within the European Commission came full circle with a series of reports called 'The Cost of Non-Europe in the Single Market (Cecchini Revisited)'.[4] Given this title, one might have expected a thorough, even definitive, analysis of why things did not turn out quite as Cecchini expected, but from its opening words the report hits a different note.

> It is well known that the Single Market has contributed significantly to economic growth and consumer welfare within the European Union. It has not, however, achieved its full potential and economic gains could be secured by better and more effective application of existing legislation and a deepening of the Single Market.

Off we go again, one is tempted to add, though it did pause briefly to mention the six studies mentioned by the UK Balance of Competences Review (these are discussed, and found to be less than conclusive analyses, Chapter 38), but then moves quickly on to urge the start of another cycle with 'the deepening of the Single Market'. The further reforms proposed will, the authors estimate, yield 'potential economic gains [which will] range between 651 billion and 1.1 trillion euro per year, equivalent to between 5 per cent to 8.6 per cent of EU GDP.'

---

3   Barry Eichengreen and Andrea Boltho, 'The Economic Impact of European Integration', Centre for Economic Policy Research Paper No. 6820, 2008, pp.30-32 http://eml.berkeley.edu/~eichengr/econ_impact_euro_integ.pdf

4   The Cost of Non-Europe in the Single Market: An overview of the potential economic gains from further completion of the European Single Market of EU GDP, PE 510.981, EPRS European Parliamentary Research Service, September2014: www.europarl.europa.eu/.../EPRS_STU(2014)510981_REV1_EN.pdf

At some point, as the years have rolled by and its achievements become part of the folklore of European elites, there was always the chance that, simply as a matter of public policy routine, some government agency or other would ask whether, given the amount of time and money devoted to it, the Single Market's performance ought not be evaluated. Her Majesty's Government could never, of course, be involved in such an investigation. Most members of the UK political elite had been speaking and soundbiting about its benefits for years. One deputy prime minister used to describe them as 'immeasurable' anyway. The 'quality' newspapers of the UK and media commentators tended to agree. So to British eyes, there could be nothing to measure.

Nonetheless, settled bureaucratic routines of the European Commission did finally notice that the performance of the Single Market had never been measured. After some 22 years, the moment had finally arrived. On 25 September 2014 a meeting of the Internal Market Committee of the European Parliament, helped by a Brussels-based consultant's report, finally addressed the question: how might the performance of the Single Market be measured?[5]

The committee has not yet answered this question, but it has given its first thoughts about what would, and would not, be a suitable measure.

It first recommended that the chosen measure of its performance should not use economic indicators for a country-based annual assessment. Those who hoped that, at long last, the electorates of member countries might be able to judge how much or how little their own country might have benefited from the Single Market, will therefore be disappointed. All the measures used in these

---

5   "Indicators for measuring the performance of the Single Market - Building the Single Market Pillar of the European Semester", presentation held during the IMCO Committee meeting of 25/09/2014. A summary of their conclusions was prepared for the Directorate General for Internal Policies by Carine Piaguet entitled Can we measure the Performance of the Single Market? PE 536.298 EN

Summary http://www.europarl.europa.eu/RegData/etudes/ATAG/2014/536298/IPOL_ATA(2014)536298_EN.pdf

Full Report http://www.europarl.europa.eu/RegData/etudes/STUD/2014/518750/IPOL_STU(2014)518750_EN.pdf

notes, such as the rate of growth of UK exports to other members, or the amount of FDI, or unemployment or productivity growth, are evidently unsuitable.

It also decided against a composite indicator, which means that it might not be quite so easy to say whether the Single Market is succeeding or not. The European Commission will evidently have several indicators and one imagines will therefore continually have a mixed 'good in parts' verdict. This will also mean that we will not be able to hold any particular Commissioner or Director-General responsible for any noticeable failure they happen to identify. Whenever it appears, this performance measure does not therefore seem as if it will mark a step forward in accountability.

Transparency and accountability were clearly not high priorities for members of this committee. Instead they recommended that 'sectoral indicators could be used to highlight where the highest potential lies', allowing predictions to be made about possible gains in the future, and hence enabling the EU tradition of propelling ever more integration on the basis of predicted future gains to continue, without having to reflect too much on the past, and having to decide whether it had been a success or a failure.

The second main recommendation is that regulatory performance might be measured by a 'Single Market Gap indicator' which could be 'directly used by EU institutions (e.g. the Commission) in the European Semester process to define EU-wide or country-specific recommendations.' In sum, the committee said that the proposed measure of performance might be a useful management tool to identify harmonization, integration and ever closer union.

27

Paradox in goods exports: non-members have been its major beneficiaries

It is a puzzling paradox that the exporters from non-member countries who do not sit at the table, and help to make the rules of the Single Market, and pay nothing for access to it, have been its main beneficiaries in terms of the growth of their goods exports

One of the most familiar arguments for remaining a member of the EU is that the Single Market is vital to the British economy. Leaving the EU would therefore be a disaster since the UK would be obliged to negotiate access to it in order to survive, and the price our former partners would require us to pay would be a high one and would entail costs and obligations very similar to those we currently pay as members. There is therefore little point in leaving the EU.

The argument rests on an imagined black and white, day and night contrast between membership, which has facilitated trade with other members enabling exporters within the market to thrive and prosper, and those outside which have faced formidable tariff and other barriers. Non-members therefore, have been engaged in an uphill struggle to make modest gains against their privileged competitors within the Single Market.

This contrast is entirely imaginary because no one who makes use of it to advance the cause of EU membership has ever bothered to measure the disadvantages of non-membership. Some empirical evidence in Chapters 17-21 showed that this contrast did not square with some known facts: the exports to the EU of both goods and services of a great many non-members have grown faster than those of the UK.

However, the evidence deserves more consideration since it is central to the entire debate. If the Single Market has not been particularly beneficial to UK exporters, there is no reason to pay the political and economic costs of membership, no reason to be especially alarmed about leaving it, and no sense at all in making great sacrifices after leaving to negotiate access to it.

Table 27.1 lists countries in order of the real compound annual growth rate of their goods exports to the first 15 members of the EU (EU-15) from 1993, the first year of the Single Market, to 2013, the most recent year for which data is available. Fourteen of the 29 are long-term members of the Single Market that had joined the EU by 1995. Luxembourg had to be omitted from the list since the OECD did not have adequate data for exports in many of these years. The other 15 countries are G20 members who are not members of the EU. The CAGR refers to each country's effective annual growth in exports to EU-15 members from 1993 to 2013.

Table 27.1: Growth of goods exports of 29 countries to 15 long-term members of the Single Market 1993-2013

in order of their compound annual rate of growth, measured in 1993US$.
14 EU members are shaded, 15 non-EU G20 members are unshaded.

Exporting Country	CAGR% 1993-2013	Exports to EU2013/2014 (2013 $bn)	Exporting Country	CAGR% 1993-2013	Exports to EU-2013/2014 (2013 $bn)
China	11.5	15.48	Spain	3.6	14.17
Russia	8.6	9.96	Netherlands	3.5	21.94
Brazil	8.5	4.22	Austria	3.5	9.22
India	7.2	3.82	Argentina	3.4	1.07
Turkey*	7.1	7.17	UK	3.1	26.84
Korea*	6.3	4.21	Belgium	3.1	20.26
Mexico	5.8	2.85	France	3.0	35.99
Australia	5.5	3.41	Denmark	3.0	4.84
S. Africa*	5.4	2.48	Germany	2.8	47.59
Finland	4.9	3.54	Portugal	2.5	4.19
Saudi Arabia	4.5	3.61	Italy	2.5	18.44
Canada	4.4	3.33	Japan	2.0	5.71
US	4.1	30.84	Indonesia	1.8	1.04
Ireland	4.0	4.23	Greece	0.6	2.02
Sweden	3.9	7.72	* Countries with which the EU has had a trade agreement.		

CAGR for 15 non-EU countries 5.7% CAGR for 14 EU countries 3.1%

www.oecdilibrary.org.OECD database Monthly Statistics of International Trade

The figures speak largely for themselves. The important conclusion is summarized in the difference in export growth between non-EU and EU countries. Non-members' CAGR has been almost twice that of EU members.

In terms of export growth, therefore, non-members have been significantly greater beneficiaries of exporting to the Single Market than its own members, with only Japan and Indonesia recording growth rates noticeably lower than the EU mean. Export growth is also the crucial measure, since it is what the Single Market was meant to deliver to its members, and that is what the Prime Minister and many others think has been the main benefit of EU membership and is the most important reason for continued membership.

The performance of all the EU members is especially worth noting. The earlier data might have left room for the all-too-common response that the poor performance of UK goods exporters had something to do with Mrs Thatcher. The poor UK performance, over these years, is in fact the same as the poor EU average.

The low rate of German growth is perhaps the most surprising. The value of German exports is significantly higher than those of every other country, despite having benefited since 1999 from the extremely low rate of exchange of the euro, its exports to fellow members have still failed to grow as fast as those of 16 other members of the G20.

This evidence kills the idea that the Single Market has put non-members at a serious disadvantage. It manifestly hasn't. Most of them have prospered mightily. This is useful to know since much, most and sometimes all, of the argument for continued membership rests on the notion that there is only a very grim future for UK exports outside the Single Market. It has not been grim for many non-members.

Many of the non-EU G20 countries have different export markets to the UK. As a result, we cannot assume that the UK would be able to equal the average performance of the other members of the G20 after Brexit. Still, there can hardly be much doubt which group it would be better to belong to.

Since the aim of the analysis was to identify the disadvantages of non-membership, similar comparisons were made with other

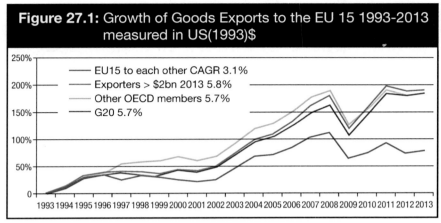

Figure 27.1: Growth of Goods Exports to the EU 15 1993-2013 measured in US(1993)$

Note: Exports of Chile to Netherlands '96-'11, Estonia to Netherlands '96-02', Iceland to Netherlands '96-'11, Iceland to Spain '97, Indonesia to Sweden '95-'02, Mexico to Netherlands '96-'11, Norway to Germany '11, Slovak Rep. to Netherlands '96-02', Slovenia to Netherlands '96-02', Spain to Greece '09 to '10, Switzerland to Ireland '02, and USA to Ireland '02 were all estimated from the proportion of exports to the same country in

OECD countries, and with other countries whose exports to the EU in 2013 exceeded $2 billion, an arbitrary ceiling intended to exclude many small, and often fast-growing, exporters who have entered global trading networks only recently.

The growth of the goods exports of all three groups to the EU-15 is compared with the growth of the goods exports of the long-term EU-15 members of the Single Market in the graph below (Luxembourg is excluded). There were a fair number of missing years, which are listed below the graph, and all of them were estimated from the proportion of exports to the same country in the missing years.

The three groups – the G20, other OECD countries, and exporters of goods over the value of $2 billion in 2013 – are rather similar to one another, perhaps not surprisingly since there is a fair measure of overlap between them. However, the main result is that, though the composition of the comparator groups changes, their growth in exports to the EU-15 is always significantly higher than that of the exports of the EU.[1]

---

1   A two-sample t-test, assuming unequal variances, shows that there is a significant difference in the 1993-2013 CAGR in exports to the EU-15 between the non-EU G20 countries and the EU-15 (exc Luxembourg). A two-tailed test gave p=0.002 and a one-tail test confirmed that the non-EU G20 growth was significantly higher giving p=0.001, well clear of the p=0.05 confidence level. The difference remained significant after removing China (p=0.0013) and all the BRIC countries (p=0.012).

They thus demonstrate that the familiar contrast, on which so much rests, between thriving secure members who have made the rules of the Single Market and non-members struggling against daunting barriers has been a figment of EU enthusiasts' imaginations, and absurdly wide of the mark.

Questions arising

Why this should be so? Why should those who sit around the table, make the rules and pay the fees not be the main beneficiaries of their own deliberations and rules? This question is examined, but alas, not answered in Chapter 29.

Why did successive UK governments not notice what was happening? Why did the leaders of these governments, Messrs Major, Blair, Brown and Cameron continue to present a quite different, ill-informed picture to the British people? Why, for that matter do they continue to do so?

These figures are taken straight from OECD databases which are available to everyone. They do not rest on clever models of what might, could or should happen in the Single Market. They are the straight record of what has actually happened. How is it possible that four UK prime ministers in succession could be so misinformed?

How, come to think of it, is it possible that specialist economic papers like the *Financial Times* or *The Economist* who routinely report OECD data, never once over all these years thought that they should point out what was happening in the Single Market, so that their readers might fairly assess the advantages and disadvantages of membership and non-membership? These comparisons should have long since been familiar to them. Instead, they look like a scoop, a startling revelation from some hitherto inaccessible source.

28

Paradox in services: non-members have been its major beneficiaries

Another paradox. The services exports to the EU of non-members who have not been 'sitting at the table, helping to make the rules', have grown as fast as those who have

When we ask the same question of services we run into the usual problem of inadequate data. The best way around it is abandon export data altogether, and rely entirely on the import figures that have sometimes been used as a substitute for missing export figures. This means that instead of using, say the reported figures of China's exports to the EU, we use the imports from China reported by EU members. For a variety of reasons these two figures are not the same, but as long as we do not mix the two kinds of figures, we will not be confused or misled. For some curious reason, import figures are often more complete than export data, and have no omissions on grounds of 'confidentiality' or anything else. There is therefore little choice, unless we wish to keep making estimates of missing data entries.

There are, however, losses as well as gains in doing this. Figures of services imports begin at a later date, but from 2004 they provide a complete return for the 35 OECD countries, and 28 non-members, and from 2006 for more than 150 countries. In the present context, the file on the EU27 is particularly useful since it includes the 27 EU countries themselves as countries from which the EU27 has imported services alongside other OECD members and non-members. It thus provides a simple means of comparing the performance of EU members and non-members as exporters to the EU 27, which cannot be done with the real export data. The only flaw in the comparison is that EU countries cannot import from themselves, hence their exports are to the other 27 EU countries, while non-members' exports are to all 28. Unfortunately, there appears to be no way of circumventing or measuring how this might bias the outcome, so we will have to live with it.

All the countries from which the EU imported services, and whose file gave full details of their imports to the EU27 from 2004 to 2012 were eligible for inclusion in this comparison, but to keep a manageable number they were subject to one filter: their imports were required to have a recorded total value of at least $1bn in the year 2012. In total 47 countries qualified, 23 of them EU members and 23 non-members. Table 28.1 presents the results, ranking the 47 countries according to the CAGR of their exports, in 2004 US dollars, to the EU over the nine years to 2012. The value of their exports in 2012 is also given. EU member countries are shaded.

If it were true that the Single Market had benefited the services exports of its members to each other, we would expect the member countries to figure disproportionately among the high growth exporters at the top of the ranking, and therefore to be disproportionately on the left hand side of the table. A slight tendency in that direction is visible, in that the top left quadrant of the table is more shaded than the top right quadrant, though it is also worth noting that countries in the top left quadrant are mainly 2004 EU entrants. Six of the 13 Single Market members on the left hand side are 2004 entrants and two are 2007 entrants, whereas nine of the 10 on the right hand side are founder members, and include all the larger EU economies – Germany, the UK, Italy, France and Spain – while the tenth, Austria, entered in 1995.

If we use the CAGR as a score of so many points, the EU member countries outscore the non-member countries. Their mean score is 4.5 versus non-members' 3.9, though it should be remembered that the EU countries enjoy an advantage over non-members that is known to be a decisive determinant of trade growth, and has absolutely nothing to do with the EU: geographical propinquity.

A two-sample, two-tailed t test shows that there is no significant difference between the mean growth rates (p=0.473). A Mann-Whitney non-parametric test on the rankings (unpaired, with two samples) agrees. There is only a 55 per cent probability that

Table 28.1: Growth of service exports of 47 EU member & non-member countries to 27 countries of the Single Market 2004-2012

as measured by reported imports to the 27 EU countries ranked in order of compound annual growth rate

	CAGR % (in 2004 US$)	2012 value (in 2012 US$bn)		CAGR % (in 2004 US$)	2012 value (in 2012 US$bn)
China	11.01	21.1	Continued		
Slovak Rep.	10.93	6.8	Israel*	4.19	3.5
India	10.51	11.3	Australia	3.72	8.6
Estonia	9.96	2.5	Germany	3.65	115.5
Ireland	9.85	35.1	Denmark	3.10	16.8
Singapore	9.25	12.8	Canada	2.81	10.8
Romania	9.07	5.9	Japan	2.61	16.4
Luxemb'g	8.89	26.9	Korea*	2.56	5.0
Poland	8.87	18.7	Turkey*	2.44	15.1
Bulgaria	8.21	4.0	UK	2.32	114.2
Chile*	6.45	1.7	US	2.10	159.2
Argentina	6.36	2.4	NZ	1.50	1.6
Slovenia	6.32	2.9	Egypt*	1.48	5.9
Russian Fed.	6.12	15.9	Belgium	1.44	38.1
Netherlands	5.74	75.2	Portugal	1.34	10.6
Czech Rep	5.73	12.9	Italy	1.31	48.4
Hungary	5.65	9.0	Norway*	1.16	13.0
Switzerland*	5.60	64.2	Austria	0.99	29.9
Sweden	5.49	24.6	France	0.84	83.4
Nigeria	5.29	2.1	Iceland*	0.74	0.8
Indonesia	5.24	2.0	Spain	0.35	54.4
Croatia**	4.88	6.3	Mexico*	0.07	3.4
Finland	4.77	9.4	S. Africa*	-0.19	4.8
Hong Kong	4.42	9.2	Greece	-2.18	13.7

*Indicates countries with which the EU had a trade agreement in force at some point in these years
** Became a member of the EU in 2014
The selection filter means Lithuania, Latvia, Cyprus and Malta are not featured on the table.

Source: OECD Dataset: EBOPS 2002 - Trade in Services by Partner Country European Union (27 countries) Total Services Imports

export growth from a random EU country will exceed that from a random non-EU country. The fact that even with their in-built geographical advantage, the growth of EU members' exports to each other cannot be distinguished from that of non-members is an important finding, leading one to wonder whether a Single Market in services actually exists.

If one sets the initial admission filter higher, and compares only those economies with exports of at least $10bn in 2012, we are left to compare 16 member countries with 10 non-member countries. The mean CAGR of the members was 3.6 per cent and that of the non-members was 5.3 per cent. Amongst high value exporters therefore, it is the non-members that have appear to have grown faster. However, this difference is not significant either. The two-tailed t test has a p-value of 0.24, and the non-parametric test gives only a 66 per cent probability that the growth of the exports of a random non-EU member will exceed a random EU member. This suggests that there are many more important determinants of the rate of growth of services exports to the EU than the advantages or disadvantages of membership. In all probability, we will only discover what they may be with much more detailed studies of disaggregated services sectors.

For the moment, we may simply note that the growth of non-members' services exports to the EU has not actually outpaced that of members, and so they are not, by this statistical measure, quite as much of a paradox as goods exports. We may fairly conclude that sitting at the table, helping to make the rules, and paying, have not helped UK services exports in the least. It is strange that anyone would think it worth paying to do so, or be terrified by the prospect of not being able to do so.

Once however, we remember that member countries enjoy the massive, inherent, and oft-demonstrated advantage of geographical propinquity, and since some of them, including the UK, must pay considerable sums to remain members of the Single Market, and that they also accept free movement of people, and other limitations of their sovereignty, there cannot be much doubt that, in value-for-money terms, they have been far outperformed by non-members. Services are therefore another example of the paradox: non-members out-perform members. They have, once again, been the main beneficiaries of the Single Market.

29

Why hasn't 'sitting round the table and helping to make the rules' helped UK exports?

The Single Market was primarily intended to improve the exports of members to each other and, in a polite WTO-compliant manner, to leave non-members at a disadvantage. Over the past 21 years it has not worked out that way. Members have sat around the table, and helped to make the rules, and some of them, including the UK, have paid substantial sums for doing so, but this has not given them any noticeable advantage in exporting their goods and services to each other.

The results presented in the previous chapters will be disconcerting, galling and puzzling to a lot of good minds and good people in Britain. Disconcerting because four successive prime ministers have repeatedly told them of the Single Market's significant economic benefits for the UK, but never mentioned that non-members would enjoy greater benefits, and galling because these same good people have been obliged to pay substantial political and economic costs despite fewer benefits.

It will be puzzling because it flies in the face of received economic wisdom. For more than 40 years the EU has been engaged in removing barriers to trade in goods and services between its members. It surely follows therefore, as night follows day, that their exports to each other over these years must have increased more than those of non-members who continued to face the barriers that members have been removing on trade between each other. The data showing that this has not happened, and that non-members' exports to members have increased faster than members' exports to each other, seems to defy common sense. It is profoundly counter-intuitive and a paradox.

This chapter does not, alas, explain or resolve the paradox but merely offers a few comments on it, in the hope that they might prompt a response that is able to suggest how it might be done. Had the UK government, or the European Commission, committed resources to continuously monitor and analyse the impact of the EU and the Single Market on the UK economy, and identified and measured the multiplicity of factors that have affected the exports both of members and non-members within the Single Market, we might well be closer to answering the question.

A similar sighting after the euro

In 2006 two Swedish economists, Harry F Flam and Håkan Nordström, came across a somewhat similar paradox when examining the early impact of the euro on trade. Like membership of the EU and the Single Market programme, the euro was intended to increase trade amongst its own members, and its supporters warned the UK and other sceptical countries of dire consequences for their trade within the EU if they chose to remain outside it.

In the event, working with limited data from the first four years of the euro, 1999-2002, Flam and Nordström found that 'contrary to our expectations, exports to the euro countries are increased to the same extent as exports *from* euro countries'.[1] They went on to describe this as a 'spillover' effect, and attributed it to increased vertical specialisation in manufacturing across national borders of eurozone and non-euro countries in Europe. In their view, producers outside the eurozone are 'able to purchase cheaper inputs from the euro countries, which makes them more competitive and can increase their exports back to the euro countries'.[2] Unfortunately, they had no data to support this comforting hypothesis.

---

1   H. Flam and H. Nordström, 'Trade Volume Effects of the Euro: Aggregate and Sector Estimates', Institute for International Economic Studies, Stockholm University, Seminar Paper No. 746, June 2006, p.10. The size of the differences between euro and non-euro countries varies with the control group. When they use a larger control group of OECD countries instead of the three non-euro EU countries, the benefits of the new currency for trade between euro countries increased to 15 per cent while the trade from non-euro countries to the euro countries increased by 7.5 per cent.

2   Ibid, p.19.

It does not seem likely that this 'spillover' hypothesis will help to explain the larger Single Market paradox of why exports of goods from non-member countries to the EU have grown more during the Single Market than those of its own members. Flam and Nordström were referring to supply chains with non-euro neighbours, rather than inter-continental ones at work over 20 years. In any case, the services exports of non-members have also grown as fast as those of members to each other.

Commission staff stumble upon the paradox in 2007

European Commission staff might be said to have stumbled upon the first signs of this paradox in 2007 when looking back at 2003 trade data. They did not want to make much of it, observing nonchalantly that,

> ...extra-EU exporters have also benefited from the suppression of intra-EU trade barriers and from the application of the principle of mutual recognition. In manufacturing since 1988 and until 2003 (latest available data) the share of extra EU suppliers... has gradually increased at the expense of domestic production.[3]

They affected no particular concern in this shift, and argued that,

> ...the slowdown of trade growth within the EU15 and euro-zone relative to trade growth with third partners is unsurprising given the already very intense trade flows within the EU15 and the large untapped opportunities for trade gains with third partners.[4]

---

3   F. Ilzkovitz, A. Dierx, V. Kovacs, and N. Sousa, 'Steps towards a deeper economic integration: the Internal market in the 21st century', Brussels, European Commission, 2007, p.48, Available from: http://ec.europa.eu/economy_finance/publications/publication784_en.pdf The diagram following the comment indicates that extra-EU imports' share in apparent goods consumption in the EU increased from 9 per cent in 1986 to 15 per cent in 2003, while intra-EU imports' share rose from 20 per cent to 24 per cent, and domestic consumption fell from 71 per cent to 62 per cent.

4   ibid, p.32.

It is a neat and happy solution to the puzzle: intra-EU trade has been so intense and successful that a slowdown is to be expected, leaving large untapped opportunities for non-members. Perhaps for members of the Commission this solution was persuasive, and even for some member countries. For the UK it is less so, since their trade or at least their exports to the EU have not been very intense, and their performance has remained inferior to that of a large number of disadvantaged non-members over many years. For UK observers at least, the paradox deserves more attention than European Commission staff cared to give it nine years ago, especially at this moment. If non-members benefit as much or more than members from the Single Market, they must now wonder why members pay the political and economic costs of belonging to it.

EU rules are a public good from which non-members benefit

There is one elementary contributory factor that deserves a mention in this context. Whatever else they may be, the rules of the Single Market are, in many respects, a public good. Those sitting round the table may intend to help only themselves but, irrespective of their intentions, by imposing uniform rules and standards on each other, they also necessarily help those who have taken no part in devising them. They allow exporters in non-member countries to comply with just one set of technical standards, and with only one set of administrative and customs procedures when exporting to members of the EU, instead of 28, thereby reducing their trade costs.

The rhetoric used to defend the Single Market often conveys a rather dated image of its rule-setting activity, much as if members were still engaged in setting tariffs, or something like tariffs, which would benefit members and leave non-members at more of a disadvantage with every new rule. The conclusion drawn from this rhetoric is that if the UK were to leave the EU, it would join the disadvantaged outsiders and therefore be obliged to negotiate re-entry to the Single Market at almost any price.

This is not the case. Non-members are, we now know, not at a disadvantage, and members are not sitting round the table devising tariff-equivalents with zero-sum consequences for members and non-members. They are more often imposing rules on each other, usually to create the Single Market's level playing field, and thereby increasing their own trade costs, while leaving those of non-members unaffected. Once we recognize that these EU attempts to harmonize, standardize and create a level playing field among its members continually raise members' trade costs, while leaving those of non-members unaffected, the success of non-members exporting to the EU begins to seem slightly less paradoxical, and the opportunity of being one of them considerably more attractive.

Making rules does not necessarily reduce trade costs

There is one piece of evidence presented by the Bank of England from 2008 that might appear to contradict this argument since it showed that 'members of the EU face lower costs of trading with each other than non-EU economies face when trading with the EU'.[5] But lower costs are hardly surprising since this measure includes transport costs, as well as regulatory and legal costs. What we really would like to know are the variations over time in the relative trade costs of goods exports of member and non-members.

Whether members enjoy much of an advantage in services trade costs is also uncertain. A consultant's report for the Commission in 2005 found no reason to distinguish between intra-EU and extra-EU firms because, among other things, 'most of the barriers will be the same for foreign intra-EU firms and extra-EU firms...', and whenever 'a (foreign) firm is established in one Member State, it automatically becomes an intra-EU firm, and it will face exactly the same legal barriers as other EU firms. Coca Cola is in reality

---

5   Bank of England, 'EU membership and the Bank of England', October 2015, p.87, Available from: http://www.bankofengland.co.uk/publications/Documents/speeches/2015/euboe211015.pdf
The data is drawn from World Bank UNESCAP Trade Costs database. This survey did not of course include the trade costs of intra-EU exporters which are paid by EU taxpayers, consumers and non-exporters

an intra-EU firm, because Coca Cola have subsidiaries in EU Member States.'[6] The very fact that members' extra-EU service exports have grown faster than their intra-EU exports, and that non-members' exports to them have grown faster than members, suggests that they may not be enjoying such a decisive cost advantage when trading within the Single Market.

All this uncertainty suggests that it is currently unsafe to assume that sitting at the table and helping to make the rules, and paying heftily for the privilege, yields any great advantage in trade costs of exporters, other than that a substantial part of them are paid by others back home.

---

6   Copenhagen Economics, 'Economic Assessment of the Barriers to the Internal Market in Services', Final Report, January 2005, p. 60, Available from: http://ec.europa.eu/internal_market/services/docs/services-dir/studies/ 2005-01-cph-study_en.pdf

30

Does a Single Market in services exist?

Since no-one in the UK has measured the Single Market in services, no-one can say whether it has been deepened or extended or by how much. In fact, no-one can say for sure that it exists

Successive British prime ministers have placed great hopes in the extension, deepening or completion of the Single Market in services. Since, however, they have never asked anyone in HMT or any other government department to measure it, it is difficult to see how they will ever know whether any of these desirable things are happening. More importantly, how would they know it even exists? In this chapter we will review some of the evidence.

Although the data on services is available only for recent years, enough is available to throw doubt on the existence of the EU Single Market in services. For instance, the proportion of UK exports to OECD countries going to 14 major EU countries between 1999 and

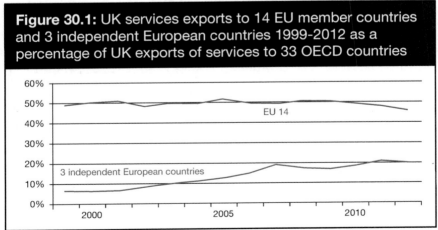

Figure 30.1: UK services exports to 14 EU member countries and 3 independent European countries 1999-2012 as a percentage of UK exports of services to 33 OECD countries

Source: Dataset: *Trade in services by partner country – EBOPS 2002*: United Kingdom. The missing entry for Australia in 2003 was taken to be midway between those of 2002 and 2004. www.oecd.ilibrary.org

2012 was virtually stable, though with a marginal decline from 48.9% to 45.9%. UK services exporters over these years do not therefore show any signs of having benefited in any way from this Single Market.

However, the proportion of UK exports going to the three independent countries who participate in the Single Market without being members of it has trebled in this relatively short period, from 6.1% to 19.8%. In real terms - US(1999)$ - UK services exports to them grew by 134%, while those to fellow members of the Single Market grew by only 58%, which is 10 points less than the 68% growth of UK exports to all 33 OECD countries. Membership of the Single Market has not brought any increase in exports to other members, but has been accompanied by a sharp increase to non-members and especially to Switzerland which has no comprehensive bilateral services agreement with the EU. This is not what one would expect if the Single Market in services was having a beneficial impact on UK services exports.

Other datasets only reinforce the doubts. For instance, as shown in Chapter 28, data on the fastest growing markets for UK services exports showed that those to 12 non-member countries, though much lower in value than those to the EU14, were growing more rapidly over the years 1999-2010. That is also disconcerting since the primary goal of the Single Market is to increase the growth of exports.

The European Commission's preferred measure

The European Commission is seldom slow to congratulate itself on its successes but on the Single Market in services it is unusually diffident. A European Commission staff report in 2007 found that 'there is little difference between trade (in services) between EU25 member states and trade between the EU and third countries.' They illustrated this finding with a histogram which showed that, in 2004, intra-EU exports were about six or seven per cent of EU GDP, while extra-EU exports were roughly nine per cent, which suggested to them, as they tactfully put it, 'that the internal market does not yet fully play its role in the services sectors'.[1]

---

1   Ilzkovitz, *op.cit.*, p.32.

In the January 2015 update of their online *Statistical Yearbook* they again refer to the ratio between intra and extra-EU exports as a proportion of GDP, noting that intra-EU trade in goods is 'two thirds higher than exports to non-member countries', from which they infer that the Single Market in goods is highly integrated. In the later section on services they observe that, by contrast, intra-EU trade is only 55.2 per cent of all exports, and imply that there had been little change over the intervening eight years.[2]

Although the ratio of intra- and extra-EU exports as a percentage of GDP is the European Commission's preferred measure of the integration of the Single Market in both goods and services, Eurostat does not provide a continuous, accessible series of these ratios.[3] However, OECD databases, allow us to construct a substitute, albeit with a good number of missing data entries. Most of these are marked 'non-publishable and confidential value', though they were, as the OECD confirmed in writing, nonetheless included in the world tables used to calculate the extra-EU exports, so that part of the calculation below is unaffected. However that leaves a good number of missing entries for particular countries, and they have been filled in the table below by giving the import figures reported by the recipient country as detailed in the note below Table 30.1.[4]

2　'Europe in Figures', Eurostat yearbook, section on international trade in goods: http://ec.europa.eu/eurostat/statistics-explained/index.php/Eurostat_yearbook.

3　After its recent lengthy investigations of the services market, European Court of Auditors the noted that it was widely recognised that the services market had not 'achieved its full potential', and criticised the Commission for its reluctance to take legal proceedings against infringements. However, it also suggested no means of measuring this market, and therefore no means knowing whether it had achieved full, half or none of its potential.
European Court of Auditors, Has the Commission ensured effective implementation of the Services Directive? Special report No 5/2016:
http://www.eca.europa.eu/Lists/ECADocuments/INSR16_05/INSR_SERVICES_EN.pdf

4　Substitutions of this kind were necessary in more than a third of all cells, 892 out of 2,508. They are far from ideal substitutes and since import and export figures are collected by different agencies, no doubt using different methodologies. And exports are usually measured FOB and imports CIF (FOB means 'free on board', separated from insurance and freight; 'CIF' means 'cost, insurance and freight' so is a different measurement.) However, they are probably better than any reconstructed estimate.

Table 30.1: Intra- and extra-EU services exports of 12 founder members of the Single Market as a proportion of EU GDP 2002-2012 in current value US$bn

	Intra-EU: exports to 19 other members	As % of EU GDP	Extra-EU: exports to rest of world	As % of EU GDP	GDP in current PPPs US$bn	Per cent difference
2002	351.6	3.58	287.5	2.93	9807.2	0.65
2003	431.7	4.30	344.8	3.43	10050.4	0.86
2004	525.1	4.99	413.5	3.93	10523.8	1.06
2005	562.0	5.08	457.6	4.14	11058.7	0.94
2006	635.1	5.30	506.1	4.22	11990.3	1.08
2007	756.6	5.98	615.2	4.87	12643.5	1.12
2008	821.5	6.25	677.5	5.16	13142.1	1.10
2009	744.8	5.79	630.4	4.90	12869.1	0.89
2010	766.3	5.83	662.5	5.04	13144.5	0.79
2011	855.0	6.25	755.7	5.53	13672.6	0.73
2012	817.0	5.87	753.3	5.41	13932.5	0.46

Note: Missing export entries were filled by imports from that country in the cases of German exports to Sweden, Finland & Slovenia 2002-12; Spanish exports to Austria, Belgium, Greece, Ireland, Luxembourg, Portugal. Finland, Slovakia, and Slovenia 2002-2005 plus Slovakia 2007 and Slovenia 2006-2012; Greek exports to Slovakia 2003-5, 2007, Slovenia, 2003, 2006; and for Irish exports to Italy in 2009, to Greece, 2002, 2006-7, to Portugal 2002, 2005.
NB five of the '19 other members' only fully joined the EU in 2004.

Sources: The export, and import, figures are taken from the datafiles of the individual member countries. OECD (2014), "Trade in services - EBOPS 2002", OECD Statistics on International Trade in Services (database). DOI: 10.1787/data-00274-en The GDP figures are taken from National Accounts at a Glance 2014 Gross domestic product, current PPPs, Last updated: 30-Jan-2014© OECD 2014. www.oecd-ilibrary.org

I would much prefer not to have to do this. However, it seems better than any other option such as estimating the missing entries from the given ones. And one must remember what is at issue. This is an attempt to give voters for the first time an impartial measure of something that their government has never bothered to measure, at the same time as telling them that it is one of the most important reasons for remaining a member of the EU.

The table shows intra-EU and extra-EU exports of the 12 founder members of the Single Market as proportion of their GDP over the years from 2002 to 2012. Intra-EU exports are to the other 11 founder members plus the eight other members for whom there is a fairly continuous set of figures over these years.[5]

---

5   Three of the eight joined in 1995 (Austria, Finland and Sweden), and five in 2004 (Czech Republic, Hungary, Poland, Slovakia and Slovenia).

The European Commission's preferred index of the degree of integration of the Single Market in services is the difference between the first two shaded columns, which is given in the third. As may be seen, the difference is a very small percentage of GDP. While intra-EU exports have always been a slightly larger percentage of GDP over these 11 years, they only climb to more than one per cent larger in the years 2004 and 2006-8. Having peeped over the horizon, so to speak, the Single Market in services thereafter trailed away, so that it was, by this index, rather less integrated in 2012 than it was in 2002.

Table 30.2: Growth of intra- and extra-EU services exports of 12 founder members of Single Market, 2002-2012

Intra is to each other and to 8 other current EU members*
extra is to the rest of the world
Compound Annual Growth Rate in US (2002) $, and value in 2012 in US(2012) $bn

Intra-EU exports			Extra-EU exports		
	CAGR %	Value in 2012 $b		CAGR %	Value in 2012 $b
Ireland	12.14	65.2	Ireland	12.58	50.8
Luxembourg	10.23	49.5	Luxembourg	11.78	22.8
France	8.50	114.9	Portugal	9.70	7.9
Germany	7.19	132.2	Belgium	9.70	37.8
Belgium	6.76	63.8	Netherlands	8.90	58.2
Spain	5.98	92.2	Denmark	8.88	38.6
Portugal	5.24	16.6	Germany	7.95	138.2
Netherlands	4.93	75.3	UK	6.48	181.2
Denmark	4.71	27.6	Italy	6.41	52.6
UK	4.32	110.7	Spain	6.30	45.5
Greece	2.30	16.7	France	5.64	101.3
Italy	0.89	52.5	Greece	4.45	18.7

*Austria, Finland and Sweden who joined in 1995, and Czech Republic, Hungary, Poland, Slovakia and Slovenia who joined in 2004.
NB five of the '19 other members' only fully joined the EU in 2004.

Source: OECD Dataset: Trade in services, www.oecd.ilibrary.org/statistics

In the light of these figures, one may reasonably doubt whether a Single Market in services can be said to exist, least of all for the UK. A doubt remains of course because the import figures we have been obliged to use may systematically depress the intra-EU export figures, in which case the intra-EU exports would be higher than those given and hence the difference in the final column would also be higher. However, most of these substitutions refer to the earlier years, so it is unlikely that it would be far from the truth about the later years.

One suspected that without any measure to guide them, Prime Ministers might get it wrong. And so it has proved. The Single Market in services has not been widening or deepening over these years in which they have been urging it to do so, and citing it as a good reason for remaining a member of the EU. It has been shrinking and subsiding, or perhaps evaporating.

The UK's extra-EU exports are not only growing at a faster pace than its inter-exports, (that is also true for every member country except France), but it is the only member country whose intra-EU exports are of much lower value than its extra-EU exports, as Table 30.2 shows.

Obviously, 19 near-neighbours collectively constitute a large and important market for the UK services, but they are not a market that has provided distinctively better opportunities for UK exporters than other world markets. The EU's Single Market differs from other world markets in that the UK has helped to write its rules, requires a hefty annual contribution and is growing much more slowly. Nothing more. France alone has found it provided slightly greater opportunities than the rest of the world. No other member country has done so.

There are questions therefore that will not go away:

- Why would the UK or anyone else bother to sit around the table, help to make the rules, and pay a hefty fee for something that it is shrinking and evaporating, and can hardly be said to exist at all?

- Why would anyone try to persuade voters that it would be a terrible fate if the UK were no longer to engage in these activities?

- Still more puzzling perhaps, why would the UK accept the rule which forbids them helping their exporters by negotiating services trade agreements around the world?

31

Services exports to the EU and other markets

'Our participation in the Single Market, and our ability to help set its rules, is the principal reason for our membership of the EU.'

David Cameron, 23 January 2013

Given that many EU enthusiasts devoutly believe that there is a Single Market in services, and the existing data suggests that it does not exist, the latest published data on UK services exports is obviously of particular interest. Maybe, it has suddenly sprung to life.

Alas, the data is infuriatingly slow to appear. As of January 17th 2016, OECD still only has a complete set of UK exports to fellow OECD members for 2012. They have been used in the graph below to compare the growth, which is reported in current value US dollars, of UK exports to the EU 14 as in 2000 with UK exports to the rest of the world over the thirteen years 2000-2012. Consistent with all of the preceding evidence, they show that exports to the Single Market have grown significantly less than those to the rest of the world. Its existence has therefore still to be demonstrated, and the rationale of buying into it remains a mystery.

Out of curiosity, the growth of services exports to the world by Switzerland and Norway has been added. In both cases this is the only data available over the same period for these two countries. Their exports to the EU 14 alone cannot therefore be shown. Switzerland, we are often reminded does not have a services agreement with the EU, but as far as one can tell from their total services exports, they do not appear to have suffered unduly. The per capita value of Switzerland's services exports to the world in 2012 were $11608, Norway's were $8662, and the UK's were $4726, so Switzerland's about two and a half times more, and Norway's almost double.

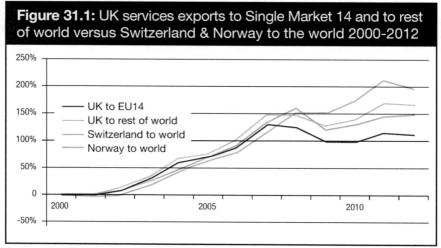

Figure 31.1: UK services exports to Single Market 14 and to rest of world versus Switzerland & Norway to the world 2000-2012

Sources: OECD iLibrary Dataset EBOPS 2002 Trade in Services by Partner Country Total services, Exports in millions of US dollars.

The interesting question is: how long will the UK wait until the Single Market in services appears? Might it not be time to take its fate in its own hands and like the Swiss negotiate trade agreements for themselves?

Ideally, it would have been interesting to compare these rates of growth with UK exports to the countries with which the EU has concluded trade agreements which include services, to see if they had made any difference. The available data do not allow us to do this.

Part Five

Trade agreements

32

The Commission as trade negotiator (I): A preference for small partner countries

The EU may be a heavyweight in GDP terms, but it has long preferred to negotiate with flyweights

The European Commission is currently negotiating a trade agreement with the United States, called the Transatlantic Trade and Investment Partnership (TTIP). The negotiations still have some way to go, and it may then be some considerable time before an agreement can be ratified, and come into force. In the meantime, this chapter will consider the record of the European Commission in negotiating trade agreements over the past 42 years.

The World Trade Organisation (WTO) database on trade agreements in force shows that EU trade agreements have three remarkable characteristics:

- They are overwhelmingly with small economies;
- Only a minority include services;
- They seldom include Commonwealth countries.

These are severe disadvantages from a UK point of view, especially when compared with the trade agreements of non-EU countries. The strategy and priorities that have guided European Commission trade negotiations over the past decades do not appear to have ever been the subject of debate in the UK or anywhere else. The Confederation of British Industries (CBI), along with many other trade federations and large companies, has warmly commended the transfer of responsibility for negotiating trade agreements from the UK to the European Commission. According to the CBI the European Commission has more 'clout' than the UK alone, though it has never bothered to conduct any assessment of what the impact of EU clout on UK exports might have been.

All the European Commission trade agreements in force in March 2016 are listed in the table below, along with the GDP in 2014 of all the partner countries. The European Commission preference for negotiating with smaller countries will be evident, and is thrown into sharp relief when compared with the agreements negotiated by Switzerland, Singapore, South Korea and Chile, none of which have much clout.

In 2014 the mean GDP of all the EU's 34 partner countries was $191.1bn. The mean of Switzerland's partners was more than three times larger ($893.2b), Chile's nearly 12 times larger ($2,964.7b), Singapore's 14 times larger ($3043.9b) and Korea's was $4396.46b, 17 times larger than that of the EU's partners.

Over the past 40 years, the European Commission has never used its clout to go head to head with large economic powers. The largest country with which it has ever concluded an agreement is the Republic of Korea. It has preferred instead to secure a large number of agreements with small countries. In 2014 the total GDP of the EU's partner countries was $6.5tn.

Table 32.1: Trade agreements in goods negotiated by the European Commission with foreign countries 1973-2016 with GDP of partner country, value in US$bn of exports in 2014, and as % of all UK services exports in 2014

Partner Country	Year in force	GDPCurrent US$bn 2014	UK Exports in US$bn 2014	as % of all UK services Exports 2014 ($511.1bn)
Albania	'06	13.37	0.03	0.01
Algeria	'05	214.06	0.79	0.15
Andorra	'91	3.25	0.01	0.00
Bosnia & Herzegovina	'08	18.34	0.04	0.01
Cameroon	'14	32.55	0.08	0.01
CARIFORUM EPA *	'08	131.38	0.66	0.13
Central America **	'13	210.90	0.51	0.10
Chile	'03	258.06	0.78	0.15
Colombia	'13	377.74	0.55	0.11

*   The CARIFORUM countries are Antigua and Barbuda, The Bahamas, Barbados, Belize, Dominica, Grenada, Guyana, Jamaica, Saint Lucia, Saint Vincent and the Grenadines, Saint Kitts and Nevis, Surinam, Trinidad, Tobago, and the Dominican Republic.
**   The Central American partner countries are Honduras, Nicaragua, Panama, Costa Rica, El Salvador, and Guatemala.
***   The East and South African EPA countries are Djibouti, Eritrea, Ethiopia and Sudan, Malawi, Zambia and Zimbabwe, Comoros, Mauritius, Madagascar and the Seychelles.

Table 32.1: Trade agreements in goods negotiated by the European Commission with foreign countries 1973-2016 with GDP of partner country, value in US$bn of exports in 2014, and as % of all UK services exports in 2014

Partner Country	Year in force	GDPCurrent US$bn 2014	UK Exports in US$bn 2014	as % of all UK services Exports 2014 ($511.1bn)
Peru	'13	202.90	0.28	0.05
Cote d'Ivoire	'09	34.25	0.13	0.03
E & S Africa Int EPA***	'12	38.28	0.22	0.04
Egypt	'04	286.54	1.73	0.34
Faroe Islands	'97	2.61	0.02	0.00
Georgia	'14	16.53	0.10	0.02
Israel	'00	304.23	1.81	0.35
Jordan	'02	35.83	0.43	0.08
Korea, Republic of	'11	1410.38	6.91	1.35
Lebanon	'03	45.73	0.82	0.16
Macedonia FYR	'01	11.32	0.89	0.17
Mexico	'00	1282.72	1.73	0.34
Montenegro	'08	4.58	0.02	0.00
Morocco	'00	107.00	0.94	0.18
Palestinian Authority	'97	12.74	0.00	0.00
Papua New Guinea	'09	15.41	0.02	0.00
Fiji	'09	4.03	0.03	0.01
Moldova	'14	7.94	0.07	0.01
San Marino	'02	1.90	0.01	0.00
Serbia	'10	43.87	0.21	0.04
South Africa	'00	349.82	3.92	0.77
Syria	'73	40.41	0.02	0.00
Tunisia	'98	46.99	0.26	0.05
Turkey	'96	799.53	6.13	1.20
Ukraine	'14	131.81	0.58	0.11
TOTAL mean of 34 agreements = $191.1bn		**$6497.0bn**	**$30.73 bn**	7.265%

*   The CARIFORUM countries are Antigua and Barbuda, The Bahamas, Barbados, Belize, Dominica, Grenada, Guyana, Jamaica, Saint Lucia, Saint Vincent and the Grenadines, Saint Kitts and Nevis, Surinam, Trinidad, Tobago, and the Dominican Republic.
** The Central American partner countries are Honduras, Nicaragua, Panama, Costa Rica, El Salvador, and Guatemala.
*** The East and South African EPA countries are Djibouti, Eritrea, Ethiopia and Sudan, Malawi, Zambia and Zimbabwe, Comoros, Mauritius, Madagascar and the Seychelles.

Sources: Regional trade agreements information system of WTO http://rtais.wto.org/; UN Comtrade http://comtrade.un.org/data; the World Bank http://data.worldbank.org/indicator/

In the same year the total GDP of Switzerland's partners was $23.2t, Korea's was $44.0 t, and Chile's was $62.3t. The total GDP of Chile's partners was more than eight times larger than that of the EU's.

John Cridland, when director-general of the CBI consistently defended the clout of the European Commission in trade negotiations. He once claimed, 'Thanks to our EU membership we have trade deals with countries across the globe, worth £15 trillion – we'd struggle to pull off deals of this scale on our own.'

He never explained where this figure of £15 trillion came from. The media never pushed him on this point. All the trade agreements in force that are listed in the WTO database are given in the table, and as may be seen they total $7.7 trillion, or about £5 trillion.[1] Even to claim £5 trillion would be exaggerating, since the worth of a trade deal can only be determined by *ex post* research on its impact. Mr Cridland declined to have the CBI conduct any research of this kind.

After asking the CBI where they acquired the £15 trillion figure, they referred me to their *Our Global Future* study's footnote, itself referring to a CBI study. It included the EU itself (GDP $13 trillion) as one of the deals 'we'd struggle... to pull off on our own.' How clever!

Details of the Chilean, Korean, Singaporean and Swiss agreements currently in force are given in Table 32.2.

The EU's preference for agreements with small or mini-states undercuts one of the familiar arguments for the UK ceding its right to negotiate FTAs to the European Commission. Supposedly, the UK alone would be unable to secure trade agreements with larger trading powers and blocs because it does not have the negotiating leverage or 'collective clout' of the European Commission.

The European Commission has preferred to negotiate with a large number of small countries like Andorra, Albania, Cameroon, Cote d'Ivoire, Costa Rica, including of course the four countries with which it is here being compared. The contrast with Korea is quite striking. Korea has only 10 agreements, but they include countries with very large markets: India, China, Canada, the US, and of course, with the EU itself. Korean trade agreement strategy is evidently very different from that of the European Commission.

---

1   p.76, *Our Global Future*: The business vision for a reformed EU, Confederation of British Industry, 2013.

And yet, one international company made this claim to the Balance of Competences Review:

> The fact that the EU, comprising the world's largest trading bloc, negotiates on behalf of the UK is a big advantage, which no individual state could hope to replicate – even assuming third countries wished to conclude such individual trade agreements.
>
> EU competence for trade policy magnifies the UK's influence into a trading block large enough to deliver the big value market access wins...[2]

---

2   DIAGEO, Evidence submitted to 2013 Balance of Competences Review, p. 2

Table 32.2:

CHILE	In force	GDP (2014)$b
Canada	'97	1786.7
Mexico	'99	1282.7
Costa Rica	'02	49.6
El Salvador	'02	25.2
EU goods	'03	(below)
EU services	'05	18460.6
US	'04	17419.0
Korea	'04	1410.4
EFTA	'04	1208.1
China goods	'06	(below)
China services	'10	10360.1
India	'07	2066.9
Japan	'07	4601.5
Panama	'08	46.2
Honduras	'08	19.4
Peru	'09	202.9
Australia	'09	1453.8
Colombia	'09	377.7
Guatemala	'10	58.7
Turkey	'11	799.5
Malaysia	'12	326.9
Nicaragua	'12	11.8
Hong Kong	'14	290.9
Mean of 21= $2,964.7b		
TOTAL $62,258.7b		

KOREA	In force	GDP (2014)$b
Chile	'04	258.1
Singapore	'06	307.9
EFTA	'06	1208.1
India	'10	2066.9
EU	'11	18460.6
Peru	'11	202.9
US	'12	17419.0
Turkey	'13	799.5
Australia	'14	1453.8
Canada	'15	1786.7
Mean of 10= $4,396.4b		
TOTAL $43,963.4b		

GDP**SACU, the South Africa Customs Union, consists of South Africa, Botswana, Lesotho, Namibia and Swaziland.

SINGAPORE	In force	GDP (2014)$b
New Zealand	'01	188.4
Japan	'02	4601.5
EFTA	'03	1208.1
Australia	'03	1453.8
US	'04	17419.0
India	'05	2066.9
Jordan	'05	35.8
Korea	'06	1410.4
Panama	'06	46.2
China	'09	10360.1
Peru	'09	202.9
Costa Rica	'13	49.6
Chinese Taipei	'14	529.0
Mean of 13= $3043.9b TOTAL $39,571.6b		

SWITZERLAND	In force	GDP (2014)$b
Turkey	'92	799.5
Faroe Islands	'95	2.6
Israel	'93	304.2
Morocco	'99	107.0
Palestinian Auth.	'99	12.7
Mexico	'01	1282.7
FYR Macedonia	'02	11.3
Jordan	'02	35.8
Singapore	'03	307.9
Chile	'04	258.1
Tunisia	'05	47.0
Korea	'06	1410.4
Lebanon	'07	45.7
Egypt	'07	286.5
SACU	'08	384.5
Canada	'09	1786.7
Japan	'09	4601.5
Serbia	'10	43.9
Albania	'10	13.34
Peru	'11	202.9
Colombia	'11	377.7
Ukraine	'12	131.8
Montenegro	'12	4.6
Hong Kong, China	'12	290.9
China	'14	10360.1
Costa Rica	'14	49.6
Panama	'14	46.2
Bosnia & H'gvna	'15	18.3
Mean of 28= $893.2b TOTAL $23,223.6b		

33

The Commission as trade negotiator (II): The neglect of services

Services have been overlooked in EU trade agreements, despite the pleas of successive British prime ministers

Figure 33.1 shows the size, in trillions of US dollars, of the markets covered by the FTAs of the EU alongside those of four small independent countries (in force as of January 2015). Each column showing the size of the markets covered by the agreements is split into two halves. The left half covers all FTAs and the right half covers those agreements that refer specifically to services.

The EU FTAs are presented in two separate columns. The first column on the far left entitled 'EU FTAs only' shows negotiations that the EU has conducted with other sovereign powers. This, however, seemed a less than fair comparison. The columns of the other four countries include their FTAs with the EU, while the EU's does not. Since the EU's efforts have been primarily directed towards creating freer trade amongst its own members, this may give a misleading impression. A second EU column entitled 'EU inc EU' includes the GDP of the EU itself as one of the markets covered by an EU FTA. As may be seen, it makes a substantial difference. The GDP of the EU is nearly three times larger than the aggregate GDP of all the countries with which it has successfully concluded FTAs which were in force in January 2015.

The main purpose of the figure is to compare the ability of the independent countries to include services in the agreements they have negotiated. The overwhelming majority of their agreements, in terms of the GDP of the countries concerned, include services. The two halves of the four columns therefore do not differ greatly. Switzerland is the worst in this respect. Just short of 90 per cent of

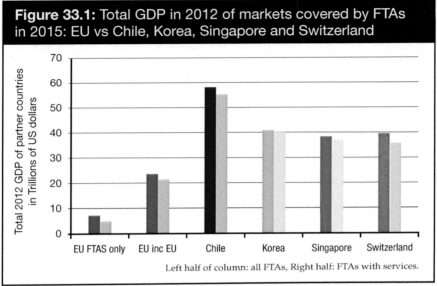

Figure 33.1: Total GDP in 2012 of markets covered by FTAs in 2015: EU vs Chile, Korea, Singapore and Switzerland

Left half of column: all FTAs, Right half: FTAs with services.

Source: WTO Database 'Participation in Regional Trade Agreements' rtais.wto.org; World Bank, http://data.worldbank.org/indicator/

the value of the markets with which Switzerland has FTAs now in force include services. The EU, including the EU itself, is just over 90 per cent.

When we turn to EU agreements negotiated with foreign countries the proportion including services drops to 68 per cent. Nearly one third of EU FTAs with foreign countries do not include any reference to services at all. In terms of the absolute size of the markets opened for freer trade in services, the EU agreements total $4.1tn, whereas Swiss FTAs have opened markets worth $35.8tn., and Singaporean, Korean and Chilean FTAs have opened markets work $37.2t, $40t and $55.4t respectively.

By this simple initial measure, the four smaller, independent countries seem to have been rather more effective than the Commission in negotiating FTAs, especially in services. The 'collective clout' and 'negotiating leverage' of the EU has evidently counted for little.

The agreements the European Commission has negotiated with a service element are shown in the table. The percentage each agreement represents of the UK's total services exports and each partner country's GDP are also included.

Table 33.1: EU Services trade agreements since 1973-2016 with date in force, 2014 GDP of partner in $b, and as a percentage of total UK services exports

Partner	in force	GDP(2014)$b	As % of UK services exports
Mexico	'00	1282.7	0.246
FYR Macedonia	'04	11.3	0.038
Chile	'05	258.1	0.101
Albania	'09	13.4	0.008
Montenegro	'10	4.6	0.015
CARIFORUM States	'08	131.4	0.294
Serbia	'13	43.9	0.024
Korea, Republic of	'11	1410.4	0.800
Ukraine	'14	131.8	0.050
Colombia	'13	377.7	0.071
Peru	'13	202.9	0.077
Central America 6	'13	210.9	0.077
Rep. of Moldova	'14	7.9	0.020
Georgia	'14	16.5	0.010
Bosnia & Herz'ina	'14	12.9	0.018
TOTAL $4,121.8b			**1.849%**

Source RT-AIS WTO, World Bank; UN Comtrade http://comtrade.un.org/data: OECD EBOPS 2010

Figures about the number of FTAs do not say anything about their content, so it may well be that the EU's FTAs secure more substantial advantages for member countries than those of the four independent countries. It may be, for instance, that the terms under which the UK services exporters can trade in the $4.1tn market that the European Commission has facilitated are much better than those the Swiss were able to obtain for their exporters in $35.8tn of markets. The EU's 'clout' may have counted for something after all.

One way of testing this idea would be to compare UK exports to countries covered by an EU agreement with UK exports to countries not covered by an EU agreement. This could show whether the UK benefits more from trade agreements negotiated by the Commission. Or we could measure the pre- and post-agreement growth of UK services exports to individual partner countries. However the available services data does not allow us to do this, and in any case many of the agreements are too recent to provide time for their impact to be felt.

Hence the only measure of their impact that we have is the final column of the table. This gives the value of UK services exports covered by each EU agreement as a proportion of the total value of the UK's total world services exports.

As may be seen, the European Commission has managed to negotiate service agreements that cover in total just 1.8% of all UK services exports. (Figures exclude the EEA countries Norway, Iceland and Liechtenstein.) This does not appear to be a remarkable effort for more than 42 years of negotiations, but then services were not high on anyone's agenda in 1973 and for many years thereafter. The European Commission began including services in its negotiations in 2000, so perhaps we should say that the EU's service agreements are a culmination of 15 years' worth of effort. It still does not appear much better.

34

The Commission as trade negotiator (III): The sidelining of the Commonwealth

The evidence in the Regional Trade Agreements Information System (RTAIS) in the WTO database shows that the European Commission has been very slow to open trade negotiations with Commonwealth countries. The first agreement to come into force was that with South Africa in 2000, some 27 years after UK accession, and the second with members of the Cariforum group of Caribbean countries in 2008.[1]

The 17 Commonwealth countries with which the EU currently has some kind of trade agreement in force are, in terms of their GDP, a small minority of the Commonwealth. These countries had an aggregate GDP in 2014 of just $473.9billion. Those with which it does not have an agreement in force are very nearly sixteen times larger, and in 2014 had an aggregate GDP of $7,491.3billion. This is only a little short of the aggregate GDP of all the countries with which the EU has negotiated agreements since 1973 ($7,713.8billion). For several reasons this contrast comes as a shock, first of all because it is seldom mentioned. But it is also counter-intuitive.

Supposedly, the UK has always pressed the case for increased free trade within the EU. One would have thought it would have done so with especial vigour on behalf of Commonwealth countries. Ties of kin, sentiment and trade with most of them long predate the

---

1   The Cariforum states are Antigua and Barbuda, The Bahamas, Barbados, Belize, Dominica, Grenada, Guyana, Jamaica, Saint Lucia, Saint Vincent and the Grenadines, Saint Kitts and Nevis, Surinam, Trinidad, Tobago, and the Dominican Republic.

Treaty of Rome, and the UK must have felt an additional obligation after leaving them to cope with the EU's common external tariff. One would therefore expect the UK government to have continuously pressed the case for negotiating with them, helped perhaps by Malta and Cyprus, the two other Commonwealth EU members, and for the CBI and trade associations to have been especially keen to build on long-standing ties.

The evidence suggests that the reasoning behind these expectations is mistaken. UK ministers have often congratulated themselves for pushing the EU in a more outward-looking and trade liberalizing direction. However there is no evidence that they have pressed the case for agreements with Commonwealth members with any particular enthusiasm. Whenever deals have been pushed for, the UK has failed miserably. Two recent trade commissioners have been British: Peter Mandelson (2004-8) and Catherine Ashton (2008-9). Neither displayed any particular interest in, or obligation towards, the Commonwealth, and perhaps were not allowed to do so by virtue of their oath of office.

The CBI and many trade federations have been equally forgetful and inert. They enthused about surrendering trade negotiations to the European Commission when giving evidence to the FCO Balance of Competences review. Only one federation among dozens, the National Air Traffic Services (NATS) raised any questions about the European Commission's negotiating priorities and strategy. It observed that the rationale for selecting countries for EU agreements is unclear, and noted that several important emerging markets seem to be missing from the information supplied, for example both Australia and New Zealand.[2]

An inescapable conclusion: the minimal British influence on European Commission trade strategy

The three preceding chapters lead to one inescapable conclusion: UK influence on the EU trade agenda and strategy has been minimal.

---

2   The Balance of Competences Trade & Investment.

Table 34.1: Commonwealth countries' trade agreements with the EU 1973-2016

With an EU agreement in force in 2015	GDP in 2014 in US$ b	Without any agreement in force in 2015	GDP in 2014 in US$b
Antigua & Barbuda	1.27	Australia	1453.77
The Bahamas	8.51	Bangladesh	173.82
Barbados	4.35	Botswana	15.81
Belize	1.62	Brunei	17.26
Cameroon	32.55	Canada*	1,786.66
Dominica	0.54	Fiji	4.03
Grenada	0.88	Ghana	38.65
Guyana	3.23	India	2,066.90
Jamaica	14.36	Kenya	60.94
Mauritius	12.62	Kiribati	0.17
St. Lucia	1.37	Lesotho	2.09
St. Vinc't &t	0.72	Malawi	4.26
St. Kitts & Nevis	0.83	Malaysia	326.93
Seychelles	1.41	Maldives	3.03
South Africa	349.82	Mozambique	16.39
Trinidad & Tobago	24.43	Namibia	13.43
Papua New Guinea	15.41	New Zealand	188.38
TOTAL	**$473.92b**	Nigeria	568.51
		Nairu (est.)	0.08
		Pakistan	246.88
		Rwanda	7.89
		Samoa	0.80
		Singapore	307.87
		Sierra Leone	3.40
		Solomon Is.	1.16
		Sri Lanka	74.94
		Swaziland	3.40
		Uganda	26.31
		Tanzania	49.18
		Tonga	0.43
		Tuvalu	0.04
		Vanuatu	0.80
		Zambia	27.07
		TOTAL	**$7,491.27b**

Notes

An agreement with Canada was concluded in December 2014 and awaits ratification by member countries, as at yet some indeterminate point in the future. Negotiations with Singapore are on-going.

GDP of Belize, Jamaica, Trinidad & Tobago, Tuvalu and Vanuatu are from 2013. That of Nairu is a CIA estimate from 2011.

World Bank, World Development Indicators, GDP in current US$

For some reason, many British participants and observers claim the opposite. Maybe this is because they attend many meetings in Brussels, are heard politely, and mistake this for influence, the actual negotiating priorities and strategy of the Commission.

The facts however do not respond to warm words and they cannot be misled. It is inconceivable that a trade policy that had been significantly influenced by the British opinion, whether from exporters, officials, MEPs, the press or the wider public could possibly have given priority to agreements i) with so many smaller countries, ii) that neglected services, iii) and that sidelined the Commonwealth.

35

Have European Commission trade agreements in goods helped UK exports? A scorecard versus Chile, Korea, Singapore and Switzerland

A post-agreement export growth league table comparing Chile, Korea, Singapore & Switzerland with the UK, finds the UK at the bottom with only four wins and 10 losses

Numerous UK political and business leaders, trade federations and businesses argue that the UK has benefited from surrendering the right to negotiate its own trade agreements to the European Commission. Not one of them, however, has ever initiated any studies to determine exactly what the impact on UK exports the agreements negotiated by the European Commission might have been, even though as prime ministers, ministers, and CEOs of large companies, they have had ample opportunity to do so.

The European Commission has only conducted one such study: on the agreement with Chile. It used a variety of methodologies, came to no clear conclusion, and had no interest in determining what the impact of the agreement on the UK might have been.

---

1   Itaqa Sarl, Evaluation of the economic impact of the Trade Pillar of the *EU-Chile Association Agreement, Final report,* for the European Commission, Directorate General for Trade, March 2012. http://trade.ec.europa.eu/doclib/docs/2012/august/tradoc_149881.pdf There was, however, an earlier study Copenhagen Economics, *Ex-Post Assessment of Six EU Free Trade Agreements, An econometric assessment of their impact on trade,* prepared for the European Commission, DG Trade, by, February 2011 http://trade.ec.europa.eu/doclib/docs/2011/may/tradoc_147905.pdf The European Commission may have considered this earlier six-nation assessment a pilot, since the Chile study refers to itself, and is referred to elsewhere by the European Commission, as 'the first wide-ranging, ex-post assessment of a specific bilateral trade agreement carried out at the request of the European Commission.' p.29, *op.cit.*

In the absence of any evidence, I decided to conduct an elementary, pilot study. It compared the growth rate of UK exports before and after the 15 EU agreements for which there was adequate data came into force, with the growth rate of Swiss exports before and after 14 agreements Switzerland had negotiated on its own behalf.[2] Partly it was an attempt to discover whether there was any truth in the oft-repeated claim that the European Commission, with all its clout, had negotiated more effective agreements than those of small independent countries like Switzerland. Also, of course, it might indicate whether European Commission agreements were bound to be more effective than any agreements the UK was likely to negotiate on its own.

The results did not support the oft-repeated claim about EU clout. The real growth rate of UK exports rose after five EU agreements came into force, but fell in the remaining 10. The real growth rate of Swiss exports increased after nine of its agreements, and fell in the remaining five. Moreover, there were striking differences in the amounts of post-agreement growth. The rate of growth more than doubled after seven of the Swiss agreements, whereas UK exports only managed this in two cases, both in the minor export markets of Syria and Lebanon.

Rules of comparison

The investigation reported in this chapter is an attempt to see whether the results of the exploratory Anglo-Swiss comparison using OECD import data could be replicated by making use of the UN Comtrade database, to extend the comparison to other small independent countries. Singapore, Korea and Chile were chosen, simply because they had an active trade negotiation policy, and the data for all three is good.

The tables below enable us to compare pre- and post-agreement export growth of Switzerland, the UK, Chile, Korea and Singapore. The rules of comparison are exactly the same as those of the pilot Anglo-Swiss study.

All agreements of all five countries for which there is adequate data are included. Adequate means that it has to show at least five

---

2   This investigation is described in full pp.45-52, Michael Burrage, *Where's the Insider Advantage?* Civitas, London 2015

post-agreement years of trade, since agreements take time to have an impact and CAGR growth rates over shorter periods can be highly erratic and misleading. Partner countries that failed to qualify are listed at the bottom of each table. In the main they are omitted because agreements with them have only recently come into force, but in some cases it is because there is no data for pre-agreement years.

Export growth is measured and compared over as many years as possible, but always with an equal number of years before and after. All the growth rates are calculated in 1993 US dollars. Unshaded cells in the final post-agreement column indicate an increase in the CAGR compared with the pre-agreement rate.

Switzerland

The results for Switzerland are consistent with the earlier study, though the countries included are not exactly the same. In the earlier study, exports to Israel showed a marginal post-agreement decline, but here they show an increase. The final score in the earlier study

Table 35.1: Swiss exports – growth rates of pre and post trade agreements with 14 countries

Unshaded cells indicate post-agreement growth exceeds pre-agreement

Final score 10 wins/4 losses				
Partner	Entry into force	Yrs pre & post	Growth CAGR % pre	Growth CAGR % post
Israel	'93	6	-4.45	1.09
Morocco	'99	11	-2.20	9.40
Mexico	'01	13	5.03	7.39
Jordan	'02	13	5.34	10.48
Singapore	'03	12	2.65	9.65
Chile	'04	11	-2.93	7.32
Tunisia	'05	10	1.06	12.50
Korea	'06	9	0.63	8.03
Lebanon	'07	8	7.10	6.70
Egypt	'07	8	-0.03	10.63
Canada	'09	6	13.45	7.27
Japan	'09	5	6.07	0.34
Serbia	'10	5	-3.19	2.35
Albania	'10	5	12.72	-2.68

Omitted: EFTA 1960; EU 1973; Turkey 1992; Faroe Islands 1995; Palestinian Authority 1999; FYR Macedonia 2002; SACU 2008; Peru, Colombia 2011; Ukraine, Montenegro, Hong Kong 2012; GCC, China, Costa Rica, Panama 2014.

Sources: https://rtais.wto.orghttp://comtrade.un.org/data/

was a post-agreement increase in 9 of the 14 countries, while here it is 10 out of 14.

UK

The overall UK score is broadly consistent with the earlier study. The post-agreement rate of growth of UK exports increased in four of the fourteen countries, and declined in the other 10.

The four 'winners' were not, however, the same in the two studies. Syria and Macedonia, two winners in the first study, could not be included because the UN Comtrade database did not have sufficient data. Two more of the original winners, Tunisia and Israel, who had registered slight post-agreement increases of two and one per cent respectively in the first study, became losers in this study. Only one country, Lebanon, registered a post-agreement increase in growth in both studies.

The three new winners were Chile, Papua New Guinea and Korea. Chile was the striking discrepancy with the earlier study, probably

Table 35.2: UK exports – growth rates of pre and post EU trade agreements with 14 countries

Unshaded cells indicate post-agreement growth exceeds pre-agreement

Final score 4 wins/10 losses

Partner	Entry into force	Yrs pre & post	Growth CAGR % pre	Growth CAGR % post
Tunisia	'98	5	15.81	2.25
Morocco	'00	7	14.16	-4.13
Israel	'00	7	9.29	2.24
Mexico	'00	7	5.56	-2.27
Jordan	'02	9	0.73	0.63
Chile	'03	10	-2.30	17.06
Lebanon	'03	10	0.19	5.05
Egypt	'04	11	2.46	1.18
Algeria	'05	10	11.52	10.56
Albania	'06	9	4.88	-1.27
Bosnia & Herz	'08	7	7.26	-1.70
Côte d'Ivoire	'09	6	8.83	6.69
Papua N Guinea	'09	6	-15.36	1.11
Korea	'11	5	0.13	11.2

Omitted: Members' Overseas Countries & Territories (10), Switzerland, Liechtenstein, Iceland, Norway 1971; Syria 1977; Andorra 1991; Faroe Islands, Palestinian Authority 1997; South Africa 2000; FYR Macedonia 2001; San Marino 2002; Montenegro, CARIFORUM States 2008; Madagascar, Mauritius, Seychelles, Zimbabwe 2009; Serbia 2010; E & S Africa States, Iraq 2012; Colombia, Peru, Central America Customs Union 2013; Cameroon, Moldova, Georgia, Fiji 2014; Ecuador 2015; Ukraine, Kosovo 2016.

Sources: https://rtais.wto.orghttp://comtrade.un.org/data/

because UK imports reported to the OECD by Chile in the tenth post-agreement year, 2012, were exceptionally low. By contrast, the UN Comtrade data shows substantial post-agreement growth of UK exports to Chile. Indeed, the difference of nearly 20 per cent, between pre- and post-agreement growth rates is the largest of the four countries. However, the post-agreement increase in exports to Korea is also striking and Papua New Guinea is also a considerable turnaround, given that prior to the agreement UK exports had been in a steady and steep decline.

Many British trade associations, large companies and the CBI came together to praise the EC trade agreements in the Balance of Competences Review in 2013, and urged HMG not to consider negotiating its own trade agreements. They did not present any evidence about any EU FTAs at all. When they next make this argument, they may want to refer to the real world, in which case they might mention Lebanon, Chile, Papua New Guinea and Korea.[3] These four countries are the only EU prima facie 'success stories' from a UK point of view, where UK exports may be seen to have grown faster after the EU agreement came into force than they had done before.[4]

Collectively, however, these four countries accounted for 1.83 per cent of UK goods exports in 2015. This suggests that the EU's heft and clout has not been particularly effective over more than forty years of negotiating. Maybe the countries listed at the bottom of the UK table, which had to be omitted, will add to this percentage when adequate evidence become available.[5]

---

3   If they found the pilot study relying on OECD import data credible, they might add Syria and Macedonia.

4   Since we have not attempted to isolate the impact of the trade agreement from other variables that might have contributed to post-agreement growth, we should perhaps call them apparent success stories. There may be other hidden success stories, countries where the growth rate of UK exports might have fallen still more than it did but for the EU trade agreement.

5   To discover whether the minimum five year before and after comparison rule might have hidden other EU and UK success stories, comparisons were conducted for some of the larger partner countries that fell foul of it and had to be omitted. South Africa UN Comtrade data only begins in 2000, the date of the agreement, but there was data for three years prior to the FTA with Turkey in 1996, and it showed a pre-agreement CAGR of 8.06% and a post-agreement CAGR of 8.36% i.e. little change. In Columbia the pre-agreement CAGR 2010-2012 was 10.6 % and post-agreement 0.8%. and Peru over the same pre-agreement years 10.2% and post-agreement 0.8%. From which one might best conclude there was some sense in the five year rule.

One noticeable difference from the earlier comparison is that the Swiss post-agreement growth rates are not markedly higher than the British in this study. The unweighted average gain in UK exports, following its four gains, was 8.6%. Switzerland has more post-agreement gains, but the unweighted mean gain following the 10 Swiss agreements was 7.9%.

Chile

At first sight, Chile appears to follow the UK in having more post-agreement declines than increases. Only six of its 18 agreements have been followed by an increase in the growth rate of its exports to the new partner countries.

Table 35.3: Chile exports – growth rates of pre and post trade agreements with 18 partners

Unshaded cells indicate post-agreement growth exceeds pre-agreement

Final score 6 wins/12 losses

Partner	Entry into force	Yrs pre & post	Growth CAGR % pre	Growth CAGR % post
Canada	'97	7	12.96	31.76
Mexico	'99	9	27.47	14.75
Costa Rica	'02	12	8.43	10.81
El Salvador	'02	12	20.17	6.17
EU	'03	12	0.30	4.28
US	'04	11	6.93	4.01
Korea	'04	11	7.23	7.37
Switzerland	'04	11	15.86	16.92
Norway	'04	11	4.56	1.74
China	'06	9	32.69	14.95
India	'07	8	41.60	9.03
Japan	'07	8	12.98	-1.60
Panama	'08	7	29.40	-9.34
Honduras	'08	7	9.26	-0.05
Peru	'09	6	17.32	3.61
Australia	'09	6	28.34	4.38
Columbia	'09	6	16.46	8.18
Guatemala	'10	5	-2.84	10.46

Omitted: Argentina 1991; Bolivia, Venezuela 1993; Mercosur 1996; EU 2003; EFTA 2004; New Zealand, Singapore 2006; Columbia 2009; Ecuador 2010; Turkey 2011; Malaysia, Nicaragua 2012; Vietnam, Hong Kong 2014; Thailand 2015.
EU refers to the 11 founding members of the Single Market with Luxembourg missing for lack of data.

Sources: https://rtais.wto.orghttp://comtrade.un.org/data/

However, it should be noted that Chile has registered post-agreement gains in export growth to Canada, Korea, Switzerland, and the EU. These are rather more significant markets than the five in which the UK has recorded post-agreement gains: Lebanon, Chile, Papua New Guinea and Korea.

Moreover, many of the falls in the post-agreement growth rate in Chilean exports follow quite remarkable growth over the pre-agreement years, such as the CAGR of 27.47% of their exports to Mexico, 32.69% to China, 41.60% to India, and 28.34% to Australia. Many of these growth rates were destined to fall, whatever the merits or demerits of their trade agreements. One cannot say the same of the falling post-agreement growth of UK exports. The two countries may have similar post-agreement success rates, but they are hardly in the same boat.

Korea and Singapore

Since we have only reported raw data, and said nothing of the other factors that might affect trade in these countries before and after their trade agreements, we cannot say what the impact of the trade agreements may have been in any of these cases.

However, since this is the best data currently available it throws serious doubt on the claim that the European Commission has, by virtue of its heft and clout, been able to negotiate beneficial trade agreements for UK exports. Three of the small independent

Table 35.4: Korea exports – growth rates of pre and post trade agreements with 5 countries

Unshaded cells indicate post-agreement growth exceeds pre-agreement

Final score 4 wins/1 loss

Partner	Entry into force	Yrs pre & post	Growth CAGR % pre	Growth CAGR % post
Chile	'04	11	0.22	12.05
Singapore	'06	9	7.65	10.49
Norway	'06	9	-7.79	6.46
Switzerland	'06	9	5.74	7.93
India	'10	5	10.80	-2.68

Omitted: EU, Peru 2011; U.S 2012; Turkey 2013; Australia 2014; Canada, Columbia 2015.

Sources: https://rtais.wto.orghttp://comtrade.un.org/data/

Table 35.5: Singapore exports – growth rates of pre and post trade agreements with 12 countries

Unshaded cells indicate post-agreement growth exceeds pre-agreement

Final score 8 wins/4 losses				
Partner	Entry into force	Yrs pre & post	Growth CAGR % pre	Growth CAGR % post
New Zealand	'01	11	5.97	15.30
Japan	'02	12	3.70	3.80
Norway	'03	11	2.84	20.72
Switzerland	'03	11	2.45	9.33
Australia	'03	11	5.69	10.16
US	'04	10	-1.03	-2.13
India	'05	9	6.62	5.88
Jordan	'05	9	10.32	20.06
Korea	'06	8	14.75	7.21
Panama	'06	8	17.10	20.04
China	'09	5	15.42	13.78
Peru	'09	5	16.60	31.75

Omitted: EFTA 2003; Brunei, Chile 2006; Costa Rica, GCC 2013; Taipei 2014.

Sources: https://rtais.wto.orghttp://comtrade.un.org/data/

Table 35.6: Final post-agreement scores of the five countries

	No. agreements examined	Pre-agreement mean CAGR %	Post-agreement mean CAGR %	No. gains	No. falls	Gain/ Fall ratio
KOREA	5	3.3	6.8	4	1	4
SWITZERLAND	14	2.9	6.5	10	4	2.5
SINGAPORE	12	8.3	13.0	8	4	2
CHILE	18	16.0	7.4	6	12	0.5
UK	14	4.5	3.5	4	10	0.4

Sources: https://rtais.wto.orghttp://comtrade.un.org/data/

countries register clear post-agreement gains. Bearing in mind the countries with which Chile has concluded agreements, and its post-agreement export CAGRs, it can hardly be considered a failure. This evidence therefore strongly suggests that independent countries can negotiate very effectively on their own behalf.

By contrast, the post-agreement growth record of the UK seems to be distinctively bad. Neither the European Commission nor HMG seem in any hurry to find out why. Indeed, it is doubtful if they are even aware of just how bad it is.

For the UK political and business leaders who have for many years been telling the British people that the European Commission is negotiating trade agreements effectively on Britain's behalf, these results raise serious questions, questions that they should have addressed years ago. Whatever the result of the referendum, it is to their discredit that they failed to do so.

36

The UK's lost years of freer trade

Switzerland and Singapore show what the UK might have done had it been able to negotiate its own trade agreements. They suggest that part of the price of EU membership for the UK has been many lost years of freer trade

In preceding chapters we have recorded the inclination of the European Commission to prefer trade agreements with small economies, which in about one third of cases do not include services. They have also been disinclined to negotiate with Commonwealth countries, which may be the most promising markets for UK goods and services.

In all these respects, the European Commission has been consistently outpaced by several small independent countries, but its failure has not attracted much interest or concern in the UK. In over forty years, the UK government has never, it seems, found fault with the European Commission's negotiating strategy. The CBI, numerous trade associations and multinationals seem never to have noticed what was happening. When asked by the Balance of Competences Review, they expressed complete satisfaction with the European Commission's performance, and were confident that by itself the UK could not have negotiated as effectively. The promise of TTIP may perhaps have distracted them.

The failings of the European Commission in trade negotiations have therefore passed without notice, but they nonetheless have costs, paid in lost opportunities, not by established multinationals, but by SMEs, start-ups and entrepreneurs who might have benefited from the additional opportunities that trade agreements can provide.

This chapter gives an initial rough estimate of the scale of the lost opportunities for UK firms, in terms of lost years of freer trade, by comparing the dates the trade agreements of Switzerland and Singapore came in to force with those negotiated by the EU which UK firms have had to live with. It assumes that an independent UK negotiating its own agreements might have kept pace with one or both of these countries. There are, of course, many differences between them, but there are also some resemblances. All three have large service sectors, within which financial services are especially prominent, all of them have very high proportions of FDI, none are self-sufficient agriculturally, and all depend heavily on foreign trade. All have high incomes, the UK being the poorest of the three.

A comparison between them is not, therefore, a total mismatch and it is not wholly unrealistic to suppose that an independent UK would have been able to keep up with them in negotiating agreements. Indeed, Switzerland provides a kind of experiment of what might have happened if the UK had remained a member of EFTA instead of joining the EU, since a number of Switzerland's FTAs were negotiated under EFTA auspices. If anything, the UK might well have run ahead of the Swiss, since UK agricultural interests are less numerous, less powerful and less protectionist than the Swiss.

Keeping pace with Singapore would no doubt have been considerably more difficult. The limited size and range of its industries means that it is likely to have fewer vested interests to negotiate over partner counties. It also has an all-powerful executive branch of government which is wholly dedicated to economic development, and can conclude agreements quickly. However, the two countries offer rather different versions of what might have happened if the UK had been free to negotiate trade agreements for itself. The table presents the result of this exercise:

Table 36.1 shows when goods and services agreements of Switzerland and Singapore came into force and the date in which the EU equivalent agreement came into force. Nil means there is, as yet, no EU equivalent. Most importantly the table shows the years of freer trade that the UK has lost by being a party to the European Commission agreements, compared with what it might have enjoyed if it had negotiated its own at the same pace as

Table 36.1: The UK's lost years of freer trade 1992-2016

Estimated by comparing dates in force of EU, Swiss and Singaporean trade agreements in goods and services up to Jan 2016

SWITZERLAND

	Goods			Services			
	Date in force	EU/UK equivalent agreement	Lost Years	Date in force	EU/UK equivalent agreement	Lost Years	GDP 2014 US$bn
Turkey	4/92	1/96	4				799.5
Israel	1/93	6/00	7				304.2
Morocco	2/99	3/00	0				107.0
Mexico	7/01	7/00	-1	7/01	10/00	-1	1282.7
Singapore	1/03	nil	12+	1/03	nil	12+	307.9
Chile	12/04	2/03	0	12/04	03/05	0	258.1
Korea	9/06	7/11	5	9/06	07/11	5	1410.4
Egypt	8/07	04	-3				286.5
SACU	5/08	nil	8				384.5
Canada	7/09	nil	6				1786.7
Japan*	9/09	nil	5+	9/09	nil	6	4601.5
Peru	7/11	13	2	7/11	3/13	1	202.9
Columbia	7/11	13	2	7/11	3/13	1	377.7
Ukraine	6/12	14	2	6/12	nil	3+	131.8
Hong Kong,	10/12	nil	2+	10/12	nil	3+	290.9
China	7/14	nil	1+	7/14	nil	1+	10360.1
Central America*	8/14	8/13	-1	8/14	8/13	-1	95.8

SINGAPORE

	Goods			Services			
NZ	1/01	nil	14+	1/01	nil	16+	188.4
Japan	11/02	nil	12+	11/02	nil	14+	4601.5
Australia	7/03	nil	11+	7/03	nil	12+	1453.8
US	1/04	nil	11+	1/04	nil	12+	17419
India	8/05	nil	9+	8/05	nil	10+	2066.9
Korea	3/06	07/11	5	3/06	07/11	5	1410.4
China	1/09	nil	6+	1/09	nil	7+	10360.1
Peru	8/09	3/13	2	8/09	13	2	202.9
Chinese Taipei	4/14	nil	1+	4/14	nil	1+	529

*Costa Rica & Panama only

Sources: Regional trade agreements information system of WTO http://rtais.wto.org/; the World Bank http://data.worldbank.org/indicator/

Switzerland or Singapore. In three cases, Egypt, Mexico, and Central America, EU agreements preceded the Swiss. Hence they are years of freer trade gained rather than lost.

In one respect the table is unfair to the EU. This count started from Swiss and Singaporean agreements to see whether the EU had managed to keep up with them. But the EU has concluded a good number of agreements before or during these years for which there are neither Swiss nor Singaporean counterparts. There are 13 goods, and 6 service agreements which have no Swiss counterparts and 28 goods and 6 service agreements without Singaporean ones.[1] So the UK has benefited rather more by EU membership than this table indicates. But not that much more, since the EU agreements tend to be with small countries. The combined GDP in 2014 of all the EU's trading partners was, as we saw in Chapter 32, only $6.5tn, whereas that of Switzerland's partners was $23.2tn, and of Singapore's was $39.6tn.

The six EU service agreements which neither Switzerland nor Singapore have matched, are with the Cariforum states, Serbia, Moldova, Montenegro, FYR Macedonia, and Georgia. Their combined GDP in 2014 was $0.22tn, which is a little more than that of Peru. But then Switzerland has had five more years of freer services trade covered by its agreement with Korea (GDP $1.41bn) and Singapore has had, so far, fourteen years of freer services trade with Japan (GDP $4.61bn).

A final comprehensive balance sheet would not therefore be quite so depressing for the EU, or the UK. The main point of this exercise, however, is to show that there is a case for a balance sheet, preferably annual, and preferably to include assessments of the contribution of agreements to the growth of exports. Thus far there has never been one. Instead we have been told by Messrs Blair, Cameron, the CBI and others that by itself the UK could not possibly match the heft and negotiating leverage of the EU in concluding trade agreements. They somehow know this without making any attempt to examine the record of the European Commission and compare it with that of any independent countries.

---

1   The 13 are Syria, Andorra, Jordan, South Africa, San Marino, Algeria, Cariforum, Côte d'Ivoire, Papua New Guinea, Fiji, East and South African states, Moldova and Georgia. The 28 are the 13 mentioned plus Lebanon, Egypt, SACU, Canada, Serbia, Albania, Columbia, Ukraine, Montenegro, Central America, Bosnia & Herzegovina, Morocco, Israel, Mexico, FYR Macedonia.

Switzerland's and Singapore's negotiators have not only matched but far surpassed those of the European Commission. The price has been paid by UK businesses that have lost many years of freer trade.

37

Obstacles impeding
EU service agreements

Compares the 'reserved rights' of EU, member and three non-member countries in the opening offers at the WTO Trade in Services Agreement (TiSA) talks in 2013, to illustrate the hurdles facing any prospective EU partner country

When surrendering the right to negotiate trade agreements to the European Commission, the UK placed an extraordinary degree of trust in a then unknown and untested body. There it has remained for over forty years. No UK government has ever evaluated its negotiation strategy, never asked any government agency to monitor its work, or to measure the impact of the agreements it has negotiated.

Evidence mentioned in previous chapters suggests that this trust was misplaced. Successive Prime Ministers have spoken frequently of the importance of services to the future of the British economy and yet the Commission has concluded rather few service trade agreements by comparison with small independent countries such as Chile, Korea, Singapore and Switzerland. In total, EU agreements with countries outside the EEA now cover just 1.8 per cent of total UK services export markets.

The neglect of the Commonwealth other than the Cariforum, which includes most of the Caribbean Commonwealth countries, almost seems like a deliberate snub; since they, along with countries like Japan and China, where English has been semi-officially accepted as the second language, seem the most promising prospects for UK services exports.

This chapter will not question why the CBI, followed by a good number of trade federations and large British companies have somehow come to believe that the UK has exercised considerable influence on EU trade strategy. When asked for their opinion by the Balance of Competences review in 2013, they strongly supported the present balance because the 'heft' or 'clout' of 'negotiating leverage' is an immense advantage in securing effective trade agreements. That's a mystery for another occasion.

Instead, it will identify two factors that appear to have handicapped their past efforts to negotiate service trade agreements and which seem likely to remain to limit effective agreements in the future.

Mixed motives: the EU has multiple goals when conducting trade negotiations

For a long time agreements seem to have been primarily seen as an instrument of EU foreign or neighbourhood policies. Its current agreements have three pillars – economic, social and environmental – which encourage its negotiators to engage in discussion about many aspects of the potential partners' society and culture, and to consider not merely the export of goods and services, but also the export of European values.[1] One imagines that, on many occasions, raising such issues will delay or even scupper any prospect of reaching a trade agreement, whatever clout the EU might bring to bear.

Because they include social and environmental issues, EU agreements are frequently described as 'deep and comprehensive', like its agreement with Ukraine; or as 'partnership agreements', as if they were half-way towards an alliance rather than mere trade agreements. By contrast, Korea, Singapore and Chile and other small countries have been far more single-minded. Their trade agreements are just that, trade agreements, and intended solely to increase their exports, which the evidence suggests they have generally been able to do (see Chapter 38). Switzerland's agreement with Ukraine came into force in 2013 without exciting any particular interest or concern in Russia.

The CBI counts itself a strong supporter of the EU's 'deep and comprehensive' trade agreements, though it is not entirely clear

---

1   Our Global Future: The business vision for a reformed EU', Confederation of British Industry, 2013.

whether it has a mandate from its members to support Commission negotiators in including human rights, gender relations and climate change as part of an agreement ostensibly intended to increase trade.[2] When it came to defending these agreements, the CBI focused on their supposed trade benefits rather than their contributions to human rights or the environment; but then it has no evidence that these agreements have been effective on any count.

The EU has failed to create a Single Market in services within the EU itself

This failure means of course that the Commission cannot offer a potential partner country an integrated services market of 500 million people. This image may be persuasive in domestic political debate, but it can hardly be a powerful bargaining chip in trade negotiations, since potential partner countries and investors could not long remain unaware of the many regulatory barriers within this supposed Single Market. There are two sources of evidence about these intra-EU barriers:

Table 37.1: Variations in restrictiveness within the EU's Single Market in services.
Aggregate scores in the OECD STRI 2014 in 18 service sectors of 21 member countries. Higher score is more restrictive.

Poland	4.562	Czech Rep	2.917
Austria	4.143	Slovenia	2.908
Greece	4.039	Spain	2.890
Estonia	3.885	France	2.782
Finland	3.783	Ireland	2.781
Italy	3.744	Hungary	2.776
Portugal	3.444	Denmark	2.772
Slovak Rep	3.363	Germany	2.449
Belgium	3.206	Luxembourg	2.428
Sweden	3.125	UK	2.347
		Netherlands	1.759

Source: http://stats.oecd.org/Index.aspx?DataSetCode=STRI
OECD Services Trade Restrictiveness Indices

2   *Ibid*, p.58

In 2014, the OECD published Services Trade Restrictiveness Indices (STRIs), which calculated and scored, on the basis of a regulatory database of comparable, standardised information on trade and investment policies in force in each country, the degree of restrictiveness in 18 service sectors of the 34 OECD members.[3]

The 18 sectors included architecture, accounting, engineering, legal services, banking, insurance construction, telecoms, computer services, air and maritime transport, road and rail freight, courier services, TV and broadcasting, sound recording, motion pictures, and distribution.

The restrictions fall into two broad categories: those common to all of them, (such as maximum foreign equity share, statutory monopolies' jurisdictions, duration of stay for temporary services suppliers, public procurement, administrative procedures regarding nationality and establishing and licensing businesses); as well as detailed sector-specific regulations.

The OECD found no reason to consider regulations of the kind that distinguish EU members from non-members, so they evidently did not rate these as discriminating or powerful enough to mark a significant divide between EU members and non-EU members. One might take this as an inadvertent, therefore highly credible, measure of the insignificance of the Single Market in services, which, in terms of this cross-national measure of trade restrictiveness, could remain an unnoticed variable. Nine years earlier, some private researchers came to a similar conclusion.[4]

That said, measures taken over many years to harmonize and standardize member countries' services in the interest of creating the Single Market may have had some effect, since member countries were, on average, slightly less restrictive compared to non-members, with a mean score of 3.15 versus non-members' 4.0. However, the variations between EU members shown in the table,

---

3   http://oe.cd/stri
4   In 2005, private researchers came to a similar conclusion on the grounds that 'most of the barriers will be the same for foreign intra-EU and extra-EU firms', which are anyway difficult to tell apart. Coca Cola, it pointed out is an intra-EU by virtue of its subsidiaries in member states; Copenhagen Economics, 'Economic Assessment of the Barriers to the Internal Market in Services', (Final Report, January 2005) pp.59-60

demonstrates that they are still far from being members of a cohesive Single Market in terms of service trade restrictions.

These variations demonstrate the difficulties facing both the Commission and partner country negotiators in trying to formulate services trade agreements. If one tries to answer the critical question of who a partner country would prefer to negotiate with, they would, one suspects, with other things being equal, choose the Netherlands over Poland. Other things are not equal of course, and if the GDP of the country is a relevant issue or a shared language, the chances are that the UK would top the list; though Poland, Austria or Greece might not be at the bottom. Probably the very worst option of all would be to negotiate with all 21 of these countries simultaneously. Yet this is what the EU expects prospective partner countries to do.

European Commission's opening 'offer' in the TiSA Geneva talks

The publication of the opening EU 'offer' in the TiSA (Trade in Services Agreement) negotiations in 2013 provides a particularly vivid demonstration of the difficulties of formulating services trade agreements in which the EU is involved.[5] The proposed agreement is intended to improve market access, and to set universal rules for services trade. The talks are being conducted under WTO auspices in Geneva, with 23 countries, including Hong Kong, Norway, New Zealand and Israel, among other small countries; as well as Japan and the United States, though not India. China is expected to join them shortly. The 28 EU countries, including the UK, are represented by the European Commission and have no independent participation.

The opening EU offer demonstrates the difficulties of negotiating a services trade agreement as a member of the EU, and may therefore help to explain why the Commission has negotiated so few, and why one should expect few in the future.

The offer begins with 31 dense pages setting out, in Section A, the 'reserved rights' of individual EU countries, as well as those of the EU as a whole which all members have in common. Like the OECD's STRIs, these pages themselves demonstrate the limitations

---

5   http://trade.ec.europa.eu/doclib/docs/2014/july/tradoc_152689.pdf

of the Single Market in services, since many of the rules restrict fellow members as much as non-members; the notable exceptions being nationality and educational qualifications.

The following chart shows, for each country, the number of conditions for sectors, sub-sectors or activities, listed in Section A, through which they claim the right to treat non-national service providers differently to national service providers. Later sections of the offer include limits on non-national providers and are identified either as all sector or sector specific limitations.

The lower part of each column shows common EU conditions (members each have some individual exceptions to these so they vary by country), and on top of these, the reserved rights or conditions that are specific to each country. On many occasions, of course, groups of EU countries reserve the same rights, but at the end of the day all 28 members have their own unique profile of national conditions.

On the far right of the chart, the reserved rights of the three non-EU members have been added, because they also published their opening offers. Their reserved rights are all of course national ones; Switzerland's oddly enough extends to fortune-telling and shoe-cleaning. However, for the sake of comparison, those that are roughly similar to the common EU conditions are distinguished from the others in a darker blue.

The full table from which this is drawn charts the profiles of the 28 members, and three non-members, on each of 140 service sectors. The UK is among those with rather few national conditions; four relate to health and social services, three to professional services, and one each to business, energy and distribution.

As a whole, the chart provides a visual indicator of the difficulties facing service trade negotiators, and the limitations of the European market on offer. Presumably, prospective partners would prefer to negotiate with Norway, if only it was not so small and did not speak Norwegian. At the other extreme is the EU. Presumably its negotiators have already tried, in separate negotiations, to reduce the number of members' reserved rights, but they are left to confront prospective partners with some 240 of them, before looking at Section B.

Figure 37.1: TiSA – EU's Initial Offer presented at Trade in Services Agreement negotiations comparing EU and Country specific reserved rights with those of Switzerland, Norway & Iceland

Source: EU – TiSA Initial Offer, September 2013,
http://trade.ec.europa.eu/doclib/docs/2014/july/tradoc_152689.pdf
Swiss – TiSA Initial Offer, January 2014,
http://www.seco.admin.ch/themen/00513/00586/04996/index.html?lang=en
Iceland – TiSA Initial Offer, December 2013,
https://www.utanrikisraduneyti.is/media/Friverslunarsamningar/Iceland_TISA_initial_offer_9_December_2013-%281%29.pdf
Norway – TiSA Initial Offer, November 2013,
https://www.regjeringen.no/globalassets/upload/ud/vedlegg/handelspolitikk/tisa_131115.pdf

To prospective partners and investors, the rhetoric of a Single Market of 500 million must all seem rather hollow, and it seems doubtful that all the 'heft' and 'clout' and 'negotiating muscle' the EU negotiators bring to the table, would make a lot of difference.

For the EU to have a Single Market in services the same conditions should of course apply to all service providers equally across the EU, and if that were the case all the conditions within the EU offer would be EU conditions. The fact that there are almost three times as many national reserved rights as there are EU reserved rights within the EU's initial offer, shows that countries within the EU have not yet created, and are almost certainly not willing to embrace, a Single Market in services. In a manner of speaking, the far left column is an index of the progress of the Single Market in services or the lack thereof.

If and when an agreement emerges from negotiations, it will either be very narrow indeed or look like a Baedeker guide with specific qualifications for each of the member countries and not quite the Single Market as advertised. The agreement reached with Mexico in 2001 gives a rough idea of what to expect, though it includes only a very small proportion of the services discussed in the TiSA talks.[6] An annex lists 85 national reserved rights, (two of which were made by the UK), which one imagines did not excite Mexican investors too much, or encourage other prospective partners to ask for a similar deal. However, appearances could be deceptive, and the efficacy of this agreement, or any other, can only be determined by regular comparative post facto assessment. The failure both of the EU and the UK governments to institutionalize such assessments makes it impossible for us, or them, to make any confident claims.

Messrs Blair, Cameron, the CBI and many multinationals, however, do make confident claims that British exporters have gained by the UK surrendering the right to negotiate trade agreements, and that the interests of British companies, and the livelihoods of the British people, have been wisely and safely entrusted to the EU, because of the 'negotiating muscle' obtained by negotiating alongside 27 other countries.

The most likely consequence has been many lost years of freer trade for UK exporters, which remain unnoticed and unregretted by the CBI, and the many large multinationals who want the present arrangements to continue unmonitored into the indefinite future.

---

6   *Official Journal of the European Communities* 12.3.2001 L 70/7Decision No 2/2001 Of The EU-Mexico Joint Council of 27 February 2001 implementing Articles 6, 9, 12(2)(b) and 50 of the Economic Partnership, Political Coordination and Co-operation Agreement http://eur-lex.europa.eu/legal-content/EN/TXT/PDF/

Part Six

Current debate

38

What does Her Majesty's Government actually know about the impact of the EU on the UK economy?

Successive governments have failed to inform the public of the impact of the EU, but they have also failed to inform themselves

There is a natural inclination to assume that when a PM says that the EU is good for jobs, trade and investment in the UK that his remark must be based on a thorough analysis of the evidence. No one thinks he did it himself of course, though one imagines his civil service advisers will have collected and studied all the available research, perhaps even commissioned some, so that when he speaks out on the EU's impact, he, and we, can be sure that he knows what he is talking about.

Is this assumption correct? Have the Treasury or other government departments commissioned, conducted or reviewed research which would entitle the PM to speak confidently about the beneficial impact of the Single Market on jobs, trade and investment in the UK?

One thing is for sure: they have not published their evidence on such topics. It may be that somewhere in Whitehall, there is a hidden cache of insightful and convincing comparative analyses of research data which, for some reason, they alone have been lucky enough to see.

What does the Treasury know?

In 2010, in response to a Freedom of Information request by an unknown person, HM Treasury released five brief internal analyses of 'third party assessments of the cost-benefits of EU membership'.[1] Could this be, one wondered, the hidden cache, or part of it?

---

1   *https://www.gov.uk/government/publications/treasury-analysis-of-third-party-assessments-of-cost-benefit-analyses-of-eu-membership*

1. EU Membership and FDI (2005 ca)[2]

According to the report, certain stylised facts support the claim that membership of the EU is a key factor in attracting investment to the UK. Unfortunately, the stylised facts were not explained, and no reason was given why they should be preferred to the unstylised facts regularly reported in UNCTAD or OECD databases. It then embarks on a rushed explanation of the benefits of FDI to host economies, and of the gains in FDI inflows to the UK that will follow 'further integration' of the EU and 'the liberalisation of services industries'.

In particular, it features a 2004 article by Pain and Young who used the NIESR[3] model to estimate that 'withdrawal from the EU would cost the UK 2¼% of GDP over time, largely from lost FDI flows.'[4] It neglected to mention one of the other forecasts in this article: 'there is no reason to suppose that unemployment would rise significantly if the UK were to withdraw from the EU.'[5]

2. The Economic Effects of UK membership for the UK: revised storyboard (August 23rd, 2005)

This begins with a review of several critical analyses of the costs of EU membership, but decides that these can be quickly dismissed because they are 'based on pessimistic assumptions'. It only assesses static direct costs and benefits and ignores second order dynamic ones. Most of the paper is therefore able to portray sunnier prospects consisting largely of forecasts of future gains of trade, FDI and even productivity, there being 'some evidence of catch-up in recent years' though these gains might be held back by EU regulation. Immigration

---

2   fn 25, *supra* HM Treasury, *EU Membership and FDI*. undated. The five papers are available at https://www.gov.uk/government/publications/treasury-analysis-of-third-party-assessments-of-cost-benefit-analyses-of-eu-member-ship
3   Footnote on the NIESR model
4   This quote is not from this report. It is from the 2005 EU membership and FDI report. Available at: http://bit.ly/1q5P1Xw
5   'The effect of EU withdrawal on employment is relatively small in relation to the change in output. After twenty years it is within 0.1% of the baseline level....The extent of the fall depends on how monetary policy operates. If policy is relaxed as the economy contracts, then the maximum decline in employment is approximately 75,000. If interest rates and the exchange rates do not fall, then employment would fall by approximately 160,000 after three years as a result of UK exit from the EU.' p.405, *ibid*.

is seen as having little impact though it acknowledges 'patterns may change with the latest accessions.'

The perils of non-membership are portrayed in one page devoted to Norway and Switzerland's dismal plight. No data is given on the growth of their exports to the EU which might have raised awkward questions.[6] Pain and Young's estimate is repeated for the same purpose, though now as an established fact, that 'GDP would decline by 2.25% permanently after withdrawal primarily because of lower FDI leading in turn to lower technical progress.'

3. EU Membership and the Drivers of Productivity and Growth (2006 ca)

This report identifies five drivers of productivity: competition, investment, entrepreneurship, innovation, and skills. It argues that the EU can strengthen the first four of these drivers, but not the fifth, since the EU has little direct input into vocational education and training.

Citing diverse published sources, it gives a generally positive account of the ways the EU could, should or has affected competition, investment and innovation, though barriers and obstacles remain. The exception is entrepreneurship on which it decides that 'the overall effect of EU membership is mixed and probably negative.'

4. EU Membership and Trade (2005)

This piece of original research tries to identify 'the observable impact of EU membership on trade flows'. It uses a standard gravity model with controls for GDP, population and real exchange rates. It finds that EU membership boosted trade of member states by 38 per cent, but the trade of the UK by only 7 per cent. However, 'after this initial boost from accession, straightforward comparisons of UK trade with the EU 15 and the rest of the world from 1970 to date do not immediately highlight the significant boost in trade amongst the EEC members that one might have expected, particularly over the period of implementation of the Single Market.' The Single Market was seen to have 'boosted intra-EU trade by a further 9% (although this may be an under-estimate)'. There is no figure for UK. While the

---

6   This storyboard is not paginated.

storyboard above says there was a 7% improvement in UK trade, it did not distinguish between imports and exports.

5. *Literature review – economic costs and benefits of EU membership 2011*

This is a limited bibliography of just seven items, with a commentary that focuses mainly on the European Commission report of 2007, published four years earlier. It manages to avoid mentioning any of the problems identified in that report.

HM Treasury's limited knowledge base about the EU and the Single Market

There is one main conclusion to be drawn from these papers: as of 2011, no significant research effort or intellectual resources have been devoted inside HMT either to document or to analyse the economic impact of the EU or the Single Market on the UK economy.

As a result, the government appears to have been about as informed as the rest of us about how EU membership and the Single Market might be affecting the UK economy. It was relying heavily on European Commission reports about the EU as a whole, and scaling them down to discover what was happening to the UK. These five reports were, it is true, 'third party assessments' but they were all written within HMT, originally for the benefit of its staff and ministers. If HMT possessed any telling sources or analyses of their own, they would have little reason not to refer to them to confirm or contest the conclusions of other publications.

They convey a sense of minds made up, and a remarkable lack of curiosity. The repetition of Pain & Young's article is symptomatic. It seems that no attempt was made by HMT, or any other department, to critically analyse this conclusion, examine other research that contradicted it, conduct research of their own, or to ask the authors to re-run, update or corroborate their conclusions.

This comes as something of a surprise. Just a few years earlier, HMT had organized a remarkable trawl of expertise from around the world to discover the likely impact on the UK economy of the adoption of the euro to answer the five tests set by the Chancellor. That exhaustive and comprehensive process had set conflicting evidence and opinions alongside one another. Because HMT was able to compare and evaluate conflicting evidence, it came to a stronger and more balanced decision.

Why the euro decision was different, and the same procedure could not have been adopted with respect to EU membership or the Single Market is not clear.

Is the Department for Business, Innovation and Skills (BIS) better informed?

In 2011 a BIS minister told the House of Lords Select Committee on the European Union in 2011 'that the Single Market has delivered substantial economic benefits'. He went on to say that 'EU countries trade twice as much with each other as they would do in the absence of the Single Market programme'. Astonished by these claims, in 2013 I submitted a FOI request for the evidence to support his claim.

I was given two references:

- Ilzkovitz et al (2007). Steps towards a deeper economic integration: the internal market in the 21st Century – a contribution to the Single Market Review, European Commission - DG EcFin; European Economy No. 27 http://ec.europa.eu/economy-finance/publications/publ ication784_en.pdf)
- Fontagne, L., T. Mayer and S. Zignago, 2005, Trade in the Triad: How Easy is the Access to Large Markets? Canadian Journal of Economics, 38(4): 1401-1430.

Unfortunately, neither of them supported his claim.[7] One from the European Commission itself, some three years earlier, included a rather candid assessment of a number of the Single Market's conspicuous failures, none of which had ever been heard in the UK debate. This contradicted many of the claims that had been made about the success of the Single Market, including those of the minister. It is included in Chapter 25.

The second, some five years earlier, was a test by three French professors of their model on border effects. It made no attempt to measure the impact of the Single Market, though incidentally it found

---

7   As explained in detail in *Myth & Paradox of the Single Market*

that Japan 'would seem almost as open to US exports as German consumers are to French exporters'. This might, on another occasion, have raised questions about the distinctiveness, or indeed necessity, of the Single Market.

Although these studies had little to say about the minister's claim, they were informative for another reason.[8] They showed the limited knowledge available to a Minister giving evidence to Parliament. He had been given no departmental or UK government sources, and instead had to rely on what were by then rather dated evidence from French academics and the European Commission. This reinforced the impression conveyed by the five HMT papers, and led to the unpalatable conclusion that two government departments, with significant responsibilities in the formation and conduct of UK government policy towards the EU, were incapable of forming an evidence-based judgement of the Single Market's merits. The opinions given by this minister and others, including the Prime Minister, must be no more than hunches or hopes, with no empirical grounding whatever.

However, in answer to my FOI request, I was referred to two UK government sources that might, it was suggested, provide some support for the minister's claim, though they could only do so retrospectively. The first was published by BIS itself.

- HM Government/CE PR (2012), Twenty Years On: the UK and future of the Single Market https://www.gov.uk/government/publications/twenty-years-on-the-uk-and-the-future-of-the-single-market/

In the preface the then secretary of state, Vince Cable, said the essays sought 'to draw together evidence about the impact that the Single Market has had to date'. Whatever their merits, they certainly did not do so, which left the 32-volume Balance of Competences Review.

---

8 The reference to these two works raised the same question as the 'five tests' research at HMT. The DBIS researchers have conducted many valuable studies of international trade, and have also conducted a number of impact assessments of specific EU policy proposals. The latter are, of course, narrowly-defined, ad hoc inquiries, but it is puzzling that these same researchers were never asked, now and then, to address the larger question of the costs and benefits of the Single Market.

- https://www.gov.uk/government/consultations/call-for-evidence-on-the-governmentsreview-of-the-balance-of-competences-between-the-united-kingdom-and-the-european-union/

This Review was a compilation of opinion rather than a research report. However it does intermittently cite research, the volume on the Single Market concludes with a table which lists all the comparative research regarding the economic benefits of the Single Market. The key part of this table is reproduced in Table 38.1.[9]

Table 38.1: Summary of study headline figures and key characteristics

		Headline results	Geographical coverage	Time period
1	Cecchini (1988)	+4.25-6.5% GDP	EU 12 (no enlargement)	5-6 years
2	Baldwin (1989)	+0.3-0.9% long-term GDP growth	EU 12 (no enlargement)	Long-term
3	Monti (1996)	+1.1-1.5% GDP; 300,000-900,000 jobs. in 1994	EU 12	Impact to 1994
4	Minford et al (2005)	-3% GDP to remaining in EU	EU15 (no enlargement)	Forward look (base-line = status quo)
5	Ilzkovitz et al (2007)	+2.2% GDP in 2006; + 2.75 million jobs	EU25	1992-2006
6	Boltho & Eichen-green (2008)	+5% GDP in 2008	EU25	Impact to date

It is a very important table, which deserves careful scrutiny and is worth reproducing, since it shows HMG's state of knowledge, as of 2013, about the economic impact of the Single Market. It will allow us to decide whether HMG as a whole was quite as ignorant as the responses of HMT and BIS to FOI requests suggest it was.

The first point worth noting is that the most recent of these studies is from 2008, some five years prior to this Review. While it is

---

9   Review of the Balance of Competences between the United Kingdom and the European Union: The Single Market 2013 p.72

dated, quality does not appear to have improved much over time. Second, more than twenty years after the inauguration of the Single Market, the government had still not conducted or commissioned comparative research on the Single Market's impact. A third point of interest is that these studies seldom refer to one another. They have evidently not been engaged in a debate, a further illustration if it were needed that the EU is without a demos.

Comments on the six studies

The first two studies are predictions, made in 1988 and 1989, and make no specific reference to the UK. They are therefore not of much help when measuring the costs and benefits of the Single Market for UK trade in 2013.

The third, Monti and Buchan, has only a single year of data to work with, 1994, a limitation which we had best put to one side. Its other limitation is that its model-derived estimates are implausible when compared with other known data. For instance, if the Single Market contributed between 1.1% and 1.5% to the EU's GDP known growth of 2.9% in 1994, then without it, we are supposed to think that it would have grown by 1.8% or 1.4%. This seems unlikely, since the World Bank database shows that 'high income OECD states' as a whole grew by 3.2% in 1994, and a large proportion of these are EU members. For some reason that Monti & Buchan do not provide, EU states would have grown, but for the Single Market, at about half the rate of the other 'OECD high income states'. In any case, their estimate of an increase of more than 1% in a single year is far above other estimates for the entire history of the Single Market, as we will see in a moment. Unfortunately, Monti did not bother to update, verify or corroborate these estimates in his better-known report published in 2010.

The fourth, by Minford et al, is mainly concerned with estimating the costs and benefits of alternative futures for the UK and the EU, rather than those already incurred by the UK specifically as a result of the Single Market. However it did suggest a cost, thus far, of 3% of UK GDP. This is, by the way, the only one of these six studies which sought to identify costs and benefits for the UK specifically.

The fifth, by Ilzkovitz et al, we have already encountered. However, the civil servant editors decided to redact their comments on many problems of the Single Market (see Chapter 25), as if they were unfit for British ears. They decided only to mention the report's speculative assessments of the Single Market's contribution to EU GDP and EU employment. Both seem highly improbable. For them to be true we would have to assume that without the Single Market, EU GDP growth would have been at, near or below zero from 2002-2006, while 'high income OECD states' as a whole were growing at 1.5 and 3.1 per cent. It is not clear why we should do this.

This study, like that of Monti & Buchan, made claims about increases in the level of employment as a result of the Single Market. They both have similar blind spots about the level of unemployment which they do not analyse, or even mention. However, to make these claims about an increase in the level of employment plausible, it is necessary to show that the level of employment within the EU increased at a *higher* rate than that of other OECD states. Neither do so, and we are expected to accept that increased level of employment growth, which is in no way different from other OECD countries and less than several, is due to the Single Market. That is not easy.

We are now left with just one, the much-cited study by Boltho & Eichengreen. It is important first to say what kind of study it is. It is not an attempt to report and analyze all the available evidence about the economic benefits of the EU. It is an imaginative, and highly speculative, experiment of 'fully specifying the counterfactual' of every stage of European integration. The study imagines what alternative policy, institution or action might have performed a similar function in the absence of those policies, institutions and decisions that determined the successive stages of integration that actually did take place. It starts from the European Payments Union in 1950. This is, as the authors say, 'no easy task', and necessarily involves guesswork every step of the way, as they readily acknowledge.

Their final estimate of 5 per cent GDP included in the table refers to this whole 60 year process of European integration. Their estimate of the Single Market is more modest: 'As an upper estimate it could, thus, be argued that perhaps half of the SMP's gains, as estimated by the Commission in 2002, might not have been obtained in its absence.'[10] They estimate that the Single Market has been responsible for a total increase of between 0.75 and one per cent of EU GDP. They say nothing about whether or not the UK shared equally in this increase, but they do point to the 'almost certainly substantial' costs of the CAP.[11]

Conclusion about HMG's present state of knowledge

The fairest conclusion from these studies would be that they tell us next to nothing about the benefits of the Single Market for the EU as whole, and nothing at all about the benefits of the EU or the Single Market for the UK specifically.

The civil servant editors saw things differently in a 2013 HMG report: 'most studies suggest that the GDP of both the EU and the UK are appreciably greater than they otherwise would be, thanks to economic integration through the Single Market.'[12] Most studies... appreciably greater. Hmm. Only one of these studies specifically addressed possible UK costs and benefits, and it decided that costs outweighed the benefits.

They lead me to conclude that HMG is indeed as ill-informed as the responses to the FOI requests suggested, and worse still, that it does not care to admit it. In the case of the EU, its civil servants have, over many years, preferred to ignore their Green and Magenta rule books on evidence-based policy, and hidden from their ministers just how ignorant they and we are.

Next time we hear a minister, ex-minister or prime minister speak confidently of the benefits of the Single Market or the EU's trade agreements, it would be foolish to trust them, on the grounds that they have been briefed by civil servant advisers who have conducted, or commissioned and reviewed all the relevant research. They haven't.

This review of the evidence available to the HMT, BIS and the FCO up to 2013 suggests they are probably relying on dated scraps of less

---

10 Which were 'of the order of 1.5 (1/2) to 2 per cent of GDP

11 Barry Eichengreen and Andrea Boltho, The Economic Impact of European Integration, (2008) p.33

12 Review of the Balance of Competences between the United Kingdom and the European Union: The Single Market 2013 pp.6,40

than relevant research, much of it drawn from the European Commission. It also seems likely that the research has been selected and arranged to suit the policy of the government of the day.

It may be that the reluctance of successive governments to monitor, analyse and report on the impact of the EU on the UK economy was to prevent the issue becoming a politically salient one. Whatever the reason, it has helped to keep the British public in the dark, but judging by this evidence, it has kept HMG in the dark as well.

39

Does the Bank of England know much more?

The Bank argues that EU membership has helped to open UK trade, labour and capital to international markets. The risks of the openness and interdependence are explained in depth, as well as the risks of future financial integration of the eurozone and of misguided 'maximum harmonisation' in EU regulation

Since the evidence collected by and available to the government is so inadequate, one may reasonably wonder whether the other main agency responsible for the UK economy, the Bank of England, might not have been collecting its own data over the years and conducting its own analyses of the impact of the EU. The answer is that it has not.

Its report, called 'EU membership and the Bank of England', issued in October 2015, makes this abundantly clear. It is not a storehouse of hitherto unpublished evidence. It has no databases of its own. It identifies eleven 'previous assessments of the impact of EU membership on the UK economy' from other sources and notes that they all 'produce a wide range of estimates by using different analytical approaches to compare the status quo of EU membership with hypothetical cases in which the UK either was not a member of, or had a different relationship with, the EU.'[1]

The report has no time for any of them saying, 'It is difficult to quantify the precise impact of EU membership on the UK economy. First, it is impossible to say with certainty what the UK economy would have looked like had the UK not joined the

---

1   http://www.bankofengland.co.uk/publications/Documents/speeches/2015/euboe211015.pdf

EU in 1973. Second, EU membership affects the UK economy in many different ways, through many different channels, at least some of which are difficult to quantify, or to separate from other changes to the UK economy taking place over the same period. Third, any quantitative assessment will necessarily depend on a wide range of uncertain economic assumptions. Fourth, the impact of EU membership is likely to have changed, and will change further, over time as the shape and structure of the framework circumscribing the UK's membership of the EU evolves.'[2]

The eleven studies play no part whatsoever in its subsequent report, which also makes no attempt to measure either the benefits or the costs of EU membership, and therefore does not make a case either for Leave or Remain. There is no support at all for the confident claims made by the present prime minister about the benefits of membership. The tone is altogether more cautious and rather than provide a balance sheet, or a recommendation, its aim is simply to show how EU membership 'affects the Bank of England's ability to fulfil its mission to promote the good of the people of the United Kingdom by achieving its statutory objectives.'[3]

Openness in trade

The main theme of the report is the role of openness to trade in goods and services, and to the movement of people and capital, have helped to make a dynamic UK economy. 'These channels from openness to dynamism operate in the EU as they do elsewhere, and it is very likely that the openness associated with membership of the world's largest economic area with free movement of goods, services, capital and labour has led to greater economic dynamism in the UK.'[4]

'Over the past forty years, the UK has become a much more open economy. This has been consistent with a general trend towards openness among advanced economies and the globalisation of the world economy since the mid-1990s. The evidence very strongly suggests that the increase in trade openness of the UK associated

---

2   Ibid. p.10
3   Ibid. p.3
4   Ibid. p.4

with EU membership has been greater than the global economic trend. Trade costs have fallen faster in the EU than internationally and the flow of trade between the UK and its partners has grown faster than might be expected based on size and proximity.'[5]

These are much the strongest words in support of EU membership to be found in the entire report, and also the most relevant to the Brexit debate. It is therefore worth stopping to consider the four items of evidence cited in support of the claim.

They are preceded by a word of warning: 'Quantifying the specific impact of EU membership on the openness of the UK economy is not straightforward. This Chapter identifies various channels through which EU membership has very likely supported greater openness of the UK economy, though it can be difficult to separate out this EU effect from that of both domestic legislation and the general trend of advanced economies towards increased openness and globalisation. In cases where the UK and other EU member states share a common experience that is demonstrably different from the experience of non-EU economies, that is taken as supporting evidence that the EU has played a role in supporting greater openness of the UK. In some areas, it is possible to establish the likely impact of the EU more precisely by comparing metrics of openness with other EU members and non-member states.'[6]

1. Total trade relative to GDP has increased in the UK from 40% of GDP in 1973 to 60% of GDP in 2014. Whereas, in contrast, it has lagged in two of three non-member countries considered, Japan and the US. In the report's view, this measure of trade relative to GDP is important as an index of trade intensity which is in turn an index of trade openness, which can be expected to yield certain economic benefits.[7]

Trade relative to GDP is a slightly odd index to use. It is, as they acknowledge, always higher in smaller countries and lower in

---

5   Ibid. p.4

6   Ibid. p.17

7   It is worth adding that in the bar charts in the Annex 3, the UK emerges by this measure to be less open in trade, than the EU15, the rest of the EU, than OECD as a whole, and about the same as NAFTA, and in services less open than all of the others except NAFTA p.89. Plainly, there is an extended debate to be had about this data, but the Bank does not have the time, in this report to enter it, but its preliminary word of warning was entirely justified.

larger self-sufficient ones, but this increase in UK trade relative to GDP is 'relative to others of a given country size', though the others are not named.[8] More importantly ONS figures show that as a proportion of UK GDP trade with Europe has been steadily declining since 1973-74, so the UK's increasing 'openness' must be with non-member countries.[9]

2. Trade costs of EU countries trading with each other were lower than the trade costs of Japan, the US and Canada trading with them, and even with the trade costs of Japan and Canada trading with third countries. This fall in trade costs is responsible, the report suggests, for the increase in trade intensity mentioned.[10]

Since the measure of trade costs included transport, as well as tariffs, legal and regulatory costs, the former is not altogether surprising. The more helpful data would have been about trade costs variation over time but that is not given. No mention is made of the fact that despite their higher trade costs, the exports of both goods and services of the United States and Canada to the EU have nonetheless grown at a faster rate than those of the EU countries to each other.

3. Service trade costs have tended to fall in the EU countries but have increased in the US. In part, they suggest, 'this reflects the EU's initiatives to deepen the integration in services over the past fifteen years.'[11]

Again, while this may be true, it seems at odds with the fact that EU services exports to each other have grown at a slower

---

8   Ibid p.18, p.87 Annex 2

9   Office for National Statistics, 'Economic Trends Annual Supplement No. 32', 2006 Edition, ed. David Harper, Palgrave Macmillan, 2006, plus the 2005-2013 figures from the ONS, show a downward trend, from 19.83 per cent in 1973 to 17.10 per cent in 2013. Williamson has similar figures indicating the peak year for integration or trade intensity with the EU was 1974 when the proportion topped 22 per cent. In 1979, it was just over 20 per cent, and in 2007 and 2008 just under. Samuel H. Williamson, 'What Was the U.K. GDP Then?' Measuring Worth, 2015: http://www.measuringworth.com/ukgdp/

10   In Annex 3, the UK trade costs in goods, are higher than those of France, Germany and Italy, and in services higher than those of Germany. p.89, Chart 3C. Once again, these measures themselves merit extended debate. Again, the report's preliminary word of warning about these measures seems entirely justified

11   Ibid p.19

rate than those of the U.S, and many other non-member countries to the EU.

4. A survey of some 300 estimates based on gravity models of trade found that, on average, trade has increased more than these models would lead one to expect.[12]

This finding depends entirely on the view one takes of the merits of gravity models, and of their margins of error which are not reported. In view of the fact, that the author of one of the most celebrated and popular applications of the gravity model, long used to extol the merits of the euro, has been withdrawn with an apology, we are entitled to be a little wary. [13]

This is the sum total of evidence which 'very strongly suggests that the increase in trade openness of the UK associated with EU membership has been greater than the global economic trend.'[14]

Whether anyone would want to take 'an increase in trade intensity and openness greater than the global trend' as a compelling argument for continued membership of the EU is doubtful. If they did, they would probably also want further reassurance and replication of the measures used, evidence that trade intensity or openness has improved UK economic performance in some measurable respect either exports, productivity or GDP, and also evidence that these improvements outweigh the costs of membership.

However, as noted, the bank's aim is not to make any such an argument for membership. It is merely to show that 'EU membership has very likely supported greater openness of the UK economy.'

Openness in the labour market

On labour mobility, the report notes the vast difference between annual inter-state mobility in the US (2.5%), and the mean inter-state mobility in the EU (0.3%)[15], while intra-EU variations in mobility

12   Ibid p.19
13   Reuven Glick and Andrew K. Rose, Currency Unions and Trade: A Post-EMU Mea Culpa: June 16, 2015. http://faculty.haas.berkeley.edu/arose/Glick2.pdf
14   Ibid p.30
15   Ibid p.30

within EU countries are considerable, with Finland, Denmark and the UK close to the US rate. A few studies are cited showing the impact of immigration on wages: one suggesting it has no impact on GDP or wage levels. others a small positive effect on GDP, another a small negative effect on wage levels, in particular on earlier immigration. It does not touch on the impact of immigration costs on education, health and welfare services. Overall, the report takes no view about the present level of immigration in the UK.[16]

Openness in the UK capital market: the contribution of membership decreases and increases risk

Openness of the UK capital market, not surprisingly, takes most of the time and attention of the report. EU membership may have contributed to it, since 'capital account liberalisation in the UK largely occurred before other EU countries so EU membership itself is likely to have played less of a role in increasing the UK's openness to foreign capital', though it 'has probably increased the openness of other EU member states to capital flows, [which] will in turn have increased the openness of those countries to the UK.'[17]

In addition, there is some evidence that the UK's membership of the EU has played a role in facilitating the attractiveness of the UK as a destination for Foreign Direct Investment (FDI) from outside the EU, as 'one of a number of factors that affect foreign investors' decisions to invest in the UK, alongside others, such as the integrity of the UK legal system, the availability of particular skills and services, and the status of the English language.'[18]

'The EU has also probably had a powerful impact on the UK's openness to financial services as a result of the Single Market in financial services and regulation of the EU financial sector.'[19] The most important of these is the passport regime which enables firms

---

16   Reuven Glick and Andrew K. Rose, Currency Unions and Trade: A Post-EMU Mea Culpa: June 16, 2015. http://faculty.haas.berkeley.edu/arose/Glick2.pdf
17   Ibid p.53
18   Ibid p.23
19   Ibid p.53

authorized in one member state to operate in another without the inconvenience and regulatory hurdles of setting up a subsidiary there.[20] None of these contributions are amenable to measurement.

Much of the report reads like a lecture course on capital markets and their contribution to creating a dynamic economy, as well as their vulnerabilities and deficiencies. It also includes detailed accounts of the global and euro-area financial crises, and of subsequent changes to the UK financial system and its relationship with the international and EU regulatory framework created in response to the crises.

These defy summation, but the main theme is that interdependence is a necessary consequence of openness and because it diversifies risks across countries, 'it should lead to lower economic volatility'. Along with increased participation of foreign institutions in the UK, this makes for 'a diversified financial system which should be more resilient and competitively intense.'[21]

However, interdependence with other economies, also means 'the UK economy is more exposed to economic and financial shocks from overseas' and open to 'channels of contagion'[22] which may 'accentuate existing imbalances'[23], as the global and euro financial crises demonstrated. Since then 'the UK's institutional framework for financial stability has been comprehensively reformed' to 'provide the UK with a coherent architecture of national macroprudential and microprudential regulators and supervisors commensurate with the scale and nature of the risks that the UK's high degree of financial openness can pose.'[24]

Openness in the UK capital market: union-wide harmonisation vs national flexibility

'Financial stability is ultimately a national responsibility. The Bank of England.... is accountable to the UK Parliament. The UK taxpayer is the ultimate backstop of the UK financial system.'

---

20 Ibid pp.23-25
21 Ibid p.4
22 Ibid p.65
23 Ibid p.68
24 Ibid p.5

However, UK authorities depend in no small part on the quality of regulation in the home jurisdictions of foreign financial firms active in the UK. The UK's membership of the EU is especially relevant in both respects.

Thus far EU membership has not prevented 'the [Monetary Policy Committee] from achieving monetary stability in the UK. Although closer integration with the EU has changed the nature and amplitude of shocks to which the UK economy is subject, and the complexity of the policy response, a floating exchange rate and the UK's institutional and monetary policy framework has enabled the UK to absorb these shocks with little impact on underlying price stability'.[26]

That said EU 'directives and rules define many of the Bank of England's policy instruments particularly in relation to financial stability'[27]. Further still, 'the majority of the legislation and regulation applying to the financial sector in the UK is determined at EU level.'[28]

So far, flexibility in applying EU rules to address the particular risks they face has in the main been respected by the European Commission. However, the general movement away from setting minimum standards in favour of 'maximum harmonisation', which prevents national authorities from strengthening regulation to meet particular risks in their jurisdiction, has in some instances been problematic.

How financial regulation in the EU evolves will be important to the resilience of both the euro area and the UK. It is important, particularly given the influence of the ECB and of the members of the single currency within the EU, that arrangements are put in place so that the future development of the EU regulatory framework aids the necessary deepening of integration in the euro area without impairing the ability of the Bank of England to meet its financial stability objective and without compromising the Single Market.

---

25 Ibid p.5
26 Ibid p.5
27 Ibid p.3
28 Ibid p.6

The bank remains neutral with both sides as winners

One of the bank's objectives is 'to support the economic policies of the government'[29], and since one of those policies is to remain in the EU, the surprising thing about this report is perhaps that it does not end up making a strong case for continued membership, but rather leaves both sides able to claim it supports their campaigns.

Its main argument throughout is for openness, which both sides would find attractive, and the Leave campaign would want to claim as its trump card.[30] The report is at some pains to say that the EU membership is not the sole means of openness. Its evidence on membership's contribution to trade openness is limited and inconclusive, even inconsequential. On labour mobility, it is selective and non-committed, and while evidence on capital mobility points to gains for the financial sector from membership, these are overshadowed by the risks posed by the future 'imbalance' between union and national regulation, with the bank confident it could better handle those risks by itself.

Leave supporters will surely see all this as making a case for independence, and indeed the prospect of allowing what is, by many measures, the world's largest financial centre to be regulated from Brussels, preoccupied by the problems of their own currency, as an especially high risk. They will also draw comfort from the report's frequent references to strengths of the UK economy, which have nothing much to do with the EU membership.

'The UK is amongst the most dynamic advanced economies in the world....The dynamism of the UK economy is the product of a variety of drivers including economic openness, flexible labour and product markets, deep human capital, well-developed physical infrastructure, a competitive fiscal regime, as well as the clarity and integrity of the rule of law.'[31]

---

29 Ibid p.3
30 Openness not Isolation is the title of a winning IEA Brexit essay prize. http://www.iea.org.uk/publications/research/the-iea-brexit-prize-a-blue-print-for-britain-openness-not-isolation
31 Ibid p.3

40

Has the EU's Single Market been a magnet for foreign investors?

EU enthusiasts still make confident claims about foreign investors' post-Brexit decisions, despite their mistaken predictions about the euro, despite the European Commission's findings, despite contrary indications and evidence, and despite the known uncertainty of such predictions

One of the more common arguments in favour of continued EU membership is that foreign investors prefer to locate in the UK because it is a member of the EU and will only continue to invest if the UK remains a member. A number of foreign investors in the UK who prefer that it remain an EU member have lent support to this idea by saying publicly that they might reconsider their investment here if the UK decided to leave.

The argument is a long-running one. It was first mentioned in the government pamphlet sent to every household before the 1975 referendum. It re-emerged in the debate about joining the euro, briefly revived in 2012, when the prime minister vetoed a new treaty to help the stricken euro.[1] It was sometimes used by those who opposed the coming referendum, on the grounds that the referendum itself would create uncertainty and frighten foreign investors.

In the cases when we can check, predictions or warnings against subsequent events proved to be correct. After the decision to stay

---

1   Robert Peston explained on BBC TV that if multinationals 'begin to see the UK as an isolated island, they will not wish to stay [so] businesses are now desperate to hear a positive statement from Mr Cameron about how the UK's position in the Single Market can somehow be buttressed.' An enlarged version of his report appeared on his website. *'Big Business Deeply Troubled By Cameron's Veto'*, Robert Peston, December 11th 2011.

out of the euro, the UK's share of inward Foreign Direct Investment (FDI) flows to 15 European countries declined very slightly, but it is difficult to attribute this to the new currency since some eurozone countries fell still more. The real winners in the growth of FDI stock over the post-euro years were three non-euro and non-EU countries, Switzerland, Norway and Iceland. After the prime minister's veto in 2011, FDI in the UK rose quite sharply while that to Germany and France plummeted.

In 2007, the European Commission itself had given up the claim that the Internal Market is a magnet for foreign investors. It admitted that, '...the Internal Market has not been able to deliver in terms of promoting further the role of the EU with respect to global investment flows.' It also noted that 'the Internal Market is also losing its attractiveness for international R&D investment.'[2] In 2012, the *European Competitiveness Report*, acknowledged that 'the EU's share of global inward FDI has declined significantly' which it attributed to 'the crisis' and to 'the attractiveness of emerging markets.'[3]

Even though the European Commission has long acknowledged the evidence, Sir John Major is among those who still think this is a useful argument to persuade the British people to vote to remain in the EU. We must, I suppose, expect their warnings, and expect those foreign investors who can be persuaded to say they may reconsider their investment post-Brexit, to be heard until referendum day. Though some on that side of the argument, like the chairman of the Remain campaign, have dismissed their argument:

> Stuart Rose, chairman of Britain Stronger in Europe, dismissed fears that leaving the EU would lead to companies leaving the UK as 'a red herring' and 'scaremongering". He said: 'I think

---

2   Fabienne Ilzkovitz et al, European Economy, Economic Papers, N° 271 January 2007, *Steps towards a deeper economic integration: the Internal Market in the 21st century, A contribution to the Single Market Review European Commission*, Dir-Gen for Economic and Financial Affairs, ISSN 1725-3187 http://ec.europa.eu/economy_finance/index_en.htm

3   *European Competitiveness Report 2012, Reaping the benefits of globalization*, European Commission (2012) pp.9,10,119: http://ec.europa.eu/enterprise/policies/industrial-competitiveness/competitiveness-analysis/european-competitiveness-report/ index_en.htm

it's ridiculous to suggest that everybody is going to suddenly go offshore, I don't believe that for one moment.'[5]

The most relevant evidence on FDI is given in the figure below. It shows the FDI stock *per capita* across Europe and a few other developed societies in 2014. At first glance, it does not suggest that either the EU itself or the euro, or the Single Market have been especially attractive to foreign investors. First, because neither EU nor eurozone countries are distinguished from others by their high FDI stock holdings. Second, because EU members differ greatly among themselves, and there happen to be good reasons to explain those with the highest holdings, having nothing to do with the EU or the Single Market. However, before drawing any conclusions from these figures, two caveats must be given about any interpretation of FDI data.

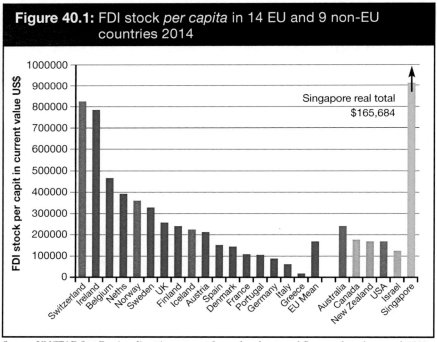

Figure 40.1: FDI stock *per capita* in 14 EU and 9 non-EU countries 2014

Source: UNCTAD Stat Foreign direct investment: Inward and outward flows and stock, annual, 1980-2014 Inward Stock, US Dollars at current prices and current exchange rates in millions

4   Sky, Dermot Murnaghan Interview with Lord Rose, 19th April 2015: <https://corporate.sky.com/media-centre/media-packs/2015/murnaghan-interview-with-lord-levy,-labour-peer-and-lord-rose,-conservative-peer-190415>

Caveat one – no-one knows

Almost everyone thinks they know why investors locate in one country rather than another, but those who have studied the evidence are not so sure. UNCTAD has been documenting and analyzing FDI flows since 1970 but has always been wary of offering explanations of their decisions on the grounds that they are influenced by a 'host of nearly unquantifiable social, political and institutional factors'.[5] In 1993, they nonetheless sought to quantify the nearly quantifiable producing their FDI Potential Index and eight factors that encourage investment.[6] In 2003 they added four more, none of which related to EU membership or the Single Market.

A few researchers have preferred to ask investors directly about their decisions. An Ernst & Young survey in 2005, for instance, included follow-up interviews with key decision-makers in 98 of the 787 multinational firms which had invested in six European countries over the years 1997-2003. The interviews were non-directive and open-ended, the informants being asked to identify any of the things that might have affected their company's decision to invest in a particular country. The proportions of items mentioned in their answers are presented in the pie chart below.

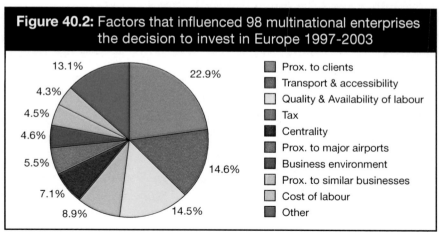

Figure 40.2: Factors that influenced 98 multinational enterprises the decision to invest in Europe 1997-2003

- Prox. to clients
- Transport & accessibility
- Quality & Availability of labour
- Tax
- Centrality
- Prox. to major airports
- Business environment
- Prox. to similar businesses
- Cost of labour
- Other

13.1% 22.9% 4.3% 4.5% 4.6% 5.5% 14.6% 7.1% 8.9% 14.5%

Source: European headquarters: Location decisions and establishing sequential company activities, Final report, Ernst & Young, Utrecht, 2005. http://ec.europa.eu/enterprise/policies/industrial-competitiveness/competitiveness-analysis/european-competitiveness-report/index_en.htm

5   http://www.oecd.org/investment/globalforum/44246319.pdf
6   *European headquarters: Location decisions and establishing sequential company activities*, Final report, Ernst & Young, Utrecht, 2005.

As may be seen, 'proximity to clients' rated number one, and several of the other answers also have a geographical dimension such as 'centrality', or 'proximity to major airports', and even perhaps 'proximity to similar businesses'. Although these company decision-makers could say whatever they wished, none of them ever mentioned either 'the world's largest Single Market', or the euro, or the absence of tariff barriers. These things did not even rate a word in the 'other' category, details of which were given in an appendix of the report.

Sir John Major seems to be among those who think that they know intuitively why foreign investors choose a particular country. He declined to commission research on the subject when in office but has spoken confidently about it with complete indifference to the research that is now available. Perhaps he thinks his conversations with a few investors are sufficient.

Caveat two – FDI data is suspect

The second thing to be said is that there is still not sufficient data about FDI flows and stocks over time that distinguishes between FDI, in the sense of investment requiring permanent presence, commitment and managerial control over time in the country in which they invest, and so-called special purposes entities (SPEs) in which capital may be nominally invested for tax purposes, or parked while awaiting real investment in some other ultimate investment country (UIC). Data that distinguishes between authentic investment and SPEs is only just beginning to be regularly collected.

There are some clues that indicate whether foreign investments are authentic or simply hosting SPEs. One is the ratio between the FDI flows into a country and its gross fixed capital formation (GFCF) in the same year, or the FDI stock as a proportion of GDP. If FDI flows or stocks exceed 100 per cent of GFCF or GDP, as they routinely do many times over in offshore financial centres (OFC), we may reasonably infer that the investment is a purely financial arrangement. A second clue is when the FDI inward flow does not merely decline, but suddenly becomes sharply negative. This suggests that investors are withdrawing or moving funds rather than closing factories and offices.

Using one or more of these clues, there is good reason to think that Luxembourg is no different, in this as in other respects, from an OFC, and for that reason it has been omitted from the figures altogether. There are also strong grounds for omitting, or at any rate sharply reducing the figures for Belgium and the Netherlands, and there must be some suspicion about the figure for Ireland. These happen to be the top three FDI stock holders in the EU, and if their real FDI stock figures were reduced, the weighted EU mean would, of course, have been still lower than it is.

A final piece of evidence

Table 40.1: A.T. Kearney FDI confidence mean of 15 rankings, 1998-2015

United States	1.7
China	1.7
UK	4.8
Germany	6.5
Italy (11)	11.6
France	11.9
Spain (13)	13.3
Neths (9)	18.9

Source: https://www.atkearne y.com/research-studies

The 2015 A.T. Kearney Foreign Direct Investment Confidence Index seeks to assess and measure how political, economic and regulatory changes will 'likely affect countries FDI inflows in the coming years'[8], and annually ranks the 25 most attractive countries for foreign investors.

The data is collected by 'a proprietary survey administered to senior executives of the world's leading corporations... The 300 participating companies represent 26 countries and span all industry sectors. All companies report global revenue of at least $1 billion.'[9] Respondents do not rate the investments prospects of their own country.

---

8   https://www.atkearney.com/research-studies/foreign-direct-investment-confidence-index/full-report

9   https://www.atkearney.com/research-studies/foreign-direct-investment-confidence-index/about-the-report

The rankings in the table are the arithmetic means of the rankings of each country in 15 reports, whose results are reported on the website, though Italy, Spain and the Netherlands were among the top 25 in less than 15 rankings. The wide difference in the ratings of EU member countries suggests that these corporate informants do not look on them as a Single Market or investment location. It seldom figures in the commentaries that accompany the assessments, though the promised EU referendum in the UK was mentioned in the 2013 and 2014 reports.

However, in 2015 respondents were asked what the most important factors were to their company when choosing to make foreign investments. 25 per cent of respondents said domestic market size, which was the most popular single answer; 11 per cent mentioned 'participation in regional or bilateral trade agreements', which was the fourteenth most popular response. Other factors mentioned included tax rates, transparency, corruption, labour costs, legal and regulatory processes, property rights, transport and telecom infrastructure and security.[10]

Two conclusions

1. It is unwise to confidently predict what will happen to FDI flows or FDI stock, and those who have previously done so to make a case for EU membership have been shown to be mistaken.

2. The publicly available evidence, like that available to the European Commission, does not suggest that the EU, the eurozone, or the Single Market have been distinctively appealing to foreign investors. One should remember that a large proportion of the investors in the non-EU countries are themselves from EU countries, and are presumably therefore well-informed about the benefits of the Single Market.

---

10 Figure 11, A.T. Kearney, *Connected Risks: Investing in a Divergent World* at: https://www.atkearney.com/research-studies/foreign-direct-investment-con-fidence-index/2015/

41

Why multinationals' opinions on the EU are less than convincing

1. They don't do cost/benefit research on membership or exit
None of those that have raised their voices to urge the UK's continued membership, and warned of Brexit's serious consequences, have conducted, or at least published, any cost/benefit analysis from the point of view of the British people. They demonstrated their indifference when asked to support their opinions with evidence to Her Majesty's Government's *Balance of Competences Review* in 2013.[1] They declined to do so, preferring to support their submissions for the status quo with assertions, anecdotes and hearsay.

The businesses who financed and guided what is by far the most thorough, rigorous and fair research on the costs of EU membership and the opportunities presented by Brexit – *Business for Britain*, with their report *Change or Go*[2] – were a maverick minority, closer in heart and mind to entrepreneurs than to managerially-controlled multinationals.

2. They have no interest in the political consequences for British people
Big business is not concerned with how the UK is governed, in the nature of its democracy, nor in the EU's democratic deficit and its lack of accountability. Hence the argument that power over the British people has been transferred to unelected appointees or to courts, whose judges are nominated by foreign governments, are not of much interest or significance. Nor are the euro and ever

---

1   https://www.gov.uk/government/collections/review-of-the-balance-of-competences

2   www.businessforbritain.org/2015/07/17/change-or-go-published-in-full/

closer union, both of which they would probably welcome from a business point of view. Brussels is not unaccountable to them. They have lawyers and lobbyists.

3. Many are foreign

Many of those who participate in the debate and fund lobby groups urging continued membership are not in fact British. It would be unreasonable to expect them to place the interests of the British people above what is convenient and profitable to themselves, or to care about British democracy.

Japanese multinationals, one must add, have distinguished themselves from others by simply stating their preference, when asked, while otherwise remaining unwilling to interfere in what is fundamentally a domestic political debate.

4. The costs of membership of the Single Market are paid by others

Financial costs are borne by UK taxpayers, consumers (tariffs), non-exporting firms (regulation) and the political costs of being governed by those they did not and cannot vote for, are paid by voters. Multi-nationals don't pay for the benefits of the Single Market. They are subsidized. If the UK were not a member of the EU, all the trade costs of selling in the Single Market, including tariffs, would have to be borne by each exporting firm, just as their competitors from non-member countries currently do. It's a choice between a subsidy and pay as you go. The EU is the low cost option.

5. They do not recognize any obligation to the UK taxpayer, consumer or voter

One might think that they would recognize that they owe the UK taxpayer and consumer who has been subsidizing membership of the club which they claim helps their business, by providing rigorous and impartial research about their own industries which shows, in terms of trade and employment, why the Single Market is worth the sums that taxpayers have invested in it, to help them to come to an informed decision. Thus far they have limited themselves to comments and sometimes warnings, off the top of their heads.

6. *An unnecessary, additional risk*
They have established a comfortable *modus operandi* with organized lobbies, professional advisers or personal contacts in the European Commission. Internal costings and procedures have been based on continued UK membership. Brexit would certainly disturb these networks, calculations and procedures for no identifiable benefit from their point of view. It might also spook markets. Hence it entails uncertainty and risk, which they would rather avoid. It would also be inconvenient.

7. *Their directors probably read the* Financial Times
Which means that over many years they have read stories and research which put the EU in a favourable light, and portrayed Brexit as a horror story (see Chapter 45).

42

Immigration, free movement and welfare

Net migration is currently the highest in British history. In 2015, net migration to the UK climbed to a record 336,000, compared to 50,000 per year in the 1990s.[1] Net EU migration accounts for half this total. All EU citizens currently have the right to reside in the UK for three months. After that, they only have the right to reside if they are in work, self-employed, looking for work, a student, or able to support themselves. Family members of an EU citizen with the right to reside in the UK also have the right to reside, including family members who are not themselves EU citizens.[2]

Until 2003 net migration from the EU averaged only 10,000 a year.[3] In 2004 the European Union was enlarged to include eight countries from Eastern Europe and immigration grew rapidly. It was interrupted by the recession in 2008 but grew rapidly again after 2012. In the year ending June 2015 it reached a new record of 180,000.[4]

According to Migration Watch UK, there are just over three million people born in the EU living in the UK.[5] 363,000 first arrived before 1973, the year the UK joined the then European Economic Community. Another 719,000 arrived between 1973 and 1993 while two million have arrived since 2004.[6]

---

1   http://www.ons.gov.uk/peoplepopulationandcommunity/populationandm-
     igration/internationalmigration/bulletins/migrationstatisticsquarterlyre-
     port/november2015
2   http://ec.europa.eu/social/main.jsp?catId=460&langId=en
3   http://www.migrationwatchuk.org/briefing-paper/371
4   http://www.ons.gov.uk/peoplepopulationandcommunity/populationandm-
     igration/internationalmigration/bulletins/migrationstatisticsquarterlyre-
     port/november2015
5   http://www.migrationwatchuk.org/briefing-paper/371
6   http://www.migrationwatchuk.org/briefing-paper/371

Of the two million immigrants living in the UK who have arrived since 2004, 1.1 million have come from the eight countries of Eastern Europe that joined in that year. About 560,000 have come from the 14 countries of Western Europe, and an estimated 250,000 people born in Romania and Bulgaria and now living in the UK have also arrived since 2004. Over 70,000 arrived in 2014, when those two nations were granted full access to the UK labour market.

The majority of these two million migrants are in work. Of the 1.33 million EU migrants in work who have arrived since 2004, 509,000 (38%) are in occupations regarded as skilled by the Migration Advisory Committee and 822,000 (62%) are in jobs regarded as low-skilled, including 28% who were in 'elementary occupations', the lowest category of skilled labour.

Opinion polls consistently show that a clear majority want immigration to be cut. Immigration was named by people questioned by Ipsos Mori in January 2016[7] as the most important issue facing Britain, eight points ahead of the next most important issue, the NHS. The 2014 British Social Attitudes Survey found that 77% of the public wanted immigration to be reduced, 56% by a lot.[8] The majority of first and second generation migrants take a similar view: 60% told the British Social Attitudes survey in 2013 that migration to the UK should be reduced.[9]

The 'emergency brake' achieved by Mr Cameron in February 2016 will have only a marginal impact on EU migration. The chief reason migrants come to the UK is not access to benefits, but because work is available and incomes are far higher than in their own country. Research by Migration Watch UK found that 75% of EU migrants are single or childless couples on arrival so are not entitled to in-work benefits such as tax credits.[10] The Office for Budget Responsibility's Sir Stephen Nickell told BBC News that changes to welfare would have 'not much' impact on net migration.[11]

---

7   https://www.ipsos-mori.com/researchpublications/researcharchive/3691/Economist-Ipsos-MORI-January-2016-Issues-index.aspx

8   http://www.bsa.natcen.ac.uk/latest-report/british-social-attitudes-31/immigration/introduction.aspx

9   http://www.natcen.ac.uk/media/205569/immigration-bsa31.pdf

10   http://www.migrationwatchuk.org/briefing-paper/373

11   http://www.bbc.co.uk/news/uk-politics-35043070

Most of Britain's population growth results from net migration. It is projected by the Office for National Statistics to reach 70 million by mid-2027.[12] This is based on net annual immigration of 185,000. The current level is 323,000.[13] The contribution of net migration (6.8 million) to the projected population increase of almost ten million over the next 25 years is the equivalent of the combined current populations of Birmingham, Leeds, Glasgow, Sheffield, Bradford, Manchester, Edinburgh, Liverpool, Bristol, Cardiff, Newcastle upon Tyne, Belfast, Aberdeen, Leicester, Coventry, and Nottingham.[14] Migration Watch estimates that this would mean adding 14 cities the size of Liverpool or Edinburgh.

The economic benefits of high net immigration are marginal and often exaggerated. The House of Lords Economic Affairs Committee reported in 2008 that they had found no evidence that net migration generates significant economic benefits for the existing UK population.[15] The OECD found, in June 2013, that in most countries the impact of migration tends to be small in terms of GDP per head and is around zero.[16] An extensive survey of the evidence can be found in a study by Cambridge economist Professor Robert Rowthorn.[17]

The economic costs of high net migration are considerable and hit the lowest-paid most. A Bank of England study reported in December 2015 that net migration had driven down pay for catering, hotel and social care workers.[18] The Migration Advisory Committee's July 2014 report acknowledged that UK school leavers were being overlooked for jobs in favour of migrants.[19]

---

12 http://www.ons.gov.uk/peoplepopulationandcommunity/populationandmigration/populationprojections/bulletins/nationalpopulationprojections/2015-10-29

13 http://www.ons.gov.uk/peoplepopulationandcommunity/populationandmigration/internationalmigration/bulletins/migrationstatisticsquarterlyreport/february2016

14 http://www.migrationwatchuk.org/pdfs/Miscellaneous-MW269.pdf

15 http://www.publications.parliament.uk/pa/ld200708/ldselect/ldeconaf/82/8211.htm

16 http://www.oecd-ilibrary.org/social-issues-migration-health/international-migration-outlook-2013/the-fiscal-impact-of-immigration-in-oecd-countries_migr_outlook-2013-6-en

17 http://www.civitas.org.uk/publications/largescaleimmigration/

18 http://www.oecd-ilibrary.org/social-issues-migration-health/international-migration-outlook-2013/the-fiscal-impact-of-immigration-in-oecd-countries_migr_outlook-2013-6-en

19 http://www.civitas.org.uk/publications/largescaleimmigration/

The most thorough appraisal of the overall impact of immigration can be found in Paul Collier's *Exodus*.[20]

Free movement rules mean EU migration is effectively uncontrolled. All EU citizens are free to come to the UK to look for work. If migrants from the European Economic Area (EEA) have not found work in six months they are supposed to leave, but very few have been required to, including those who have committed crimes. The National Audit Office has acknowledged that sheer inefficiency played a role in the failure to remove at least a third of 1,453 foreign national offenders in 2013/14, but also cites some 17 grounds of appeal that can be used to delay deportation.[21]

What sort of immigration policy would be feasible after British exit?

There are five tiers under the current points-based system. Tier 1 is for 'high-value migrants' from outside the EEA and covers entry of entrepreneurs, investors, and the very few people who have 'exceptional talent'. Tier 2 is for 'skilled workers' from outside the EEA with a job offer in the UK. It includes skilled workers who are transferred to the UK by an international company, and skilled workers required when there is a proven shortage in the UK. Many employers and organisations based in the UK, including the NHS, are suffering from skills shortages. Under this new system the UK could increase the amount of tier 2 immigration, for example, by 10,000. Tier 3 was designed for low-skilled workers, but the government has so far not allocated any visas under this scheme. Tier 4 is for students aged over 16 from outside the EEA who wish to study in the UK. Applicants must have a place at a registered UK educational establishment before they can apply. Tier 5 contains six sub-tiers of temporary worker including creative and sporting, charity, religious workers, and the youth mobility scheme, which enables about 55,000 young people (aged 18 to 30) every year to work in the UK on working holidays. The visas are

---

20   Collier, P. (2013) Exodus: Immigration and Multiculturalism in the 21st Century. Oxford: Oxford University Press.
21   https://www.nao.org.uk/wp-content/uploads/2014/10/Managing-and-removing-foreign-national-offenders-summary.pdf

awarded to young people from countries that have reciprocal arrangements with the UK.[22]

There are five tiers under the current points-based system. Migration Watch has suggested some guidelines for a carefully controlled immigration policy. What would such a policy mean for each of the current tiers?[23]

---

22 https://www.gov.uk/browse/visas-immigration/work-visas
23 http://www.migrationwatchuk.org/briefing-paper/371

Table 42.1: Immigration: what is and what might be

	Current points-based system for non-EU migrants	Post-Brexit managed system of migration based on suggested Migration Watch guidelines[24]
Tier 1	'high-value migrants' from outside the EEA and covers entry of entre-preneurs, investors, and the very few people who have 'exceptional talent'.	Extended to cover all EU nationals.
Tier 2	'skilled workers' from outside the EEA with a job offer in the UK. It includes skilled workers who are transferred to the UK by an international company, and skilled workers required when there is a proven shortage in the UK.	Expanded to cover EU citizens, which would mean unlimited intra-company transfers of existing staff and the option to recruit skilled staff from EU countries. The current annual cap for non-EU staff of 20,700 would have to be increased.
Tier 3	For low-skilled workers, but the government has so far not allocated any visas under this scheme.	If it were put into effect, and the same rule applied to low-skilled migrants from the EU, they would no longer be able to seek work in the UK, unless they could support themselves without welfare benefits. The Seasonal Agricultural Work-ers Scheme was used for many years to bring in about 20,000 workers for a period of up to six months. It was ended in 2013 when Romanian and Bulgarian nationals gained full access to the UK labour market. A similar scheme could be re-introduced for seasonal workers.
Tier 4	Students aged over 16 from outside the EEA who wish to study in the UK. Applicants must have a place at a registered UK educational establishment before they can apply. No number limit.	There would continue to be no limits on the numbers of EU citizens admitted for study in the UK. They would have the same right to work as non-EU citizens, currently 20 hours per week.
Tier 5	Contains six sub-tiers of temporary worker including creative and sporting, charity, religious workers, and the youth mobility scheme, which enables about 55,000 young people (aged 18 to 30) every year to work in the UK on working holidays. The visas are awarded to young people from countries that have reciprocal arrangements with the UK.[25]	Offered to the citizens of EU countries as to non-EU countries.

Source: https://www.atkearney.com/research-studies

---

24   http://www.migrationwatchuk.org/briefing-paper/371
25   https://www.gov.uk/browse/visas-immigration/work-visas

43

An academic illusion: research depends on an EU 'pot of money'

Analyses the EC financial statements over the 15 years 2000-2014 and shows that the notion that the UK gets more research grants than others, or 'more than we put in', is merely the folklore of the research community

In May 2015, Matthew Freeman, a cell biologist and head of the Dunn School of Pathology, University of Oxford, contributed an article to *The Guardian* headed 'EU science funding: the UK cannot afford to lose out on this pot of money'. It went on to claim that British scientists have earned more back in grants than the UK has contributed in every year of the scheme's existence.[1] He then pointed out that 'British labs were awarded over €1bn between 2007 and 2014. Again, we receive more than we put in, as we received almost double the amount of money than the next best funded country, Germany... By sheer numbers, the biggest impact is probably the Erasmus exchange studentships, which fund tens of thousands of undergraduate and diploma students to move in each direction every year. Many end up doing research in British labs, and those that go abroad bring back training and skills.'

On 25 September 2015, the Vice-Chancellor of the University of Cambridge, Professor Sir Leszek Borysiewicz said that '17 per cent of last year's research income at the University, totalling £68 million, had come from the EU's Horizon 2020 scheme.' Referring to the vast Innolife Knowledge and Innovation Community involving 144 companies, research institutions and universities across nine EU countries, he observed that 'In today's competitive

---

1   http://www.theguardian.com/higher-education-network/2015/may/13/eu-science-funding-the-uk-cannot-afford-to-lose-out-on-this-pot-of-money Wednesday 13 May 2015 10.04 BST

world we cannot stand alone... scale is exactly what is needed if we are to overcome society's grand challenges. Put simply, we cannot access the talent, develop the infrastructure or provide the funding at a national level.'[2]

These views have apparently become today's academic conventional wisdom.[3] More than 150 Cambridge researchers have followed their Vice-Chancellor and claimed that Brexit would be 'a disaster for UK science and universities' on the grounds that EU funding has 'raised greatly the level of European science as a whole and of the UK in particular'. Also, according to these researchers, 'because we now recruit many of our best researchers from continental Europe', there might be a 'loss of freedom of movement of scientists between the UK and Europe.'[4]

None of these 150 academics have evidently looked at the evidence about EU funding for research in the UK, so their letter would appear to merit an entry in the *Guinness Book of Records* as the largest number of distinguished scientists to have simultaneously made a claim before examining any evidence.

The initial flaw in the reasoning of these distinguished intellectuals is to assume there is a pot of research money in Brussels. There isn't. UK universities do not receive a penny of European Commission money, because it has virtually none of its own, unless you care to count tariff and VAT receipts, which it is pleased to call its 'own resources'.

All of the funds these research scientists receive from the European Commission are in fact from the pockets of their most long-serving and long taken-for-granted patron whose intelligence they have just insulted: the UK taxpayer. Funds from the UK taxpayer have been paid by the UK government to the European Commission as part of the UK's membership contribution.

---

2   Speaking at 'Excellent research in the UK: Do we need the EU?' See more at: https://www.cam.ac.uk/news/vice-chancellor-says-staying-in-the-european-union-is-vital-to-maintain-the-uks-role-in-world#sthash.MflYtITZ.dpuf

3   Universities UK launched a campaign 27th July 2015 making similar claims http://www.universitiesuk.ac.uk/highereducation/Pages/UniversityleadersmakethecaseforEUmembership.asp
    For campaign updates: www.universitiesforeurope.com

4   'Hawking leads 150 Royal Society scientists against Brexit', *The Times*, Sat March 19, 2016

These funds, or part of them, are then re-branded, and returned to the universities and other recipients in the UK by the European Commission, and are apparently greeted rapturously at Oxford and Cambridge, as if they were generous and far-sighted contributions to scientific endeavour in sharp contrast to the miserly and grudging, less-than-expected contributions from the UK government.

The idea that the European Commission has a pot of money which it grants to eager British recipients was first conjured up by Harold Wilson to persuade the British people that they would receive numerous grants from Brussels if only they voted to remain in the European Common Market. Even at the time, this seemed to show a rather cynical view of the intelligence of the average British voter, and it is improbable that many fell for it. That 40 years on, the brightest in the land could fall for it, or at any rate use it, comes as a bit of a shock, and suggests they also have a rather low opinion of the intelligence of their ultimate benefactor, the UK taxpayer. But let us look at the relevant data about research funding, which these eminent scientists preferred to ignore. It comes from the European Commission annual financial reports on its budgets over the past 15 years.[5]

The evidence that Cambridge research scientists didn't look at

The actual amounts of research and technology funds distributed by the European Commission, under all its programmes, to the 11 member countries who have received the most substantial amounts over the 15 years 2000-2014 are shown in Table 43.1. The last line gives the percentage of each member country's total annual contribution that has been repaid to them by means of these grants for research and technology, though Belgium and Spain have in fact made no net annual contribution over any of these 15 years.

The table gives the total amounts distributed to member countries 2000-2014 for research purposes. The figures are taken from the EU Financial Statement 2000-14 which reproduces the annual

---

5   EU expenditure and revenue 2000-2014 http://ec.europa.eu/budget/finan-cialreport/2014/annex/2/index_en.html

Table 43.1: EU payments for research and technology to 11 member countries in millions of current value €s over 15 years, 2000-2014

	Austria	Belgium	Denmark	Finland	France	Germany	Italy	Netherlands	Spain	Sweden	UK
2000	56.1	211.7	70.5	53.6	443.4	473.6	391.0	195.9	146.4	92.3	546.6
2001*	58.3	250.8	69.4	53.8	383.4	471.7	344.0	187.9	139.9	91.9	482.2
2002*	58.3	250.8	69.4	53.8	383.4	471.7	344.0	187.9	139.9	91.9	515.8
2003	63.4	272.0	55.7	60.9	404.9	490.0	328.2	213.3	145.6	89.1	436.9
2004	75.2	428.0	73.2	78.4	483.3	647.4	386.2	256.0	184.2	114.8	510.2
2005	92.9	446.6	79.3	68.1	497.9	693.7	454.7	228.7	197.6	133.0	538.6
2006	115.2	475.7	91.4	71.2	488.2	803.7	495.7	294.9	199.1	145.6	606.6
2007	80.7	416.4	56.2	57.8	481.2	561.4	452.9	216.8	159.1	118.4	422.4
2008	152.8	519.9	116.8	117.3	645.3	953.9	546.9	411.9	422.8	206.4	826.1
2009	132.1	550.8	116.8	94.0	688.9	877.5	483.6	354.8	433.4	177.4	817.7
2010	136.6	473.4	111.1	109.9	762.5	909.5	521.2	379.9	572.2	184.6	722.7
2011	146.5	603.6	119.0	105.8	791.1	947.0	553.4	403.9	634.9	203.1	840.8
2012	157.7	610.1	142.1	119.1	883.7	1047.2	570.1	475.3	783.4	210.9	980.0
2013	172.9	753.3	163.9	118.4	910.7	1143.2	596.6	560.3	795.7	241.2	1114.0
2014	119.2	670.2	126.2	78.8	584.2	844.1	459.0	368.3	417.2	167.0	796.5
15 yr total	1617.9	6933.4	1461.0	1240.7	8832.0	11335.8	6927.5	4735.9	5371.3	2267.6	10157.1
% 15 yr contrib.*	18.6	Nil	25.4	32.3	14.4	7.3	26.1	9.1	Nil	12.2	14.0

From EU expenditure and revenue 2000-2014 http://ec.europa.eu/budget/financialreport /2014/annex/2/index_en.html

Financial Statements on the Budget. From 2000 to 2006, line items are not numbered, the one reproduced in the table is described Internal Policies: Research and Technological Development, and excludes Euratom and educational programmes such as Erasmus. From 2007, funds distributed to member countries for research and technological development are listed under Sustainable Growth item 1.1.1, and named as the Seventh Research Framework, but distinguished from TEN (Trans-Europe networks), Galileo, Marco Polo, nuclear decommissioning, and from 'earmarked', 'other' and 'non-EU'. This format continues until 2013. In 2014, the labels and line item identification change. Sustainable becomes Smart and Inclusive Growth and line item 1.1.1 now refers to large infrastructure projects already mentioned plus EGNOS (satnav), ITER (nuclear fusion), Copernicus (earth Observation) Galileo, Marco Polo, nuclear decommissioning, as well as and from 'earmarked', 'other' and 'non-EU', with 'other having grown to a spectacular €1.7 billion.

Table 43.2: Funds contributed by UK & funds received back by UK for Research and Technology, 2000-2014

Year	Gross UK contribution in market value €m	EU grants to UK for research & technology in €m	Grants as % of contribution
2000	13866.97	546.6	3.94
2001	7743.392	482.2	6.23
2002	10152.83	515.8	4.75
2003	9971.531	436.9	4.38
2004	11682.52	510.2	4.37
2005	12157.06	538.6	4.43
2006	12380.63	606.6	4.90
2007	13428.95	422.4	3.15
2008	10113.94	826.1	8.17
2009	10111.6	817.7	8.09
2010	14659.37	722.7	4.93
2011	13825.23	840.8	6.08
2012	16177.48	980.0	6.06
2013	17068.37	1114.0	6.53
2014	14072.31	796.5	5.66

EU expenditure and revenue 2000-2014
http://ec.europa.eu/budget/financialreport/2014/annex/2/index_en.html.

Line item 1.1.3 is 'Common Strategic Framework (CSF) Research and Innovation', and it is this line which is reported in the table, Beneath on line 1.1.31 is Horizon 2020. It is distinguished 1.132 Euratom and 1.1.31 from Education, Youth & Training which incorporates the Erasmus programme. However, Horizon 2020 is over 97% of the CSF.

All the claims made by the head of the Dunn School of Pathology at Oxford that 'British scientists have earned more back in grants than the UK has contributed in every year of the scheme's existence', that 'we receive more than we put in', and that 'we received almost double the amount of money than the next best funded country, Germany', though often repeated by EU enthusiasts, are completely without foundation.

The total funds received by UK recipients for research and technology from the EU over the 15 years equal a small percentage of the UK's gross contribution as shown in Table 43.2. The mean over the 15 years is 5.44 per cent. The bottom line of Table 43.1 shows that these funds equal 14 per cent of the total net contribution by UK taxpayers over the same period. The 15 year total in Table 43.1 shows that the UK has received €10.1b which is less than €11.3b received by Germany. There are, however, a bewildering variety of EU programmes, so it is entirely possible that in one or other of them the UK might have received more than German recipients. The table, however, is drawn from the aggregate figures in the annual EU budget Financial Reports, and therefore gives the total expenditure apart from separately itemized projects such as Egnos & Galileo satellite navigation systems, and the European Commission's contribution to ITER, the international nuclear fusion research project.

Belgium and Spain have most reason to believe that there really is an EU 'pot of research money', since their net contribution to EU revenue over these years has been zero, but they have nevertheless received substantial research funds, more than five contributing countries and far more than four of them. All of the remaining 16 member countries have also been recipients of the grants for research and technology, even though they also have not contributed to EU funds. Since funds collected from nine contributing countries have been re-distributed among 28 countries, it may be seen that one important function of European Commission research and innovation policy has been to redistribute funds to support scientific resources and research effort within the EU away from the nine contributing countries to the 19 who contribute nothing.

In Table 43.3 below, annual payments made to individual countries are shown as a percentage of the total funds distributed in each year. This is not the same as the total budget since about 35% of the expenditure on research and innovation is 'earmarked', or otherwise not available for annual distribution.[6]

Although there is considerable stability in the shares, we can observe a few shifts over time. Between 2000-2002, for example, the UK received the largest share of these funds, but since then has been displaced by Germany. A more dramatic shift has been the continual increase in the share awarded to Belgium, and the corresponding falls in those of France and Italy. By 2014 Belgium received a larger proportion than every contributing country except Germany and the UK. The share being given to Spain, the other non-contributing country, also increased quite sharply from 2008, but fell back in 2014. Even so, its share has routinely exceeded those of five contributing countries. The shares of the other 16 members, receiving small percentages and not included in the table individually, have tended to increase steadily over time.

Some further insight into these decisions on the distribution of research funds can be obtained by showing them as expenditures per qualified researcher in each of the 11 member countries over these years 2002-2013, since the numbers of researchers for 2014 has not yet been published. In Table 43.4, all the figures have been converted to €s (2013) by the European Central Bank's euro deflator, since that enables us to see real changes without being distracted by inflation. The three bottom rows show other important information regarding recipient member states: the sum total of the amounts awarded to member countries over the 14 years, their means, and the ordinal rank in terms of both.

---

6   Or designated 'other' or for non-EU expenditures. In 2014 the 'earmarked' totalled €835.5m, the 'other' was €1.031b and the 'non-EU' €444.1m. The EC Budget Office has did not respond to my request for further details.

Table 43.3: Percentage of the total funds distributed for research & innovation going to 11 member countries, 2000-2014

	Austria	Belgium	Denmark	Finland	France	Germany	Italy	Nether lands	Spain	Sweden	UK	Other 16	Total €m
2000	2.0	7.4	2.5	1.9	15.5	16.6	13.7	6.9	5.1	3.2	19.2	6.9	2852.2
2001	2.2	9.3	2.6	2.0	14.3	17.5	12.8	7.0	5.2	3.4	17.9	7.0	2688.0
2002	2.2	9.3	2.6	2.0	14.3	17.5	12.8	7.0	5.2	3.4	17.9	7.0	2688.0
2003	2.3	10.0	2.0	2.2	14.8	18.0	12.0	7.8	5.3	3.3	16.0	8.8	2726.8
2004	2.1	12.2	2.1	2.2	13.8	18.5	11.0	7.3	5.3	3.3	14.6	7.9	3503.1
2005	2.5	12.0	2.1	1.8	13.4	18.6	12.2	6.1	5.3	3.6	14.5	8.2	3723.4
2006	2.7	11.3	2.2	1.7	11.6	19.1	11.8	7.0	4.7	3.5	14.4	10.4	4213.0
2007	2.5	12.7	1.7	1.8	14.6	17.1	13.8	6.6	4.8	3.6	12.9	8.0	3284.8
2008	2.8	9.6	2.2	2.2	11.9	17.6	10.1	7.6	7.8	3.8	15.2	9.2	5417.5
2009	2.5	10.6	2.2	1.8	13.2	16.8	9.3	6.8	8.3	3.4	15.7	9.4	5216.2
2010	2.5	8.8	2.1	2.0	14.2	16.9	9.7	7.1	10.6	3.4	13.5	9.1	5373.1
2011	2.5	10.3	2.0	1.8	13.5	16.2	9.5	6.9	10.8	3.5	14.4	8.6	5851.5
2012	2.4	9.3	2.2	1.8	13.5	16.0	8.7	7.2	11.9	3.2	14.9	8.8	6558.9
2013	2.4	10.4	2.3	1.6	12.6	15.8	8.2	7.7	11.0	3.3	15.4	9.0	7237.0
2014	2.3	12.7	2.4	1.5	11.1	16.1	8.7	7.0	7.9	3.2	15.2	11.8	5256.7
Mean	**2.4**	**10.4**	**2.2**	**1.9**	**13.5**	**17.2**	**11.0**	**7.1**	**7.3**	**3.4**	**15.4**	**8.7**	**66,590.2**

EC Financial statement 2014, http://ec.europa.eu/budget/financialreport/2014/ https://www.ecb.europa.eu/stats/prices/hicp/html/inflation.en.html

Belgium, a non-contributing member country, has been the runaway winner in terms of sums awarded per researcher, receiving more than double that of the second-placed country, the Netherlands, and more than four times as much as the UK, which is in 8th place. Italy remains a rather large recipient of funds, even though the amounts have declined slowly over the 14 years. The largest contributor of funds, Germany, has received a rather low amount per researcher. Only Finland has received less.

Enthusiasts for EU membership, like the Head of the Dunn School at Oxford, are for some strange reason fond of claiming that the UK has received more research funds than Germany, that it has been the largest recipient of research funds, and even that it is a net beneficiary because its awards exceed its contributions to European Commission programs. These misperceptions seem to be due to looking at the data selectively, and of not comparing like with like.

For the record:

- There is no EU pot of money filled by other countries or from other sources. The funds that UK research has received from the EU have been paid by UK taxpayers.

- The UK has not been a net beneficiary from the European Commission redistribution of funds, getting out more than it paid in.[7] On the contrary, research grants have been on average a mere 14 per cent of the UK's net annual contributions to the EU.

---

7   *The Guardian* seems especially fond of this argument which it supported in a special feature on October 9th 2015, by saying that 'In total, the UK – which contributes about 11.5% of the EU budget – receives about 16% of all EU science funding.' The former (€150bn) is more than 20 times the latter (about €7bn in last FP7 funding year). So what these percentages are meant to show is a mystery. http://www.theguardian.com/politics/2015/oct/09/would-brexit-damage-british-universities-science-and-research

On November 11th 2015 it repeated the same argument. http://www.the-guardian.com/politics/2015/nov/11/leaving-eu-would-be-a-disaster-british-universities-warn What, one wonders, do the researchers it is supporting make of this?

Table 43.4: European Commission Research expenditure per researcher in 11 member countries 2000-2013 in constant €2013

	Austria	Belgium	Denmark	Finland	France	Germany	Italy	Netherlands	Spain	Sweden	UK
2000	3308	9117	4831	2021	3388	2415	7777	6106	2512	2824	4214
2001	3263	10107	4633	1895	2808	2318	6699	5353	2269	2597	3439
2002	3139	10624	3528	1810	2671	2305	6272	5564	2181	2509	3161
2003	3120	10840	2757	1797	2588	2245	5749	6000	1939	2279	2484
2004	3513	16024	3393	2318	2897	2906	6505	6414	2212	2854	2703
2005	3934	16237	3389	2073	2962	3071	6643	5759	2170	2910	2611
2006	4605	15918	3696	2055	2705	3352	6542	6475	2007	3048	2787
2007	2916	13129	2134	1696	2483	2210	5576	4861	1486	2958	1914
2008	4946	15791	3654	3205	3166	3521	6379	9069	3605	4590	3663
2009	4171	15765	3472	2516	3216	3025	5195	8267	3544	4115	3493
2010	4006	12441	3186	2847	3359	2975	5407	7590	4559	4016	3022
2011	4150	14861	3191	2779	3336	2939	5479	7264	5123	4394	3516
2012	4115	14300	3564	3022	3503	3052	5289	6862	6346	4395	3929
2013	4331	16871	4012	3021	3434	3173	5057	7748	6457	3873	4295
total	53,517	192,024	49,441	33,056	42,517	39,508	84,570	93,333	46,410	47,361	45,231
mean	3823	13,716	3532	2361	3037	2822	6041	6667	3315	3383	3231
rank	4	1	5	11	9	10	3	2	7	6	8

Source: UNESCO Instit of Stats Science, Technology & Innovation Researchers (FTE) total http://data.uis.unesco.org/
EC Financial statement 2014, http://ec.europa.eu/budget/financialreport/2014/ https://www.ecb.europa.eu/stats/prices/hicp/html/inflation.en.html

- The UK has not received more research funds in absolute amounts than Germany, though if funds received by member countries are compared per researcher, the UK has received more.

- However, by this measure both the UK and Germany have received less than most other member countries.

The continuous redistribution of funds for scientific research on which the European Commission has been engaged over the past 15 years has been away from both Germany and the UK. The full extent of this redistribution and its impact has, as far as I know, never been analysed, explained or justified.

The truly baffling aspect of this examination of EU research funding is the failure of distinguished academics to examine any available evidence before making categorical pronouncements. One can understand that handsome grants for cherished projects and institutions and gifted colleagues and students, which they have received via the EU, might have distracted them. However, they owe it to their ultimate benefactor, the British taxpayer, to use their first-rate minds to give an honest, accurate and thorough appraisal of the relative merits of indirect EU or direct UK funding of their research. Thus far, their contribution to the EU referendum debate has failed to do that.

44

Scaremongering to keep the UK in

It is difficult to keep track of all the problems that will occur should the British people vote to leave the EU since a new story appears almost every day. There will be increases in mortgage rates, in air fares, in mobile roaming charges, a bonfire of workers' rights, cuts in R&D funding, European Health Insurance Cards will be void, and there will be problems on the Irish border.

They leave one wondering how the UK ever survived as an independent country, or how independent countries elsewhere in the world manage to cope. These notes examine a small sample of these stories to frighten the voters, some of them extending back a few years.

1. Leaving the EU would mean the break-up of the United Kingdom

William Hague, the former Foreign Secretary, has joined EU enthusiasts in arguing that a vote for Brexit will mean the break-up of the United Kingdom. Their argument depends on a string of contingencies: that a majority of Scots will vote to remain while the majority of English voters choose to leave, that they will then have an irresistible argument for another referendum, that the UK government will not be able to resist, and that in this second referendum they will reverse the vote of the first, and decide to leave.

An answer in a letter to the *Daily Telegraph*, 24 Dec 2015

> SIR – William Hague's assertion that Brexit would lead to the break-up of the United Kingdom is as illogical as it is scaremongering. It is not Government policy to offer a second independence referendum to Scotland.
>
> If the UK leaves the EU, Scotland would actually be less likely to leave the UK for three reasons.

First, as part of Brexit, major powers of great relevance to Scotland – such as farming, fishing, trade and environment – would be returned to the UK and could then be further devolved to Scotland.

Secondly, Scotland could not be sure it would be allowed back in the EU alone. Even if let in, after Turkey and Serbia's accession in, say, 2025, it would be forced to adopt the euro and lose the rebate.

Thirdly, an independent Scotland would be born bankrupt. Oil prices are $36 a barrel now, while Scottish National Party economics relied on a figure of $100, and 65,000 jobs have been lost in the Aberdeen area recently. It would also lose £1,700 per head in UK public spending.

The Scots are canny and are more Eurosceptic than is often claimed; a third of the SNP is pro-Brexit and the only area of the UK to vote against joining the European Economic Community in 1975 was the Highlands and Islands.

David Campbell Bannerman MEP
Co-Chairman, Conservatives for Britain

Numerous bloggers have made the same points less succinctly, some even predicting that the second referendum will include all Scots wherever they may be residing in the United Kingdom.

2. David Cameron, Prime Minister, on the huge number of asylum seekers that would come to Britain overnight, February 2015

The Prime Minister said that voting to leave the EU would result in migrant camps such as "the Jungle" in Calais moving to southern England, and that a "huge number" of asylum seekers could come to Britain "overnight" because France would pull out of current border arrangements in the aftermath of an EU exit. A vote to leave would give French politicians the chance to "tear up" the deal, which lets UK border guards check passports at Calais.

France responded saying it would not pull out of its border arrangements with the UK even in the event of Britain voting to leave the European Union.

The importance of this instant contradictory news report is not whether or not France would in the end reconsider its border agreement or not. It is that it demonstrates that the Prime Minister had not earlier sought advice of the French government's likely future actions, and is himself actively engaged in making up scare stories off the top of his head.

The normal procedure for governments that control their borders is to advise air or marine carriers of the documents passengers will require on entry, and to warn them that if they are not supplied at the point of entry, the would-be entrant will be returned to their point of departure at the carrier's expense, and with a possible fine. There is no reason why this procedure should not be applied post-Brexit. It is already applied to passengers arriving in the UK from non-EU countries.[1]

3. Dominic Grieve, a former Attorney General on the dangers of Brexit for expats, 2015

'EU exit would make 2m Britons abroad illegal immigrants overnight.'[2]

Dominic Grieve, March 2015, former Attorney General

'Spain might demand that British retirees on the costas pay for their own healthcare or it may try to limit migrants' access to healthcare…Their healthcare is costly to the Spanish treasury, which is struggling to balance its books'.[3]

The Centre for European Reform

The International Law Commission told the UN in 1959: 'Private rights acquired under existing law do not cease on a change of sovereignty.'

The Vienna Convention on the Law of Treaties 1969 refers to 'acquired rights', which individuals build up over time and hold despite any changes in future treaties enacted by their nation. Article 70 states that the termination of a treaty "does not affect

---

1   'France contradicts Cameron over Calais migrant camps', *Daily Telegraph*, 9 Feb 2016
     http://www.telegraph.co.uk/news/newstopics/eureferendum/12147334/France-contradicts-Cameron-over-Calais-migrant-camps.html
2   www.theguardian.com/politics/2015/mar/18/dominic-grieve-brexit-2m-britons-abroad-illegalimmigrants-eu-echr.b
3   For a full discussion and these and further references p.382-3, Change or Go

any right, obligation or legal situation of the parties created through the execution of the treaty prior to its termination.'

A House of Commons Library note clarified: 'Generally speaking, withdrawing from a treaty releases the parties from any future obligations to each other, but does not affect any rights or obligations acquired under it before withdrawal. Therefore, the EU's freedom of movement rights would be honoured for all those citizens who reside in other EEA nations prior to any Treaty changes'.[4]

4. Peter Mandelson on the impossibility of the UK negotiating trade agreements on its own, 2014

'India would laugh in our faces if Britain tried to negotiate a free trade agreement outside Europe... They would walk away and leave us whistling in the wind.'[5]

He declined to explain why India, apart from the collective agreements in which it has participated or negotiated, has also concluded bilateral agreements with Singapore, Chile, Korea, Malaysia and Japan, and did not leave any of them 'whistling in the wind'. Why, for that matter, is it currently negotiating an agreement with EFTA, as well as the EU? EFTA's combined GDP is smaller than that of the UK. The WTO Regional Trade Agreement Information System has many examples of small countries that have been able to conclude agreements with large ones including China and the US. The largest economy of the present 20 trading agreement partner countries of the US is Australia.[6]

5. Sir John Major, on the loss of foreign investment in the UK post-Brexit

'If the UK left the EU, 'foreign-owned companies would then migrate to the EU.'[7]

- Chatham House, 14 February 2013

---

4   House of Commons Library, Leaving the EU, Research Paper 13/42, 1 July 2013

5   'Lord Mandelson: Britain 'bonkers' to leave European Union', Angela Monaghan, *The Guardian*, 1 April 2014:
    http://www.theguardian.com/business/2014/apr/01/lord-mandelson-britain-bonkers-leave-european-union

6   https://www.wto.org/english/tratop_e/region_e/rta_participation_map_e.html

7   www.johnmajor.co.uk/page4370.html

'We would lose inward investment – ask Japan or Korea, or even America.'[8]

Institute of Directors, 28 November 2013

In 2007, the Commission decided that 'the internal market has not been able to deliver in terms of promoting further the role of the EU with respect to global investment flows.'[9]

As it happens, some of Ernst & Young's researchers in 2013 accepted Sir John's invitation and, in a manner of speaking, did 'ask Japan or Korea or even America'. They reported 'that European companies regard the UK's integration into the EU as being important to the country's attractiveness for FDI, while those in the US and Asia do not.'[10]

Earlier in the same survey, they identified 14 factors that make the UK attractive for existing or potential investors, none of which refer, even vaguely, to the EU.[11]

6. Peter Mandelson, on the impossibility of trading 'at will' in the EU without being a member, 2013

In May 2013, in an article in *The Daily Telegraph*, Peter Mandelson, a former EU commissioner, sought to discredit what he chose to call the 'anti-Europeans' argument... that we can continue trading at will in Europe, with the same privileges as now, without being part of its policy-making, its regulatory rules and its policing of the market's openness. This is a grave deception.'[12]

A good many countries 'trade at will' in Europe more successfully than the UK without the privileges of membership,

---

8   www.johnmajor.co.uk/page4364.html

9   Fabienne Ilzkovitz et al, Steps towards a deeper economic integration: the Internal Market in the 21st century: A contribution to the Single Market Review, by the Directorate-General for Economic and Financial Affairs, N° 271, January 2007, ISSN 1725-3187: http://ec.europa.eu/economy_finance/index_en.htm. For an extended discussion pp.728-733, Business for Britain, Change or Go, How Britain would gain influence and prosper outside an unreformed Europe, London, 2015.

10 *Ernst & Young's attractiveness survey*, UK 2013, No room for complacency, London, 2013. p.35 http://www.ey.com/Publication/vwLUAssets/Ernst-and-Youngs-attractiveness-survey-UK-2013-No-room-for-complacency/$FILE/EY_UK_Attractiveness_2013.pdf

11 *ibid*. p.26

12 Peter Mandelson 'David Cameron must not cave in to the UKIP threat', *Daily Telegraph*, 16 May 2013

without being part of EU policy-making, without helping to make its regulatory rules or policing its openness. As a result, the exports of goods and services of many of them have grown more rapidly over the life of the Single Market than those of the UK. Who is deceiving whom?

7. Robert Peston, on David Cameron's veto of a treaty to defend the euro, 2011

At the time, BBC TV's Business Editor, Peston explained to his national audience that if multinationals 'begin to see the UK as an isolated island, they will not wish to stay. So it would really matter if the UK's place in the world's biggest market ... were somehow in doubt. Which is why... businesses are now desperate to hear a positive statement from Mr Cameron about how the UK's position in the Single Market can somehow be buttressed.'

This is a variation on the long-running argument that FDI in UK depends on EU membership. The UK share of FDI inflows to Europe increased significantly over the year following his veto, while that of France and Germany plummeted. A euphoric UKTI report on 23rd July 2013 noted the spurt in FDI in the UK.[13]

8. The Economic Research Institute and Bertelsmann Foundation predictions of economic costs to the UK of Brexit, 2015

This is a very short report, (published 27 April 2015) and needless to say, only its worst case scenario was reported. The institute is partly responsible since it headlined its worst case scenario in which the UK had no trade agreements with the EU to 2030. However, its main conclusion is that 'depending on the extent of the UK's trade policy isolation its real GDP would be between

---

13 An enlarged version of his report appeared on his website. *'Big Business Deeply Troubled By Cameron's Veto'* Robert Peston, December 11th 2011.

14 https://www.bertelsmann-stiftung.de/en/topics/aktuelle-meldungen/ 2015/april/brexit-could-be-expensive-especially-for-the-united- kingdom/Brexit – potential economic consequences if the UK exit the EU. There is a second, slightly longer version of this paper called Policy brief#2015/5 which ends with an editorial paragraph saying Brexit must be avoided! http://www.bfna.org/sites/default/files/publications/Brexit%20- %20potential%20economic%20consequences%20if%20the%20UK%20exits%20 the%20EU.pdf

0.6% and 3% lower by 2030.' Since they put Britain's EU budget payment at a low 5%, they conclude that Brexit 'could not compensate for economic losses, even in the best case scenario.'[14]

If trade meaning 'total isolation' was more severe, and 'dynamic economic consequences such as weakening of innovative power as well as London as a financial centre are taken into account' then we get the headline figure that the loss 'could reach 14 per cent' by 2030. But this 14 per cent depends on the arguments of another economist and is, the second paper explains, only a 'theoretically conceivable value'. The press reports did not notice that. Raoul Ruparel, head of economic research at Open Europe, described this report as "one-sided", "short on detail" and using assumptions, such as the 14 per cent of GDP potential loss to the UK economy, that had been pulled "out of nowhere". Open Europe has itself placed the costs between 0.8 per cent of GDP, and in the best case scenario predicted a gain of 0.6 per cent of GDP.

The curious thing about these model-based predictions is that they have realistic means of incorporating the probable reactions of the actors involved between 2016 and 2030. For instance, when 'dynamic consequences are taken into account Germany's estimated GDP losses would come in between 0.3% and 2%'. But are German automotive manufacturers merely spectators watching the decline of their best market? Is the UK, the most globally-connected society on the planet, likely to descend into severe isolation?

45

We have been here before!

There are more than a few echoes in the present Brexit debate from the earlier campaign to join the euro. As that campaign began, the UK political elite who favoured entry discovered that they had to win support for membership before they could begin to persuade the electorate about the merits of the euro.

That campaign, for both euro and for membership, had a cross-party elite profile, much like the current Remain campaign, and indeed with some of the same figures leading the media presentation of the case: Tony Blair, Kenneth Clarke and Michael Heseltine. Multinational corporations bankrolled a pressure group called Britain In Europe.[1] It found distinguished academic support from LSE.[2] It commissioned a report from a Berkeley professor whose adapted gravity trade model had predicted prodigious growth of UK exports and GDP after the UK joined the new currency. Fifteen years later, he published a *mea culpa*, saying that if anything 'EMU has a smaller trade effect than other currency unions and is often estimated to be negligible or negative.'[3] Or negative? Ouch!

Britain in Europe's contemporary equivalent, Business for New Europe, has not revealed its financial support though it has listed

---

1   Britain in Europe https://en.wikipedia.org/wiki/Britain_in_Europe #List_of_backers
2   Richard Layard, William Buiter, Christopher Huhne, Will Hutton, Peter Kenen and Adair Turner with a forward by Paul Volcker *Why Britain should join the euro*, Britain in Europe, London, 2002 www.britainineurope.org.uk. Christopher Huhne and Nick Canning, *Crystal Balls: false prophecies from anti-European economists*, Britain in Europe, nd, 2002ca
3   The original paper was A.K. Rose 'One money, one market: The effect of currency unions on trade', *Economic Policy*, 15 (30) (2000), pp. 7–46. The apology was Reuven Glick and Andrew K. Rose, Currency Unions and Trade: A Post-EMU Mea Culpa * Revised Draft: June 16, 2015 Comments welcome http://faculty.haas.berkeley.edu/arose/Glick2.pdf

the executives and officers who 'participate in a personal capacity'[4] amongst which one may see some of the same companies that supported Britain in Europe fifteen years ago. Alongside this lobby, there is a research-oriented think tank called Centre for European Reform with a still longer list of corporate backers, a number of whom have publicly entered the debate to urge continued membership. CER claims to be working to improve the quality of the debate on the European Union which seems to mean research to ignore eurosceptic voices. In 2014 it organized a 'commission' to examine the merits of EU membership, and presented its own adapted gravity trade model, which happily found that the membership had increased UK trade by an astonishing 53 per cent. Strange how obliging these models are.

As this article from *The Independent* in 2000 demonstrates, there was also a resemblance to the contemporary scaremongering. This story was carried by the BBC and other papers. For *The Independent*, eight million unemployed was evidently not quite scary enough, so it sketched a scenario in which 'exports would halve... and as the effects of lower demand feed through... 30 per cent of the workforce would be unemployed which is more than the total number of people working in manufacturing, retailing or the entire public sector.'[5]

The Independent report was totally bogus. The NIESR report, which it quotes, had in fact found that British withdrawal would have no long-term impact on employment. On seeing this NIESR's director said 'It's pure Goebbels ...a wilful distortion of the facts.'[6] His response led to scaling down the figure, and the story continued as it does to this day, as three and half million jobs that 'depend' on Europe.

Brexit campaigners seem to have a more difficult task on their hands, since a new scare story appears almost every other day. Last time around, however, there was a verbal assault on those who opposed the new currency as some columnists competed to

---

4   www.businessforneweurope.org/our_people

5   Andrew Grice, *Eight million jobs would be lost if Britain quit EU*, The Independent, 18th February 2000.

6   Andrew Pierce, Pro-euro group acted like Goebbels to distort figures, *The Times*, 19th February 2000.

see who could abuse them in the cleverest manner. They were 'loony tunes' (Andrew Rawnsley in *The Observer*), 'assorted maniacs' and 'buffoons' (David Aaronovitch in *The Independent*) and men 'weighed down by the baggage of phobia, sentiment and illusion' (Hugo Young in *The Guardian*).[7] Brexit supporters seem to be spared this kind of treatment, though Niall Ferguson is trying.[8]

Eight million jobs 'would be lost if Britain quit EU'

BY ANDREW GRICE
Political Editor

EIGHT MILLION jobs would be lost if Britain were to leave the European Union, according to a study by academics to be published next week.

The report by the National Institute for Economic and Social Research will be seized on by Tony Blair and other ministers as they launch a campaign to turn the Eurosceptic tide among the British public.

Supporters of the single currency admit they need to "go back to basics" and win support for Britain's continued membership of the EU before they can start to swing public opinion behind joining the euro. Although the Conservative Party

Robin Cook: Concerned about Eurosceptic tide

does not support withdrawal from Europe, its opposition to the single currency has helped turn opinion against membership, with polls suggesting one in three people now wants Britain to pull out.

The National Institute's study will conclude that Britain's exports could halve if it withdrew from the union. If there was no change in prices and wages, "employment would fall by around eight million as the effects of lower demand feed through the system", it will say.

If that happened, 30 per cent of Britain's 27.2 million workforce would be unemployed, more than the total number of people working in manufacturing, retailing or the entire public sector.

The knock-on effects for firms working for companies exporting goods or services to EU countries would be even greater than for the exporters themselves, according to the study. There are 750,000 small firms which depend on trade within the EU.

The survey was commissioned by the Britain in Europe group, the embryo 'yes' campaign for a single currency referendum, which will be addressed by Kenneth Clarke, the former Tory chancellor next week as it launches a fightback against its Eurosceptic opponents.

Mr Blair, meanwhile, will make a keynote speech on Europe in Ghent, Belgium, and visit the Brussels-based European Commission. He will echo the institute's warning on job losses and call for sweeping economic reforms by EU member states.

Pro-euro ministers, including Robin Cook, the Foreign Secretary, are concerned about the growing public hostility to Britain's EU membership.

"The country is tipping further and further towards the precipice," one pro-EU campaigner said yesterday. "We have got to draw a line in the sand and say 'thus far, no further'. At the bottom of this slippery slope, we would end up with eight million people out of work."

Britain in Europe is to adopt a more aggressive approach in an attempt to counter the Eurosceptic propaganda of the rival Business for Sterling group, which published a study suggesting the transition cost of joining the euro could be £36bn.

---

7   Documented in detail in Peter Oborne and Frances Weaver, *Guilty Men*, Centre for Policy Studies, 2011.

8   Niall Ferguson, Brexit's happy morons don't give a damn about the costs of leaving, *The Sunday Times* April 17 2016

46

A *Financial Times* editor apologises for urging entry into the euro

Most of those in the UK political, industrial, and media elites who favoured joining the euro have chosen not to comment on their woeful miscalculation, and on their efforts to sell this disastrous project to the British people. Many of them have quietly resurfaced, and are now intent on selling the Single Market and EU membership to the British people, much as if the euro was no more than an optional extra, and that British participation in the project could and should continue much as before, without any searching re-examination of the assumptions of the project, and without too much regard for the misery it has already inflicted on millions, with more to come.

The euro was in fact an integral part of the Single Market driven by the same logic and rationale as the other policies it has inspired and justified. Its failure might therefore have provoked a careful reconsideration of what the Single Market entails and what it has achieved thus far. It has not, and some of the notes in this handbook are intended to make good that deficiency. Andrew Gowers is one fervent and influential supporter of the euro, and editor of the *Financial Times* when the euro debate was at its height, who did not take the view that we should simply forget it and move on. In 2011 he reflected on his part in the campaign.

'Why I should have foreseen the euro inferno' by Andrew Gowers, editor of the *Financial Times* 2001-2006, writing in the Sunday Times, 13 November 2011

> It's confession time. Exactly 10 years ago, I was cheering as the preparations to launch notes and coins for Europe's bold new

single currency reached their climax. For more than a decade before that, mine was among the voices egging on Europe's leaders as they agreed to pool control over their money and form an economic and monetary union (Emu). In the years that followed, with the euro establishing itself as an instrument of European power and integration, I was one of those celebrating its success and urging Britain to join the party.

I now believe I was wrong...

After describing the crises in Italy, Greece, Portugal and Ireland, he decided:

It is possible that apocalypse will be avoided and that the EU will find a way of muddling through to save the euro in some form...

But even so, for me something fundamental has changed. The travails of the euro have done irrevocable damage to the political assumptions I have carried around for most of my adult life – that the evolving "European project" is, for all its much-discussed faults, by definition a force for good; that economic integration driven by the EU is the essential motor for peace, prosperity and economic development across the continent.

In fact, watching Europe's leaders floundering and fumbling for the past 18 months and more, it is hard not to conclude that the single currency is achieving the precise opposite of what its progenitors intended.

Where they promised greater economic stability, the euro has exacerbated uncertainty and volatility. Where the single currency was supposed to promote trade and integration, it has instead created new divisions. Where it was portrayed as a vehicle to enhance Europe's influence in the world, it has reduced the EU to an international laughing stock, or worse. Where it was promoted as a forge for closer political co-operation in Europe, as part of the formula to end the wars and bloodshed of the 20th century, it has fuelled conflict, undermined democratic structures and reawakened age-old national resentments...

What makes this litany all the more humiliating is that we should have seen it coming...

...it is a comprehensive and devastating failure of political leadership and economic understanding — Europe's worst fiasco since the second world war. Its roots go back to the origins of the project and, to me regrettably, its consequences now threaten the long-term future of the European Union...

All of those involved — the political leaders who signed the 1992 Maastricht treaty that created Emu, the central bankers, officials and policy experts who designed the common currency and its institutions, the cheerleaders in the worlds of journalism, economics and business — bear a share of it. All of us paid too little attention to the arguments of those who opposed the project in principle and of those who worried about its viability.

For there were enough voices, both in continental Europe and in Britain, warning of the economic and political risks inherent in the euro's conception and design as the project gained momentum in the 1980s and 1990s...

Too often, their arguments were drowned out by the political imperatives driving the project forward and, frankly, by a tendency among euro supporters, including myself, to lump together the critics — the die-hards who had always opposed European integration and who had been mostly wrong, and those who saw the point of Europe but worried about the euro — under the prejudicial label "sceptics". It was, in that sense, an epic-scale exercise in "group-think".

In the remainder of the article he reports the random reflections of euro enthusiasts, most of whom prefer to remain anonymous, from which Gowers attempts, with some difficulty, to draw four points.

First, most insisted that for reasons of economic structure and competitiveness, the idea of a common currency remains right in principle – with or without Britain...

Second, all agree that the design of the euro as launched 10 years ago was fatally flawed, largely for political reasons involving those former bitter enemies France and Germany...

Third, even the project's staunchest supporters concede that since the launch, member states' management of the euro has been somewhere between miserable and catastrophic…

[The fourth point] …is that having set out down the road, Europe is doomed to carry on. There can be no turning back. It may be messy, but the consequences of failure and the collapse of the single currency would be much worse.

And one by one he knocks down all the proposed solutions which he decides either won't be accepted by the parties involved or will have disastrous consequences. He therefore finally decides that:

…there is nothing for it but to overlook the history of this mis-shapen creation and throw money at it. The political consequences, though, hardly bear thinking about.

47

How difficult would it be for post-Brexit UK to replace existing EU trade agreements?

Claims have been made that post-Brexit UK would face near insurmountable difficulties having to renegotiate the EU extra-Europe trade agreements from which it currently benefits, but the evidence suggests that the problem for post-Brexit Britain would be far more manageable than many have suggested

The *Financial Times*, the CBI and many others have argued that it would be an arduous, problematic and lengthy process for the UK to conclude alternative trade deals to replace those that the EU has negotiated over 42 years with 58 countries around the world. In part this is because there are so many, in part because the UK alone does not have the 'clout', 'heft' or 'negotiating leverage' of the European Commission to persuade these countries to open negotiations, and also because it does not have people with appropriate skills to conduct such negotiations.

However, the task that post-Brexit, newly-independent UK would face can only be accurately assessed after documenting the number and scale of the EU trade agreements, both for goods and services, with other foreign countries which are currently in force. The FT and CBI declined to do this, but this paper will do so.

Goods exports

The 33 EU trade agreements in goods that the EU has negotiated with 58 foreign countries are listed in the following table, excluding those with the EEA, Switzerland and 14 Overseas Territories & Countries linked to EU members.

Table 47.1: Trade agreements in goods negotiated by the European Commission with 55 foreign countries 1973-2016

Partner Country	1 Year the agreement came into force	2 GDP 2014 US$bn	3 UK goods Exports 2014 US$bn	4 % of all UK goods exports ($511.1bn)	5 % value of MFN non-ag goods duty free	6 Average MFN weighted tariff, (%) non-Ag goods	7 Est value of UK exports subject to a tariff post-Brexit US$bn
Albania	'06	13.37	0.03	0.01	57	3.1	0.013
Algeria	'05	214.06	0.79	0.15	2	13.5	0.774
Andorra	'91	3.25	0.01	0.00	Not WTO	-	0.000
Bosnia & Herzegovina	'08	18.34	0.04	0.01	30	6	0.028
Cameroon	**'14**	**32.55**	**0.08**	**0.01**	**1**	**13.2**	**0.079**
CARIFORUM EPA (14)	**'08**	**131.38**	**0.66**	**0.13**	**63**	**10.6**	**0.244**
Central America (6)	'13	210.90	0.51	0.10	40	5.1	0.306
Chile	'03	258.06	0.78	0.15	0	5.9	0.780
Colombia	'13	377.74	0.55	0.11	56	8.1	0.242
Peru	'13	202.90	0.28	0.05	57	1.6	0.120
Cote d'Ivoire	'09	34.25	0.13	0.03	2	5.9	0.127
E & S Africa Int EPA (4)	'12	38.28	0.22	0.04	28	8.2	0.158
Egypt	**'04**	**286.54**	**1.73**	**0.34**	**11**	**10.1**	**1.540**
Faroe Islands	'97	2.61	0.02	0.00	0	0	0.020
Georgia	'14	16.53	0.10	0.02	93	1	0.007
Israel	'00	304.23	1.81	0.35	65	1.9	0.634
Jordan	'02	35.83	0.43	0.08	56	7.6	0.189
Korea, Republic of	'11	1410.38	6.91	0.80	17	3.7	5.735
Lebanon	'03	45.73	0.82	0.16	42	4.3	0.476
Macedonia FYR	'01	11.32	0.89	0.17	44	6.2	0.498
Mexico	'00	1282.72	1.73	0.34	55	3.3	0.779
Montenegro	'08	4.58	0.02	0.00	30	3.2	0.014
Morocco	'00	107.00	0.94	0.18	0	8.1	0.940
Palestinian Authority	'97	12.74	0.00	0.00	0	0	0.000
Papua New Guinea	'09	15.41	0.02	0.00	81	1.6	0.004
Fiji	**'14**	**4.03**	**0.03**	**0.01**	**5**	**12.7**	**0.029**
Moldova	'14	7.94	0.07	0.01	52	2.4	0.034
San Marino	'02	1.90	0.01	0.00	0	0	0.010
Serbia	'10	43.87	0.21	0.04	1	5.1	0.208
South Africa	'00	349.82	3.92	0.77	64	5.5	1.411
Syria (2007)	**'73**	**40.41**	**0.02**	**0.00**	**12**	**15.3**	**0.018**
Tunisia	**'98**	**46.99**	**0.26**	**0.05**	**38**	**11.2**	**0.161**
Turkey	'96	799.53	6.13	1.20	25	3.5	4.598
Ukraine	'14	131.81	0.58	0.11	43	2.4	0.331
Total for 34 Agreements		**$6497.0 bn**	**$30.7 bn**	**6.0%**	**Weighted Mean 33.2%**	**Weighted Mean 5.0%**	**$20.51bn**

Sources: Regional trade agreements information system of WTO http://rtais.wto.org/
UN Comtrade http://comtrade.un.org/data;
WTO Trade Profiles 2015 http://stat.wto.org/CountryProfile/WSDBCountryPFHome.aspx?Language=E;
The World Bank http://data.worldbank.org/indicator/

With these figures we can see the problems that would face post-Brexit UK goods exporters more precisely than has been attempted thus far. The table is presented in seven columns for which we provide comment. The shaded rows indicate partner countries with which the UK runs a trade deficit.

The GDP of each partner country in 2014 (Column 2)

The data shows that the majority of EU trade agreements have been with small partner countries. The EU may be a heavyweight in GDP terms, but until TTIP it has preferred to negotiate, in the main, with flyweights. The average GDP accessed by each trade agreement is $191.1bn, whereas that of Switzerland's partners is more than four times larger (at $893.2bn), of Chile's 15 times larger (at $2964.7bn), of Singapore's 18 times larger at ($3597.4bn) and Korea's partners 23 times larger than that of the EU's partners (at $4396.46bn).

The largest economy with which the European Commission has concluded an agreement is Korea, which in 2014 had a GDP of $1.41tn, slightly less than that of Australia, slightly more than that of Spain, and around half that of the UK.

The value of UK goods exported to each partner country (Columns 3 and 4)

Column 3 shows the sum total of all UK exports to all 58 of the countries covered by the EU's 33 agreements was $30.7 billion in 2014 which Column 4 shows accounts for only 6 per cent of the total world exports of UK goods in 2014, which had a value of $511.1bn.

The percentage of non-agricultural goods admitted duty free and the average WTO tariff on non-agricultural goods that are not duty free (Columns 5 and 6)

The WTO Tariff Profiles show that the proportion of EU non-agricultural goods exported tariff-free into each of these countries is nearly always 100 per cent, as a result of its agreements, and for that reason it is not listed separately in the table. What column 5 shows is the proportion of goods for every country designated a

MFN (most favoured nation), which is virtually all countries with which they trade without an agreement. A post-Brexit UK would fall into this category if it took no steps to negotiate new agreements.

If we take the first line as an example, we may see that 57 per cent of non-agricultural goods exported to Albania are duty free, but 43 percent would face a tariff of, on average, 3.1 per cent. Taking only countries to which more than one per cent of UK exports go: 83 per cent of UK exports to Korea would face an average tariff of 3.7 per cent, and 75 per cent of UK exports to Turkey would face a tariff of 3.5 per cent. The weighted mean of all 33 countries is almost exactly a third (33.2%) meaning on average one third of UK exports to these countries would be tariff free, and two thirds subject to a tariff of, on average, five per cent.

The estimated value of UK exports subject to a tariff post-Brexit (Column 7)

Since Column 3 shows the total value of UK exports to each country, Column 5 shows the proportion of non-agricultural goods on which each country levies a tariff, and column 6 shows the average value of that tariff, it is not difficult to calculate the actual value of UK goods exports to each of the 58 countries that would be subject to a tariff. As such Column 7 provides an estimate of the value of UK exports which would be subject to a tariff, based on the hypothetical that Brexit had occurred in 2013, and the UK had not negotiated an agreement.

The sum total for all 58 countries is $20.56 billion, which means that almost exactly two thirds of UK goods exports to these 58 countries, which amount to 4.02 per cent of total UK goods exports, would face a tariff of, on average, 5 per cent, if the post-Brexit UK government does not negotiate any new agreements.

There are six tougher cases where it can be seen they would face a tariff of 10 per cent or more: Cameroon, CARIFORUM, Egypt, Fiji, Syria, and Tunisia. Together they constituted, in 2014, 0.69% of total UK goods exports, though slightly less, of course, if we subtract the average proportion of their goods imports which are duty free.

Services trade agreements

A similar analysis can be conducted for UK services exports, though since the European Commission has been much less successful in concluding services trade agreements, we are dealing with only 15 agreements, covering 33 countries. These agreements ease regulatory non-tariff barriers rather than tariffs.

The 15 agreements currently in force are listed in Table 47.2, as before with the GDP in 2014 of the partner country, followed by the value of UK services exports to that country in 2014, which, in the final column, is expressed as a proportion of total UK services exports in that year.

Table 47.2: Trade agreements in services negotiated by the European Commission with foreign countries 1973-2016

Partner	in force	GDP(2014)$b	UK services exports 2014 in US$bn	as % of total UK services exports ($361.6bn)
Albania	'09	13.4	0.03	0.008
Bosnia & Herz'ina	'14	18.34	0.07	0.018
CARIFORUM States 14	'08	131.4	1.06	0.294
Central America 6	'13	210.9	0.28	0.077
Chile	'05	258.1	0.36	0.101
Colombia	'13	377.7	0.26	0.071
Georgia	'14	16.5	0.03	0.010
Korea, Republic of	'11	1410.4	2.89	0.800
Mexico	'00	1282.7	0.89	0.246
FYR Macedonia	'04	11.3	0.14	0.038
Rep. of Moldova	'14	7.9	0.07	0.020
Montenegro	'10	4.6	0.05	0.015
Peru	'13	202.9	0.28	0.077
Serbia	'13	43.9	0.09	0.024
Ukraine	'14	131.8	0.18	0.050
Total for 15 Agreements		**$4121.8bn**	**$6.69bn**	**1.849%**

Source:.The regional trade agreements information system of WTO http://rtais.wto.org/
World Bank; http://data.worldbank.org/indicator. The export data is from OECD Statistics on International Trade in Services (database) EBOPS 2010. www.oecd-ilibrary.org

As may be seen at the bottom of the final column, all the EU service agreements currently in force cover just 2.4 per cent of all UK services exports, an even smaller coverage than that of the EU goods agreements.

Conclusion 1: On small markets and tolerable tariffs

First, the argument that post-Brexit UK would find it an arduous, decade-long task to replace the EU trade agreements from which it currently benefits is surely wildly exaggerated. These EU agreements cover only a small proportion of UK exports: six per cent of all UK goods exports and 1.8 per cent of all UK services exports in 2014. Moreover, about one third of non-agricultural goods exports to these countries are tariff free. If we assume British exports to these countries do not depart from the average distribution of their imports by which the tariff is weighted, it would mean that, in 2014, $20.1bn or 4.1 per cent of UK total exports would face, on average, a 5 per cent tariff in these 55 countries.

Supporters of continued membership, like the CBI and the *Financial Times* (FT), have for years been exaggerating the efficacy of the EU's 'clout' and 'negotiating leverage' when negotiating trade agreements and therefore also exaggerating the difficulties of replacing the agreements it has managed to conclude. According to the CBI, the post-Brexit UK government, would face 'uncertainty and dislocation', 'would first have to build up national capacity', might find other countries 'unwilling to negotiate', and would lack the clout to conclude agreements.

One of its former director-generals, who is also an ex-editor of the *FT*, Sir Richard Lambert, emphasized what he considered 'a vital point' by claiming that 'according to CBI data the EU has negotiated trade agreements that cover around 30 per cent of trade outside the EU area', which would amount, if it were true, to exports of around $80 billion.[1] On Feb 22nd 2016, the *FT* argued that post-independence 'the UK would have to negotiate

---

1   Sir Richard Lambert 'The UK and the new face of Europe' Gresham College lecture, 6 June 2013

agreements with non-EU countries including the US, China, India, Japan and Australia. This would be a matter of urgency (since)... sales to and from 60 other countries are governed by agreements struck with the (EU) bloc.'

The WTO/UN statistics presented above are more credible than those of the CBI. They indicate that it would be rather more simple to negotiate agreements than the CBI or the *FT* pretend, and it would hardly be a devastating blow even if the post-Brexit UK government decided to do absolutely nothing. There would be an average 5 per cent tariff on 4.1 per cent of UK exports. No doubt there would be some tough cases, in particular to the six countries mentioned above. However, five of them, as may be seen from the table, happen to have a trade surplus with the UK which they would no doubt wish to preserve, and therefore would be pleased to negotiate to do so. Exporters to all the other countries would face an average tariff of less than 5 per cent. In March 2016, the value of the pound sterling fluctuated by more than 5 per cent.

Even if the UK was determined to replace all the EU goods agreements, it would only require amendments to the existing agreements with Korea, Turkey and South Africa, which together now take 3.32 per cent of UK goods exports, and that new agreements be negotiated with, say, Hong Kong (2.6 per cent) and United Arab Emirates (2.06 per cent), and these would more than compensate for the potential loss from tariffs on 4.1 per cent of UK goods exports.

If none of these work out, there are of course numerous other options including Australia, Singapore, New Zealand and other countries with which the European Commission has been unable to strike a deal, often for reasons that have nothing whatever to do with the UK. The FT chose to mention the US, China and India, even though these are all countries with which the Commission has not yet managed to conclude an agreement, presumably so that it could exaggerate the daunting task that would face post-Brexit Britain. The reality is far less worrisome, and full of incidental opportunities to extend the coverage of freer trade given the inadequacies of so many EU trade agreements, which is the great promise of Brexit.

To replace the services agreements would be simpler still. Switzerland currently takes 5.74 per cent of all UK services exports, so an agreement with Switzerland alone would mean that post-Brexit Britain would more than double the coverage of all the service trade agreements that the EU has been able to obtain over the past forty-two years. Given the very limited coverage of EU services trade agreements, there are once again considerable opportunities for post-Brexit Britain to extend the very poor coverage of EU agreements that facilitate services exports.

Conclusion 2: On negotiators and partners

The idea that the UK currently lacks the negotiating expertise to do this seems to be another example of EU enthusiasts thinking that to make a case for EU membership they have to belittle Britain's resources and capabilities.

First, one might ask how it is that Chile, Korea, Singapore and Switzerland have been able to find the skills that the UK lacks to secure far more trade agreement partners, in both goods and services, than the EU, and partners with far larger economies.

Second, one might first ask how a country, like the UK, that trades globally in both goods and services, largely with countries with which the EU has no trade agreement, could conduct that trade, especially the services trade, without having a considerable cadre of experts in negotiating terms and conditions, and anticipating and handling problems. Moreover, when the Commission is negotiating agreements it normally makes use of external consultants, some of which are UK based, such as LSE, and the University of Manchester. There is no reason why post-Brexit UK trade negotiators, should not, if need be, use consultants in the same manner whether from the UK or elsewhere.

Third, the tables above show that with most of the partner countries the UK runs a trade deficit in goods.[2] Is it likely that countries running a surplus in their trade with the UK would

---

2   There are not quite as many UK deficits as the table suggests since 9 of the 14 Cariforum countries, 2 of the 6 Central American countries, and 1 of the 4 Eastern and Southern African states had deficits on their UK trade. In the services agreements, the UK ran a trade surplus with 7 of the 14 Cariforum countries.

decline to negotiate with post-Brexit UK to enable that trade to continue without interruption. Mexico has already indicated that it would not.

Conclusion 3: Is 'clout' and 'negotiating muscle' important?

Overall, the claim that 'the negotiating muscle' of the EU (to use Mr Cameron's phrase) has brought substantial gains for the UK exporters in trade agreements which the UK could not replicate is not supported by this, or any other, data. Over the past 42 years EC negotiators have mainly concluded agreements with small countries, which have therefore affected only a small proportion of UK exports. Any benefits they may have brought to UK exporters must have been correspondingly small.

It is a pity that neither the Commission, nor the UK government, nor the CBI and the *Financial Times*, have ever sought to measure these benefits before talking about them. What the UK currently lacks is not experts to conduct negotiations, nor clout to conclude them, but research to inform policy-making and public opinion on trade issues.

Note: HM Treasury's take on the EU trade agreements analysed above

In 2016 a Treasury report on the economic impact of EU membership outlined what the UK government sees as the benefits of EU membership in negotiating trade deals with the rest of the world.

> Membership of the EU also facilitates trade through the EU's negotiation of trade deals with the rest of the world. With an economic weight 5 times the size of the UK, the EU is able to negotiate access to global markets through multilateral trade agreements and, increasingly, bilateral agreements with other countries.

> Through these trade agreements, the UK currently has preferential access to markets covering around a third of the world economy.

If the UK left the EU it would no longer have the right to benefit from the EU's Free Trade Agreements (FTAs) with third countries. While these FTAs fall short of the Single Market in terms of breadth and depth, they are some of the most advanced in the world. Just to maintain what the UK enjoys through the EU would mean renegotiating new trade arrangements with the EU and over 50 other countries around the world, while commencing trade negotiations with a further 67. There is significant uncertainty about how long this would take and how much access the UK could achieve, as the UK's ability to negotiate beneficial deals as part of a large bloc would no longer exist.[3]

---

3   pp.44, 45, 85, *HM Treasury analysis: the long-term economic impact of EU member-ship and the alternatives*, HM Government, April 2016
     https://www.gov.uk/government/uploads/system

48

Why the UK would negotiate better services FTAs by itself

The UK has considerable comparative advantages when negotiating services trade agreements. As a member of the EU they have been ignored. After Brexit, they could be put to use

Concluding better services FTAs than the Commission, as previous chapters have shown, is setting a rather low bar. As has been shown in Chapter 33, the Commission has concluded a fair number of service trade agreements, but most are with small economies, which take only 1.8 per cent of all UK services exports. It has largely overlooked the Commonwealth where the prospects for UK services exporters would seem most promising.

In earlier chapters, we sought to understand this failure, and noted the inherent difficulties that arise when negotiations are conducted with prospective partner countries on behalf of 28 member countries. The Commission negotiators themselves might well have difficulty making sense of the still diverse regulatory/ legal systems, business practices and educational credentials of 28 member countries. Even if they do, the prospective partner might then find it difficult to recognize what constitutes an attractive offer, or an acceptable compromise.

Negotiating on its own, and for itself, the UK would not face these problems, since, for a variety of historical reasons, it enjoys a number of significant comparative advantages which are described below. They make the mutual recognition of professional qualifications and rules, of regulatory systems, of tax regimes, of accounting and legal practices easier than it is in any other EU country. In all probability, most prospective partners have a greater familiarity with the educational qualifications of British service providers than those of any other member country. This makes it easier for them to recognize them as acceptably equivalent and compatible with their own.

The first advantage might easily be taken for granted.

1. A world language and a true Single Market

First, the UK would be negotiating a simple, familiar bilateral format in its own Single Market, and using the world language of trade, business and diplomacy which happens to be, in many of the most attractive markets for UK services exports, either the first or the second language. Indeed, the English language itself may well be a marketable asset.

Table 48.1: Annual value of extra-EU services exports of the 12 founder members of Single Market, 2012 in $bn

UK	181.2
Germany	138.2
France	101.3
Netherlands	58.2
Italy	52.6
Ireland	50.8
Spain	45.5
Denmark	38.6
Belgium	37.8
Luxembourg	22.8
Greece	18.7
Portugal	7.9

OECDstat

2. The extra-EU exports of UK services are larger than any other member

As a result, it probably already knows more about marketing services in the rest of the world, about where and what are the UK's best prospects, and about the obstacles that impede the growth of services trade, than the Directorates-General of Trade in the Commission, or any other member country, could have acquired.

The annual report of Lloyd's the insurance market provides an example since it has negotiated licences to operate in 75 jurisdictions including China, India, Japan and the United States, none of which the EU has yet been able to conclude an agreement with.

In all probability therefore, UK negotiations to improve services trade would adopt a more intelligent and informed strategy than that of the EU over the past 42 years.

3. The global ties of UK educational institutions

The UK has, for many years, been the favoured European destination for students from around the world seeking to acquire higher educational and professional qualifications. They may do so either by coming to the UK to study or by registering in a UK university extension or extra-mural programme.

Table 48.2: Top 20 countries of origin of higher education students in the UK 2014

China	81,776
India	22,155
Nigeria	17,325
United States	14,652
Germany	14,192
Malaysia	13,322
China, Hong Kong	12,946
Ireland	12,579
France	11,494
Cyprus	10,928
Greece	10,881
Saudi Arabia	9,344
Italy	8,238
Pakistan	7,154
Romania	6,440
Canada	6,132
Bulgaria	6,051
Thailand	5,983
Singapore	5,946
Spain	5,900

UNESCO Institute of Statistics

Internal students: Large numbers of students from other continents study for degrees in the UK, more than in any other

EU country.[1] They come from all over the world. Table 48.4 shows the 20 countries, from which the largest numbers of students come. Nine of them are fellow EU members, the other eleven are countries with which, as luck would have it, the EU has never negotiated a trade agreement.

Table 48.3: Higher education students from abroad	
UK	416,693
France	239,344
Germany	196,619
Italy	82,450
Neths	68,943
Spain	56,361

UNESCO Institute of Statistics

Extramural students: UK universities and colleges have run extramural programmes for generations. These enable students all over the world to study for their degrees and diplomas in local institutions with the help of local teachers, but to curricula, to standards, and with lecturers and examiners from their registered university in the UK.

In 2014, there were 636,675 students around the world registered with a UK university. Their distribution by their country of origin and by their UK university is given in the table below.[2]

There does not appear to be any similar body of external students in other EU countries, though DAAD, the German Academic Exchange Service, estimated that there were 23,400 such students registered at German universities in 2013-14, with some 10 per cent of them, 2,129, coming from other EU countries.[3] The proportion of students from other EU countries at British universities is about the same, 12 per cent, but the number is of course, larger, 35 times larger, at 75,170. The UK is, therefore, far

---

1   http://www.uis.unesco.org/Education/Pages/tertiary-education.aspx
2   https://www.hesa.ac.uk/stats
3   The closest competitor of the British programs appears to be the similar extension of programs of Australian universities, which in 2013-14 had 111,404 registered students, and perhaps, if they really are a competitor, public and private MOOCs (massive open on line courses) emanating mainly from the United States. https://en.wikipedia.org/wiki/Massive_open_online_course

Table 48.4: Higher Education students studying wholly overseas for a UK undergraduate or postgraduate degree by top 20 countries & top 20 universities countries in 2013/14 World Total is 636,675

Students are from	Number	And are studying with	Number
Malaysia	76,600	Oxford Brookes University	162,045
Singapore	50,070	London	42,140
China	49,680	The Open University	23,520
Pakistan	43,400	Wales	13,005
Nigeria	28,455	Leicester	12,620
Hong Kong	28,385	Heriot-Watt University	11,220
Ghana	17,130	Greenwich	9,125
Oman	15,490	Bradford	8,220
U Arab Emirates	14,885	Middlesex University	8,125
Egypt	14,710	Staffordshire University	8,010
Ireland	13,640	Sunderland	8,005
Sri Lanka	13,615	Nottingham	7,550
Greece	13,220	Liverpool	6,580
Mauritius	12,845	Hertfordshire	4,605
Trin. & Tobago	12,815	East London	4,410
India	12,750	Northumbria at Newcastle	4,315
Kenya	11,085	Manchester	3,695
Russia	9,435	Central Lancashire	3,445
Zambia	8,160	Edinburgh Napier University	2,965
Saudi Arabia	8,110	Strathclyde	2,870
Total (Top 20)	**454,480**		
Total (World)	**636, 675**	All numbers are rounded up or down to the nearest multiple of 5.	

Source: The Higher Education Statistics Agency (HESA) http://bit.ly/1VBwX0H

and away the favoured distance learning headquarters in the EU, both for EU students and for students around the world.

In 2014, there were in total over one million students (1,053,368) from abroad studying in or through British universities. Students do not negotiate trade agreements, but former students do, and, since these programmes have been running for generations, there must be probably considerable number of graduates in every country to which the UK exports services which would be helpful when negotiating an agreement. Nelson Mandela and Robert Mugabe are among London's graduates, which like the Inns have cabinet minister alumni aplenty. As a result, in most prospective partner countries, there is likely to be a comparatively high degree of familiarity with British educational institutions and credentials. In trade negotiations, that familiarity is an advantage which no EU trade negotiator, endeavouring to reconcile the qualifications of 28 members with that of the prospective partner could expect to find.

4. *The global reach of UK professional bodies*

Many UK professional institutions have a similar global reach, especially those which act as training and qualifying associations and entail lifelong membership. In many cases, they have been the model or prototype for sister institutions in other countries. India, for example, has institutes of Civil, Mechanical and Electrical Engineers which perform functions similar to British engineering institutions. The Bar Association and the Law Society of Hong Kong likewise bear a close resemblance to their English counterparts. There are others in Australia, New Zealand and other Commonwealth countries. And the United States has a large number of Inns of Court.

The ties among professionals tend to be stronger than those of any commercial or educational affiliation simply because the socialization is indelible and the membership lifelong. In foreign settings, fellow members are probably the better guides and interpreter to their home societies than any consular service. Professional networks necessarily penetrate every significant institution in a society and at all levels, though we hear more about those at the top. Among the 2,261 overseas members of the Inner Temple are His Majesty the King of Bhutan, the Chief Justices of Pakistan and Singapore, two Justices of the present US Supreme Court, the President of the Caribbean Court of Justice, the former Chief Justice of Nigeria, the Governor-General of Barbados and many more.

The table lists some of the better known UK professional associations and gives their total membership and the proportions of overseas members. In some cases their overseas members are themselves organized. The Chartered Institute of Arbitrators, for example, has 37 overseas branches. Judging by its 2014 accounts those in UAE, Singapore, East Asia, Nigeria, Kenya and Australia were the busiest.[4] RIBA has active chapters in the United States, the Gulf States and Hong Kong.[5]

There appear to be few professional bodies with a similar global reach anywhere else in the EU. The French *ordres des avocats* may be an

Table 48.5: The global ties of 24 British professions, 2015

	Membership in 2015	of which overseas	% overseas
Association of Chartered Certified Accountants	165,625	85,138	51
Association of International Accountants	8545	7035	82
Chartered Institute of Management Accountants	95,925	20,999	22
Chartered Institute of Public Finance and Accountancy	13,328	399	3
The Chartered Institute of Arbitrators	14,000	8960	64
Chartered Insurance Institute	122,014	13,262	11
Inns of Court Lincolns	14913	5823	39
Inns of Court Inner Temple	19,201	2261	12
Institute of Chartered Accountants in Eng & Wales	142,334	21821	15
Institute of Chartered Accountants of Scotland	20,109	2892	14
Institute of Marine Engineering Science &Technology	16,800	5,100	30
Institution of Chemical Engineers	42,000	18,480	44
Institution of Civil Engineers	88,810	22,313	25
Institution of Engineering and technology	165,000	41,388	25
Institution of Gas Engineers and Managers	4002	430	10
The Institute of Materials, Minerals and Mining	18000		
Institution of Mechanical Engineers	111,408	7200	6
Law Society	133,367	6863	5
Royal College of Physicians of London	32,186	5523	17
Royal College of Phy'cns & Surgeons, Glasgow	12,854	4242	33
Royal College of Surgeons of England	24828	5234	21
Royal College of Veterinary Surgeons	29,369	2860	10
Royal Institute of British Architects	27,468	4182	15
Royal Institution of Chartered Surveyors	74,885	13,401	18
Royal Pharmaceutical Society	28,905	2328	8

A few of the figures were obtained from websites, but most were kindly supplied in response to an email or telephone request

Source: The Higher Education Statistics Agency (HESA) http://bit.ly/1VBwX0H

4   https://www.hesa.ac.uk/stats
5   The closest competitor of the British programs appears to be the similar extension of programs of Australian universities, which in 2013-14 had 111,404 registered students, and perhaps, if they really are a competitor, public and private MOOCs (massive open on line courses) emanating mainly from the United States. https://en.wikipedia.org/wiki/Massive_open_online_course

exception, but continental professions do not have practice-based, practitioner-controlled training and qualification, or of self-regulation, like the British. For the most part they are state-regulated and primarily concerned with protecting the interests of their current members, which may explain why they are less collegial than their British counterparts. However, comprehensive comparative research on the professions which the EU has been seeking to harmonise is lacking.

5. The UK is the preferred location in the EU of foreign investors from around the world, and is itself the EU's largest investor in other parts of the world

The UK has more inward FDI stock than any other member country. For many generations, it was the favoured European destination of American investors, and then was similarly preferred by Japanese investors. It may yet also be the first choice of Indian and Chinese investors. The figure below gives the amounts of FDI stock held by 24 EU countries in 2014.

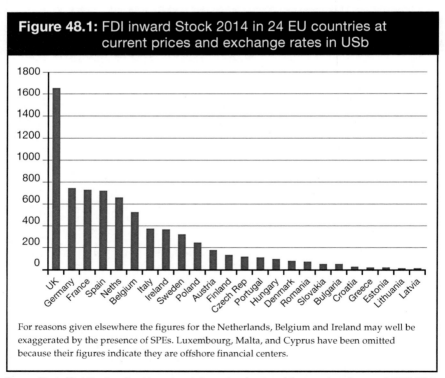

Figure 48.1: FDI inward Stock 2014 in 24 EU countries at current prices and exchange rates in USb

For reasons given elsewhere the figures for the Netherlands, Belgium and Ireland may well be exaggerated by the presence of SPEs. Luxembourg, Malta, and Cyprus have been omitted because their figures indicate they are offshore financial centers.

Source; UnctadStat Foreign direct investment: Inward and outward flows and stock, annual, 1980-2014

There are of course many reasons why foreign investors choose a particular location, but it seems likely that, among other things, they are stating a preference about which member country they prefer to operate in. And of necessity, after operating in the UK they acquire some understanding of, and familiarity with, UK service providers of all kinds.

Outward FDI flows perform the same function. Per capita, the UK remains one of the world's largest foreign investors. It follows that when the UK opens negotiations for a services agreement, the negotiators of many prospective partner countries are already familiar with UK services; either because some of their own companies operate in the UK or because UK companies operate in their country. Negotiations need not, therefore, start from scratch.

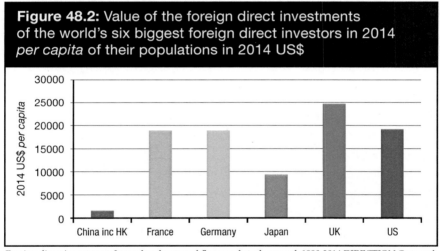

Figure 48.2: Value of the foreign direct investments of the world's six biggest foreign direct investors in 2014 *per capita* of their populations in 2014 US$

Foreign direct investment: Inward and outward flows and stock, annual, 1980-2014 DIRECTION Outward MODE Stock MEASURE US Dollars at current prices and current exchange rates per capita www.unctadstat.org

Conclusions

How the British overlooked their own decisive comparative advantages in services

The evidence presented above suggests that there are a considerable number of managerial and professional people across the globe, who are familiar with British educational and professional institutions, and have contact with British services either as employees of British companies abroad or of foreign companies in the UK. When, therefore, negotiations about services enter into legal and medical issues, or audit and accounting procedures, or engineering standards, or have to match institutions and qualifications in these and other fields, the British standards and qualifications are likely to be less foreign to the negotiating partner country. Indeed, given the reach of British universities and professions, there is a chance that the negotiators for some partner countries will themselves be graduates of a British university or members of a British professional body.

Familiarity and recognition constitute significant advantages in negotiating service trade agreements, which the European Commission has plainly failed to recognize. When it surrendered the right to negotiate its own trade agreements, the UK was clearly thinking solely of trade in goods and had no regard for the distinctive comparative advantages it was already accumulating in services. It is now time perhaps for them to recognize these advantages, and to consider ways in which they might be best deployed to contribute to the further extension of the UK's services export markets.

Speculation about a radical form of subsidiarity

It seems unlikely that they would ever be able to do so if they remain members of the EU. However, it is worth considering what would be required if they were to do so while still a member, because while speculating in this manner we are better able to see how present structures and practices prevent member countries making the most of their strengths, and thereby also prevent them making their best contribution to the advance of the European Union as a whole.

In this particular case, the ability of the Commission to negotiate effective service trade agreements is holding back the abilities of the Union's foremost service trade exporter to extend its world markets for those services. The UK must instead defer to the Commission which in this particular area (negotiating service trade agreements) is demonstrably less than competent.

To enable the British to make the most of their comparative advantages in services, it would first be necessary for the European Court of Justice to be able to adjudicate whether the

Commission has made effective use of rights entrusted to it by a member state, and if not, to require that they be returned to the member states. This would bring to an end the Commission's monopoly of negotiating service trade agreements, and make subsidiarity an active principle of Union government which would enable a member country, or a group of member countries, to be lead negotiators for agreements in which they have particular skills or interest, and, as in this case, significant comparative advantages. This member country, with others of similar skills and interest would, with the full oversight of other members and of the Commission, and on behalf of the Union, might then strike a deal which they would put into force in their own jurisdictions. This would be on the understanding that, when any other members feel they can live with the terms of the agreement, they too can become a party to it. Services trade, in other words, would no longer be governed by rules devised for goods.

Obviously, this requires an EU with very different institutions and mindset than at present; one in which solidarity cannot be used to restrain members from seizing economic opportunities for which their comparative advantages best prepare them; one in which subsidiarity has become a working principle of government; and one where the Union leaves members free to play to their strengths because it recognizes that even if a few sometimes obtain some temporary economic benefit before others, it is not at the expense of others, and much to the advantage of the Union as a whole.

This speculation was prompted by the British experience, but it is surely not only of relevance to the UK. In the case of services agreements, it seems likely that Luxembourg would also wish to be a lead negotiator, along with the Netherlands, and the other English-speaking member countries Ireland, Cyprus and Malta. Other groups of member countries no doubt have analogous comparative advantages in other settings. The odds are that a joint Spanish and Portuguese team would both devise and pilot better service trade agreements and relationships with Latin America, than could a Commission team that had first to present the reserved rights of 28 countries.

Part Seven

The future

49

Uncertainties of staying

Although some of those who want the UK to remain a member of the EU suggest that the referendum is a choice between the comforting security of the status quo and a dangerous leap into the unknown, it is clear that there are uncertainties whichever way the referendum goes. One of the best think tanks, Open Europe, made 'There is no such thing as the status quo' something of a slogan. This and the final chapter attempt to provide a checklist of post-referendum uncertainties, whichever way it turns out on both sides.

1. Little influence in the EU in the short term

At this particular moment, on the brink of the possible departure of the UK from the EU, and the termination of its substantial financial contribution, the UK's influence within the EU is at its high point, and over the last few months its negotiating hand has been as strong as it has ever been, or is ever likely to be.

If it votes to stay in, it seems likely that its negotiating hand will be weaker for some considerable time, either because the majority vote of the British people will be taken as a reassuring mandate for EU policies that British governments have been resisting for some while, or because other members will have grown a little weary of listening to and trying to accommodate the concerns of this especially troublesome member, that claims 'a special status' and will expect it to be quiet, for a little while at least, since it has nowhere else to go.

No-one knows of course what promises or quid pro quos the Prime Minister may have made to secure the concessions he did announce, modest as they have been found to be. We will only learn about them after the referendum, if that is, the vote is to remain.

2. Free trade agreements

The European Commission's abysmal record in negotiating agreements to the benefit of British exporters has been documented in the notes. However, the case for remaining in the EU does not appear to depend much on the EU's record, but entirely on the promise of TTIP, even though no one knows its terms, or can say when it will be finally concluded, or if it will finally be ratified by both parties. TTIP has already provided an illustration since a French veto on these negotiations was only lifted after the exclusion of audio-visual and media services, a sector which might have been of considerable benefit to the UK. That, however, was part of the price of solidarity. We will have to wait and see if there have been any more.

In his report to the House of Commons Mr Cameron also announced that 'We have secured commitments to complete trade and investment agreements with the fastest growing and most dynamic economies around the world, including the USA, Japan and China, as well as our Commonwealth allies, India, New Zealand and Australia.' After 42 years of being sidelined in EU trade negotiations, and despite Britain's alleged considerable influence within the EU, the Commonwealth is suddenly produced like a rabbit from the Prime Minister's hat. What this commitment might be worth remains to be seen.

3. Immigration from other member states will continue at an unpredictable rate

Even if all the measures Mr Cameron renegotiated, and which he hoped would reduce immigration from EU countries, (such as the temporary limitations on the welfare benefits new EU immigrants can claim, as well as the measures against criminals from EU countries, and sham marriages by EU nationals) all worked well, immigration from the EU will still continue at an unpredictable level. His renegotiation made it abundantly clear that the UK cannot be exempt from one of the cardinal principles of the Union.

Immigration from member states with significantly lower incomes and social services than the UK will continue, placing extra unpredictable pressure on UK housing, schools and medical services into the indefinite future. One major uncertainty therefore is whether that level will prove to be acceptable or unacceptable to the British people.

4. Increased regulation of financial services seems certain

The Bank of England has expressed its fears about the risks of future financial integration of the eurozone and of misguided 'maximum harmonisation' in EU regulation. The Prime Minister claims to have negotiated protection for the City of London, but apart from mentioning that it will not be forced to relocate to conduct euro-denominated trades, gave no specifics to the House of Commons.

He also claimed that 'we have guaranteed British business will never face any discrimination for being outside the eurozone' but it is difficult to see how there could be any guarantees for protection against as yet unknown measures that the new EU regulatory authorities (European Banking Authority, European Insurance and Occupational Pensions Authority and European Securities and Markets Authority), may decide on, or steps the eurozone may take to safeguard its own financial stability which incidentally adversely impact the City of London.

The greater part of EU financial law is based on the treaties' Single Market articles, and therefore decided by QMV, so the UK cannot veto them. The eurozone also has an inbuilt majority in both the Commission and Parliament, and all seem set to continue on a path of more stringent regulation without any particular regard for the interests of the City of London.[1] The European Court of Justice offers no protection since it is committed to further EU integration. The UK has lost three of four cases it has brought to the Court, and won the fourth, on the ocation on euro-denominated trading, on a technicality, not on the principle itself, so it might well be resurrected.[2]

In 2012 George Osborne secured a so-called double majority lock in the European Banking Authority so that measures had to pass a majority of both eurozone and non-eurozone members. At the

1   The 13 major items on the EU reform agenda since 2013 are described pp.328-330, Business for Britain, Change or Go, London 2015. businessforbritain.org/2015/07/17/change-or-go-published-in-full/
2   Europe Economics, EU Financial Regulation, 2014, p. 40. forbritain.org/EUFinancialReg.pdf

time there were 18 eurozone members and 10 non-members. Now there are 19 eurozone members and five of the present nine non-members have indicated they will join the euro before or by 2020. It is implausible to expect 24 eurozone members to allow four non-members to veto their decisions.[3] The UK is the only country that is permanently committed to retaining its own currency, so it had best be prepared to be a minority of one. Whether Mr Cameron's words to the House of Commons will then be of much help is unclear. But by that time he will probably have retired.

5. *Financial Transaction Tax, and other new or 'harmonized' taxes are on the cards*

For a very long time, the EU has sought to impose a tax or taxes across all member countries that would substantially increase its own resources, so that it would have an income of its own in addition to that from tariffs and a proportion of VAT, and render it less dependent on the outcome of discussions in the European Council every seven years, preceding agreement on the multi annual financial framework. It is an aspiration that, if it succeeds would render it even less dependent on member governments and of the peoples it hopes to govern.

The near certain prospect in the not too distant future is a Financial Transaction Tax. Although this has been accepted by eleven eurozone members. It was opposed, unsuccessfully, in the European Court of Justice by the UK, on the grounds that it would adversely affect non-participating member countries. One study had claimed that it would add £4b to the annual costs of issuing UK debt.[4] After a positive referendum result in the UK, the chances are that it will be re-launched and receive enthusiastic support from the European Parliament and public opinion in member countries, including the UK.[5] It is, after all, a tax on other people, and such taxes are usually acceptable.

---

3   p.333, *ibid.*

4   Andrew Trotman, 'EU's Financial Transaction Tax would hit City, says study'. *The Daily Telegraph.* 3 April 2013.

5   'Final decision on financial transaction tax expected in June' *The Guardian*, 8 Dec 2015
     http://www.theguardian.com/business/2015/dec/08/decision-financial-transactions-tax-june-eu

There are other possibilities. Given the EU's permanent interest in new sources of revenue, it will no doubt support proposals like that of German Finance Minister Wolfgang Schäuble's proposal for a petrol tax to cover the costs of the refugee crisis, which might gain traction, and even popular support if the fall in pump prices continues.[6]

More importantly, over the longer run the proposed common consolidated corporate tax base (CCCTB) will be the preliminary to tax harmonization. In itself the CCCTB is intended to enable cross-border companies to make just one calculation of their taxable profits in the EU, and thereby tackle base erosion and tax shifting to low tax jurisdictions. Almost all member states support the idea, other than its two offshore financial centres, Luxembourg and Ireland, since it will ensure greater tax transparency and illuminate opaque and preferential tax regimes. Once established, it will be a platform for the policy which both the European Commission and German government have long supported of reducing tax competition and 'competitive distortions in the Single Market', and finally dealing with low corporation tax rates that have attracted FDI to Ireland in particular but also to the UK.[7] In the last budget negotiations, the UK had to resist pressure for new EU-wide taxes as a new 'own resource' for the Commission.

6. The rebate will come under renewed attack
The reduction or elimination of the UK rebate has long been an objective of a number of member countries that contribute to it.

---

6   *Sueddeutshe Zeitung* 16 Jan 2016.
7   Article 188c of the Lisbon Treaty already provides legal grounds for such intervention. It reads 'The common commercial policy shall be based on uniform principles, particularly with regard to changes in tariff rates, the conclusion of tariff and trade agreements relating to trade in goods and services, and the commercial aspects of intellectual property, foreign direct investment, the achievement of uniformity in measures of liberalisation, export policy and measures to protect trade such as those to be taken in the event of dumping or subsidies. The common commercial policy shall be conducted in the context of the principles and objectives of the Union's external action.' For the moment, however, action under Article 188c appears to require unanimity. 'France and Germany want to see common basic corporation tax rates across the EU', according to a report by Matthew Holehouse, and Christopher Williams, in the *Daily Telegraph*, 26 May 2015

Mr Blair proved unable to resist this pressure during the UK presidency, a concession for which he obtained nothing. By 2014, his concession had cost the UK taxpayers some £10bn.

The likelihood is, especially after a vote to remain a member, it will almost inevitably, come under renewed attack. Unless the UK continually finds especially resolute leaders, and as long as it has no other goal for which it is willing to make a concession, then it is difficult to see it maintaining its present level. In all probability, it will be asked, and perhaps already has been asked, for a reduction in the rebate in return for the UK's 'special status'. How would a victorious, and soon to retire, Mr Cameron be able to refuse?

7. Subsidiarity: will it happen?
In his report on his renegotiations to the House of Commons, on 22 February the Prime Minister said:

> We have a new mechanism finally to enforce the principle that, as far as possible, powers should sit here in Westminster, not in Brussels, so now, every year, the European Union must go through the powers that it exercises and work out which are no longer needed and should be returned to nation states.

There are no recorded cases of the fundamental principle of subsidiarity even being used to return powers to national governments. Presumably the Prime Minister meant that the Commission, rather than European Union, 'must go through the powers that it exercises' etc, but he said nothing about how this 'mechanism' would work. We will therefore have to wait and see how this annual review is conducted.

8. A long-term decline of UK influence within the EU seems likely
A great many of the most fervent advocates of membership Messrs Major, Blair, Brown, Heseltine, Clarke and Mandelson take the view that the UK should stay and fight in the EU and make allies, win hearts and minds, and fight for the reforms that they want to see. Gordon Brown like Blair before him even thinks that the UK should 'lead in Europe – with progressive British values to the fore.'[8]

---

8   Gordon Brown, The truly patriotic British view on Europe? We must lead from within, *The Guardian*, 9th March 2015

Unfortunately, their own careers negotiating with or working in the EU do not offer a single example of how this might best be done, that is to say, of reforms which they proposed, fought for in EU meetings, found allies for, and finally brought to fruition. If there are any such cases, it is odd that they themselves have never brought them to our attention, either in their speeches or in their memoirs, and that no one else can identify them either.

Over the long term one must expect a continuous decline in its influence within the Union bearing in mind that the UK is not a member either of the euro or of the Schengen area and has therefore been unwilling to participate in the rescues following the crises that both of these ill-considered projects have precipitated: bailouts of eurozone countries and EU quotas for the redistribution of refugees and immigrants. The Prime Minister is proud of these achievements which cannot endear him or the UK to other members. The UK has now emphatically stated that it does not wish to participate in the drive to ever closer union, and expects its reservation on this score, not only to be taken for granted but formally acknowledged by other members in the next Treaty.

Since these three things are among the primary defining characteristics of the European Union, it seems unlikely that the UK could in the future exercise much influence on policy making within it. Moreover, in all probability, there are more UK opt outs to come. UK participation in EU military endeavours has been perfunctory to say the least, and it has frequently made known its resistance to the idea that the European Defence Agency should evolve into the EU Ministry of Defence, though for founder members it would be the capstone of the project on which they have been engaged since the Treaty of Rome in 1957.

One must also recall that the largest party group among the representatives the British people elect to the European Parliament are committed to leaving the Union and have little respect for its leaders and its institutions. That may, of course, change in the future, but for the moment, this combination of many opt outs, and a large number of MEPs hostile to the whole project makes it unlikely that other members would want a Brit to ever again hold one of the significant offices of the Union, president of the Commission, of the Central Bank, of the Eurogroup, or of the Parliament. It is therefore unclear how this influence might be exercised, and to what end.

However, Messrs Major, Blair, Brown, Heseltine and Mandelson are accomplished political operators so they may perhaps explain how this might be done, and why other members would be inclined to heed the influence, let alone accept that leadership, of a member that is clearly at odds with the goals of other members.

9. A question about the legitimacy of the EU authority

The EU flies in the face of the primary principle of political legitimacy in the modern world which is that those who make laws and give orders should be co-cultural with those who they expect to obey them. This is a principle that underpins every democratic polity and every non-democratic polity in the modern, post-imperial world. Indeed, it is precisely because it is universal that it remains all but invisible.

The EU alone stands firmly against this principle, in the belief that there are European values enunciated in its charters and treaties that transcend the cultures of member nations. Whether cultures can be transcended easily, is not so certain. These superior European values are enunciated by elites, usually on special occasions, when they all speak the same language. Culture, by contrast, is embodied in the daily habits, interactions and vernacular of the people, and not just in their quaint popular customs and folklore. It informs the whole apparatus of government, lawmakers, judges, policemen, civil servants, every professional, business and family relationship. No one can quite ignore its preferences and demands.

As the scope of EU laws extends, and enters people's lives more directly, one might expect its legitimacy to become increasingly uncertain, since these laws are voted by a Parliament which can and does easily outvote entire national delegations of MEPs, even if they happened to be unanimous, and its executive and judicial branches are led by unknown foreigners, who speak another language. Thus far, the authority of this emerging state has not been questioned because the peoples of the EU have been protected from direct contact with its alien authority by national elites who have accepted it, and who re-enact its legislation, and use national institutions to impose its will on their own people. The EU itself is never questioned or threatened because it has willing agents or proxies in the elites of member countries. It is not certain that this can continue indefinitely, and provide a foundation for a permanent form of government.

50

Uncertainties of leaving

Post-Brexit uncertainties are fairly clear, since it has been in the interest of the Government to identify and reiterate them over many years. As the referendum approaches, it has multiplied and enlarged on them apparently to frighten voters, and suggest the risks of independence are too great.

1. What kind of future trade relationship with the EU?

Unquestionably, this is the number one issue for any British government following a vote to leave. The way it is resolved will have repercussions on other post-Brexit uncertainties. Some of those who hope the UK will remain a member have suggested that our former partners, keen to discourage any further defections will be vindictive and difficult negotiators. Others take the view that 'rationality will prevail', and that they will act in their own self-interest, and therefore be willing to conclude an agreement that provokes as little disturbance to existing patterns of trade as possible.

Some reassurance may be found in the OECD and UNComtrade data reported in this handbook, since it has repeatedly demonstrated that the benefits of membership have, for many years, been much exaggerated in the UK. The exports to the EU of many non-members, including many with no agreements with the EU, have grown faster than those of the UK and those of other members over the life of the Single Market, despite the tariff and non-tariff barriers they face. The idea that a country has to 'sit at the table and help to make the rules' to export successfully to the EU is plainly absurd, as therefore is the idea that it would be necessary to pay substantial membership fees or to allow free movement of labour to all EU citizens to export to it.

2. Can the UK replace EU trade agreements with other countries

None of the trade agreements that the EU has negotiated with other countries will be automatically transferred to the UK as an independent country. It will be a matter of negotiation in each and every case, which depend in some respects on the outcome of the negotiations with the EU. This is sometimes presented as a daunting task extending over many years.

However, the UNComtrade and WTO data reported in this handbook has also shown that the benefits of these agreements have also been exaggerated. While there are a large number of agreements their scope in terms of UK exports is limited. Aside from the EEA and EFTA agreements, they cover 6% of UK goods exports and 1.8% of services exports, and the tariffs on exports to those goods markets for all WTO members is low, on average 5%. Second, the evidence that we have suggests that a majority of these agreements have not been effective in increasing UK goods exports. The post-agreement rate of growth of UK goods exports has increased in four of the fourteen in which data allowed a pre-and post-agreement comparison: Chile, Lebanon, Korea and Papua New Guinea.

The agreements with Korea and Chile have been the spectacular success stories of the past 42 years of EU trade negotiations, (together 1.5% of all UK goods exports in 2014) but most of the other agreements would probably not be a post-Brexit UK priority. They are with small countries, often do not include services, and have slighted the Commonwealth over many years.

Hence, Brexit provides an opportunity for the UK to adopt a trade agreement strategy geared to its own comparative advantages and interests. Many small independent countries have shown that it is possible to conclude agreements with large economies, which include services. This must be counted one of the main economic opportunities of Brexit.

3. What sort of immigration system?

If there is an agreement with the EU, which entails freedom of movement for all EU citizens, then there will be little change from the present unpredictable flows. If there is no such agreement, immigration will be managed, in all likelihood become qualification-based and equally open to immigrants from all countries rather than restricted to the EU, plus such provision for refugees as the government of the day considers appropriate, and UK public services and communities seem able to manage.

The financial and scientific research communities will be the most deeply affected by the outcome of the agreement with the EU. However, once immigration is under control, and the public backlash removed, it will be easy for a post-Brexit government to ensure not only that immigration from the EU to their workplaces continues, but that they have exactly the same freedom to recruit equally freely from around the world. Some Remain campaigners suggest that Brexit campaigners are xenophobic or anti-European, but there does not appear to be any significant body of opinion that wishes to restrict free movement of scientific research labour, nor even financial experts.

4. FDI
Supporters of continued membership have often predicted that foreign investors will leave the UK, if it votes to leave the EU, and that new investors will decline to come. The evidence does not support these confident claims. The EU itself has long since abandoned the claim that the Single Market is or has been a magnet for FDI. However, the post-Brexit government will have to consider how to ensure that the UK continues to be attractive for foreign investors, and the outturn of the preceding three questions will therefore be important. It will be even more important to continue the present policy of reducing corporation tax.

5. The scope and scale of de-regulation
One of the trickier issues of a post-Brexit government will be to decide what regulation is no longer considered necessary. Expectations on this score run very high, since even the Prime Minister and many others who wish to remain members of the EU are among those who think there is much to be gained by reducing EU regulation, even more so at times than those who wish to leave. There are therefore bound to be disappointments. Many of these

regulations, as has often been pointed out, stem from global regulations which the EU has merely transposed. Others have considerable support in the UK, and would have been adopted, even if the UK were not a member. No doubt there will be many expectations that will not be fulfilled.

Open Europe conducted a detailed analysis of eight distinctive types of regulation from the EU and found that the likely UK response of a post-Brexit government to each type differed.[1] Some, bearing in mind their domestic political support, it would probably prefer to leave alone. Others it would repeal and make considerable savings, while in a few cases it might consider amending or even strengthening. In short, it would not be a bonfire, but a deliberate and considered choice of the regulations that are most appropriate and effective in the UK.

The estimated total savings in their 'politically feasible' scenario would be £12.8b while under an 'extremely liberal' one they would be £24.4b. Under the former they estimate no savings at all from regulation in consumer protection, competition and public procurement, product standards, and life sciences, while the biggest savings under both scenarios are amending regulations of employment health and safety and in environmental and climate change.

6. Will the UK be less influential in the world?

Tony Blair has argued that 'the case for the EU today... is that, in this new world, to leverage power, you need the heft of the EU'. This is true in economics, in trade, in defence, foreign policy and global challenges such as climate change. It gives us a weight collectively that on our own we lack. It enables the UK to perform what he called 'our global leadership role', our meaning the UK, not the EU. The first major disadvantage of leaving the EU, in his view, is therefore that we would be unable to perform this role.

In a similar vein, the former Deputy Prime Minister, Nick Clegg, has often claimed that EU membership enables Britain 'to walk tall in Beijing, New Delhi and Washington'. And presumably outside the EU, Britain would walk more diffidently in these cities.

---

1   Annex 3, Stephen Booth, *Open Europe, What if...? The Consequences, challenges & opportunities facing Britain outside EU*, Report March 2015 http://openeurope.org.uk/intelligence/britain-and-the-eu/what-if-there-were-a-brexit/

President Obama has now added his voice to this argument by saying 'the European Union doesn't moderate British influence it magnifies it….it enhances Britain's global leadership.'

One problem with this argument is that there is no acceptable index of influence in the world. It seems to depend on a variety of ill-assorted, incommensurate factors. The size and strength of an economy, nuclear weapons and/or conventional military resources which can be deployed across the globe, representation on significant global bodies, and the English language itself seems to be a powerful influence. The present UK government, like many others, thinks that foreign aid increases influence. How, alongside all these things, and membership of NATO and numerous global bodies, should we assess the impact of EU membership?

The second, more important, problem is that it is uncertain whether the British people want to play 'a global leadership role', or want their global leadership 'enhanced' as President Obama puts it.

Putting these questions aside, surrendering as the UK has done, the right to speak for itself in the WTO, and other global bodies, and allow EU representatives to speak on its behalf, while simultaneously speaking on behalf of the other 27 members, seems, on the face of things, a curious way of 'magnifying' or 'enhancing' the UK's influence. Inevitably, it must often require that the UK qualify or amend its initial position to reach an EU consensus. How could this magnify Britain's influence in the world?

The logic of this argument is that Britain should also surrender its seat on the board of the IMF to an EU representative, as has been discussed at EU Ministers of Finance, and then go on to surrender, as has also occasionally been suggested, its permanent seat on the UN Security Council, since this will still further increase the UK's influence in the world.[2]

Meanwhile Norway, has not chosen the more conventional method of increasing its influence in the world, by energetically speaking up for itself on all the issues that matter most to it (fishing and shipping, oil rigs, food exports and climate change) at all the relevant global bodies, including the WTO, the WHO codex

---

2   p. 318, *op.cit.*

alimentarius, the FAO, the ILO, the High North & Arctic Council. Not infrequently, it plays a leading role upstream, not merely of EU member countries, but of the EU itself.[3] Might not post-Brexit UK do the same?

---

3   pp. 30-40, Jonathan Lindsell, *The Norwegian Way, A case study for Britain's future relationship with the EU*, Civitas, London 2015